IVY C

CW00584614

North Yo Within Living Memory

Compiled by the North Yorkshire Federations of Women's Institutes from notes sent by Members in the County

Published jointly by
Countryside Books, Newbury
and
NYEFWI, Thirsk
NYWFWI, Ripon

COUNTRYSIDE BOOKS
3 Catherine Road
Newbury, Berkshire

ISBN 1 85306 375 4

The cover photograph shows a view of York in 1913.

Designed by Mon Mohan
Produced through MRM Associates Ltd, Reading
Typeset by Acorn Bookwork, Salisbury
Printed by J.W. Arrowsmith Ltd., Bristol

Contents

North Yorkshire

NORTH
YORK
MOORS N.P.

A
Moors Cross

NORTH
SEA

Whitby

Scarborough

Filey

Malton

R. Derwent

York

R. Ouse

Wharfe

Selby

R. Ouse

M. Chapman

N
W O E
S

Acknowledgements

We have thoroughly enjoyed reading all the many fascinating and entertaining contributions, with their accompanying photographs, which have come from North Yorkshire members.

Memories have been sent to us by 281 members representing institutes from our two Federations, and our heartfelt thanks go out to them all.

Obviously there has been some duplication in the contents, and therefore it was not possible to include all submissions. Nevertheless, without exception, all the material has been of great value in shaping the finished book.

Margaret Chapman
Pat Smith
Co-ordinators

Foreword

Although the sterotype of the Yorkshire character persists, there is endless variety in the personality and customs of the people living here. There is elegance in the spa towns of Harrogate and Scarborough; an international flavour in the historic city of York; a coastline shaped by the weather, often rugged, alway beautiful; and there are hundreds of acres of countryside consisting of the Wolds, the Dales, the Moors and the Fells for which the county is noted. These correspond in some degree to the characteristics of our people. There is a resilience and a resourcefulness shaped by years of working with nature in all its vagaries: a determination and perseverance with the capacity to cope and adapt to changing circumstances.

So huge is the county of North Yorkshire that it has been divided into two federations with the A1 providing the dividing line. Both still remain largely rural with widely spaced communities, the villages and towns have developed their own character.

The preparation of this book was undertaken by our hardworking co-ordinators, Margaret Chapman and Pat Smith, to whom our thanks and appreciation are due. Bill Evans (a WI husband) provided the illustrations that head each chapter, Yvonne Bennett prepared the drawings and Margaret Chapman drew the county map. Keith Smith did much of the typing. We are grateful to them and to all our members who shared their reminiscences with us. We trust that our readers will enjoy these glimpses into our past.

Olive Davey
County Chairman, North Yorkshire East
Ann Martin
County Chairman, North Yorkshire West

TOWN & COUNTRY LIFE

SOME TOWNS AND VILLAGES REMEMBERED

It is not really so long since there were lamplighters on the streets, the only telephone in the village was at the local post office, cars were rarely to be seen, and ships in distress off the Yorkshire coast were rescued with the aid of horse-drawn equipment. Here are just a few memories of some of our towns and villages as they were.

BECKWITHSHAW

'Villagers at Beckwithshaw during the early decades of the 20th century experienced the gradual winding down of the former congenial semi-feudal system. The Williams family of Moor Park Hall estate owned the church with its vicarage, the village hall and the Smith's Arms public house, the landlord of which also had to be the farrier, to look after the estate horses. Farmers of the surrounding district attended six-monthly "Rent Dinners" at the local pub, when they paid their dues via the estate agent. Some nicknames remembered from those days are "Peg leg Charlie" for obvious reasons, "Diggle" the cobbler, "Tack Hammer" the joiner, "Pa" a handyman, and widow "Ma" with twelve children whom she ruled with a rod of iron and who went to church on Sunday morning and chapel in the afternoon.

Typical wages were, for a farm labourer 30 shillings, a tradesman 50 shillings and the schoolmistress the luxury of £5 weekly. Mothers made most of their own and their children's clothing using a hand or treadle sewing machine and the village dressmaker, with one assistant, sometimes made special Sunday coats and dresses.

Reliable weekly deliveries, by flat cart and later van, set a certain pattern, such as greengrocer on Thursday – bananas for tea; fishmonger on Fridays – fishcakes next day; Saturday the butcher with weekend meats; and Monday the grocer regulated biscuits, jellies etc and flour for baking day on Friday. Other delivery regulars were coal by the cart and barrels of beer by drayman's heavy horses and cart to keep the pub supplied. The daily postman never failed, even on Christmas Day, albeit by cycle.

Well attended social activities centred on the church, with its harvest festival and suppers, parochial tea and concerts, garden parties and choir trips to the seaside by charabanc. Other activities were the village hall's Christmas parties, whist drives, dances, bonfires, pantomimes, dramas, musicals and year round sports including billiards, football, tennis, hockey and cricket, with the vicar and squire's son members of the latter team. The chapel authorities arranged their own "Bright Hours" and seasonal events and everyone supported one another's activities.

Coincidentally adhering to the close-knit pattern of village life, the last squire ("Joss" to all) married the local schoolmistress around 1920 and properties were then gradually sold off, which included the manor house itself.

Upon his death in 1945 the owner bequeathed the church, vicarage and village hall to the people of the district, under appropriate trusteeships. The post-war period saw a new pattern of village life emerge, in the hands of the sons and daughters of former residents, who in the early 1950s arranged their first traditional Gala Day, which has been a fine example of "from little acorns grow" as, without a break, this continues today. However, by the 1960s gone were the smithy, joiners and cobbler's business, the post office and village shop where the children spent their Saturday pennies. The increase of car-owning families diminished the aspect of close-knit village life forever.'

EASINGWOLD FROM THE VILLAGE SHOP

'My mother had the village shop at Easingwold from 1937 to 1963. She sold most things as well as being the postmistress. At Christmas she sorted and delivered mail twice daily for ten days before Christmas Day. The shop was open from 8 am to 6 pm but really was "open all hours". People came to our back and even front door, evenings and weekends. They would "pay tomorrow" but some never did.

When I look back, the shop was a place for news and gossip. I can remember Mother listening patiently but not getting involved. If the doings of children and young people came up, she would say, "I have two girls of my own". In those days there were people who knew absolutely everything that went on in the village.

Mother was a Sunday school teacher in the 1940s. For Mothering Sunday she made little posies of snowdrops from the churchyard for children to give to their mothers. If snowdrops were early she cycled on her "sit up and beg bike" up to Manor Farm and gathered crocuses from Eleanor's garden. This was quite an uphill journey of well over a mile each way.

During the Second World War the villages held raffles and dances to raise money for the boys and girls returning from the Forces.

9

The village green was the place to meet and mull over local affairs. Ted and George Metcalfe, Jim Terry and Robert Heseltine met regularly on the green at Thoralby in the 1940s.

When the money was presented they each gave back £1 for the village children to have a treat. Mother wrote to the Major who lived at the local Hall asking if he would give a raffle prize for funds to provide the children's meals on this outing. He wrote back and offered to pay for everything. This annual outing to Redcar continued for several years. The children each had lunch and tea, and one shilling to spend. I remember these outings Mother organized, it was the only outing to the seaside during the year for many of us. There could be three coaches (charabancs) with some sitting on stools in the aisles and sometimes a taxi for the overspill.

Mother used to lay people out when they died. The lady who did this job once sent for Mum to help her, and then she did the job herself. My friend asked her recently if she had any training, she said that she was shown the job once and then just did it when asked. She didn't like the job but always did her best for people. This service was free, of course, as were a lot of things she did.

The telephone number of the village kiosk was the same as the post office. If Mother answered the phone she could be asked to go to the box about 25 yards away and if the person needed was not nearby, she would deliver a message or even go and fetch them. In some cases there was quite a distance involved.'

THE LAMPLIGHTER AT ALNE

'When I was a young girl we had a street lamp right outside our front gate. It was a gas lamp and it was my daily pleasure to look out for the lamplighter. He came at dusk every day and I loved to watch him push his long pole up into our lamp to the mantle and see the light come on. I don't know how many lamps he had to visit each evening, but he had to go round them all again to put the lights out later.'

THE INN AT COVERBRIDGE

'Life in a small country inn was rather special before the Second World War. Alongside a road, at a river crossing, the inn at Coverbridge was built in the mid 17th century, and extended in 1838 and 1906. There were four bedrooms for visitors and three attic bedrooms for the family.

The small, cosy bar, with a coal/log fire was an inviting prospect, but for men only. Any lady customers came to the back door and sat in a busy kitchen. Bar seating was on high backed settles with highly polished long and round tables. The stone floors were scrubbed each morning, the loose mats shaken and the sawdust-filled spittoons emptied. Glasses were washed by hand, after sterilisation in boiling water. Dominoes and darts were available, with keen competitions, and a raffle organised at Christmas and New Year. Clay pipes were popular, along with twist tobacco, among the more elderly locals. Opening times were rigidly kept from 11 am to 3 pm, and from 6 pm to 10 pm, when time was called by the landlord.

The cellar was cool and ideal for keeping beer in perfect condition. Eighteen and nine-gallon barrels of mild and bitter, set up on a stone gantry, were corked and tapped in turn. Each pint of beer was brought, to order, straight from the wood and served from a tin tray. The head was always perfect to satisfy the discerning regular customers.

The kitchen was large and high, with a shallow stone sink and a hand pump to draw the cold water from a deep well on the opposite side of the road. There was a blackleaded fireplace with an oven on one side and a water boiler on the other, and a large black kettle always on the boil above the coal fire. A paraffin stove was later available to supplement the meagre cooking arrangements. Lighting was by oil lamps, Tilley lanterns and candles in large, brass candlesticks.

Catering was for residents only. Breakfast, lunch and dinner were served in a small dining room, with a big extendable table to seat up to twelve guests. Fishermen came for a week, or a fortnight, each year, often travelling by train. The same shooting parties came for two days on most weekends. They were served with great joints of beef or ham to carve for themselves, with home-grown vegetables; home-produced milk, cream, butter and cheese were served and large apple pies and rich fruit cake. Lunches were transported by horse and cart, to the nearby moors for the grouse shooting, and to local farmhouses for the pheasant shooting season.

The bedrooms were furnished with feather beds, and a jug and a bowl on a marble-topped washstand, with hot and cold water delivered to the rooms each morning and evening. The earth closets – two seaters – were outside in the garden, so the chamberpot under the bed had to be emptied each morning. The landlord (as at most country inns) also farmed a smallholding of 40 acres, this was meadow and pasture grassland, and there was also a kitchen garden and orchard. Five or six cows were milked by hand, the milk was separated twice a day, and the skimmed milk fed to the calves. The spare cream was made into butter on Thursdays (churning day), and when surplus milk was available cheese was made and stored in the cool cellar. Monday was washing day with the copper in the farmyard washhouse being lit by 7 am, and the clothes hung out in the farmyard.

Two or three pigs were reared on kitchen waste and pigmeal and killed in the autumn. The hams and sides of bacon, after curing for three weeks in the cellar, were hung from the kitchen ceiling. The various surplus cuts of pork were given to friends and neighbours after each pig-killing. Poultry and sheep provided further variety for this almost self-sufficient unit.

Haytime, with horse-drawn implements, ensured a busy July, followed by hedge slashing, manure spreading, thatching on haystacks, and the harvest of fruit from the orchard and vegetables from the kitchen garden. It was a distinctive way of life, with hard work and a rigid routine which was little changed over many years. Holidays were virtually unknown, and the whole family were involved in the work of the inn and the farm.

The Second World War, the private car, modernisation, new machines and labour saving devices, and the contrasting social climate, brought about many changes, and the traditions of the old country inn have disappeared for ever.'

RAVENSWORTH IN THE 1920s

'My first recollections of Ravensworth are of helping my sister to push the pram down the top road, and passing a man with a hammer, breaking up stones and filling in the potholes in the road. He was kept fully occupied at this job as cart loads of stone came from the quarries. He used a small hammer with a long handle and wore a pair of mesh goggles to protect his eyes.

That day we were moving house, from a cottage on the low green, that has now been pulled down, to a house next door to the Bay Horse Inn. The cottage had a small field which enabled us to keep poultry. This house, I found out later, was the oldest house in the village, about 400 years old. It was called a cruck house, because of its construction.

At one period it had had a thatched roof. To support the roof were three timber crucks, made in the shape of large wish-bones, joined at the top with wooden pegs. The sides came three-quarters of the way down and were built into the wall; the first floor rooms were supported by ceiling joists 16 inches square, and the floors of the bedrooms were covered with boards twelve inches wide by one inch thick. The bedrooms were so low at the outside wall sides that it was difficult to stand up and the windows were at floor level. All the timber was solid oak.

Downstairs two large fireplaces divided the main rooms. One had a hot air oven with a boiler at the side. The floors were flagged and laid on clay, and on a wet day they struck up damp. One of my mother's main problems was getting the oven sufficiently hot on baking day. To do this she would resort to using oven sticks, pushed under the oven, and sometimes so long that they met you at the door as you came in.

The early 1930s were hard times for the villagers with an average weekly wage of only £2 coming in. Some men were self employed – masons, joiners etc – others worked at the three main farms in the village. The largest number of men would work at the Forcett Limestone Company, and prior to the advent of the bicycle would walk to work. The path led up the new road, over a stile by the little wood, and over the fields to run by the Foxhall Inn. The A66 road was then crossed, and down a lane at the other side. It then followed a track as straight as the crow flies to the quarry which was four miles away. I could imagine the men's wives would be very pleased when their husbands were able to have a bicycle, for the Foxhall Inn was a great temptation, and when Friday night came along some wages were greatly depleted by the time the men arrived home. At the quarry the men worked on a bonus system, blasting the rock and then breaking it up with a hammer, small enough to go through a six inch metal ring. It was then loaded on trucks and sent by rail to the ironworks on Teesside.

Lunch, or bait as they called it, would be bread and cheese, but on Monday they might have a beef sandwich if the Sunday joint had been large enough. This would be followed by cold tea before the introduction of the vacuum flask.

On arriving home at night one of the first jobs would be bringing water from the Far Lark; this was the old water supply for Ravensworth Castle, previously known as Hungarams Well. I never knew this to run dry. The men went armed with two buckets and they took a wooden square which was to prevent the buckets from swaying, and so losing half the contents. It would take at least three quarters of an hour to do this job.

In the centre of the village was a giant sycamore tree, which when in full leaf would cover about 90 yards circumference. This was known as the Cross Tree. Next to it was a square stone with evidence that at some time a Saxon cross had been embedded in the centre. Services were held there by travelling evangelists or Ranters, the name being self-evident. About 1935 the tree fell down in three different stages, and the villagers spent days sawing it up with crosscuts and axes, for winter fuel.

One night, by the tree, near the road a hole suddenly appeared in the ground, and when I looked down it next day a well-built, stone faced well of about 20 feet deep was evident. The council came and filled it up the next day. I thought it seemed unusual for a well to be on sloping ground.

A new Cross Tree was planted at the instigation of the Girl Guides, led by Miss Brown of Dunsa Manor and the names of all the Guides were placed in a jar under the roots of the new tree.

Water first came to the village in 1938, from a small reservoir at Flatts Bank, and piped to five taps in the village. Electricity did not arrive until 1946. To serve the 200 or so people the tradesmen included four masons, two joiners and undertakers, one butcher, two farriers and blacksmiths, one dressmaker, a post office with shop, a midwife, two pubs and over a period three fish and chip shops.

A wooden hut behind the Hare and Hounds was used for the local dances – the sixpenny hops – to music from a fiddle and an accordion: eventually the church relented and let the school be used for these purposes. As children we provided our own entertainment and top of the list was "bows and arrows". Willows were cut from the beckside and the test was to shoot one over the Cross Tree. Marbles and cricket were popular, and we spent Saturday afternoons watching our local cricket team who played to quite a good standard.'

UNEARTHING THE PAST

'Robert Greaves was born in 1904, the sixth of seven children, into a family that had been farmers for several centuries. Robert farmed in Grafton, then up the road in Marton, from 1934 to 1972.

He remembers the quarry at Grafton which gave work in the 1930s to many men who could no longer find jobs on the farms. A large

14

deposit of first-class gravel was excavated. It was good, clean stuff, smelling of the sea under which it had formed aeons before, Robert recalls. Remains of an Iron Age village were found on the hill top, and several indications of Roman occupation were revealed, including an urn which was removed to the museum at nearby Aldborough. The quarry closed in 1946 and the company gave the land back to the village. Robert was clerk of the parish council at the time and involved in the energetic money-raising that went on to have the quarry filled in, grassed over and turned into the splendid recreation field which is still used today.

There was a pond on Robert's own land which had a six foot wide causeway running through it. It was paved with egg-shaped pebbles, evenly matched and beautifully laid, and widely believed to be of Roman origin. The close proximity of the old Roman road, Dere Street, leading to Aldborough with its well-preserved remains of a Roman settlement (Isurium), would support the theory. Robert is also convinced that the semicircular, tiered garden rising up behind a neighbouring farm marks the site of a Roman amphitheatre.

In 1960 Robert's pond was filled in using material from the excavations involved in widening the A1 trunk road. He watched as truck loads of earth were tipped into his pond and was amazed to discover that it took 3,000 tons to fill it up – "Oh, it won't take much to fill up that little pond," his fellow farmers had said. Amongst the stones and rounded pebbles typical of the area there appeared in one truckload a large blue rounded stone like a big fat cushion, weighing at least two hundredweight and of a most amazing colour – a beautiful azure blue. It is all grassed over now with no sign of stone, pavement or pond and only Robert's memories remain.'

LIFE IN GLAISDALE

'In the village of Glaisdale in the 1920s and 1930s there was not much need to go to town. We were quite self-sufficient with our own doctor, dentist, butcher, baker, draper, blacksmith, tailor, cobbler, grocer, builders and joiners.

The doctor had a surgery in a cottage next to the post office. He visited it three times a week; there was a waiting room, surgery and a small dispensary. Further along lived the tailor. He could be seen through the window sitting cross-legged on a big table sewing, with a black stove behind him for warmth. One of the three village postmen was also a tailor and also the Registrar for Births, Deaths and Marriages. The post arrived by rail each morning and was sent each evening to Whitby the same way.

The station was a busy place. Always lovely fires in the waiting room in winter and spotlessly clean. The gardens were immaculate and the station was awarded a "best kept" certificate. There were always animals going to market and goods trains passing through. Railway coaches for campers in the summer were stationed just above the cricket field beyond.

Travellers came through with their wares. A draper who came round with his packs of clothes caused many a smile with his well known remark, "My wife wears those". Another called Zacky Swales came with a huge basket of pots balanced on his head. It was well known that he spent most of his time in one of the three local hostelries. One of "mine hosts" wives always wore a man's flat cap with her hair hanging down in a pig-tail. Another old character who sold his wares around the farms was called Cunny Dale. He was a little bent old man who dressed in black, complete with a bowler hat and a button-hole, and invariably a dewdrop on his nose. In his spare time he collected old broken pots with which he made a path that was known as the China Path.

In the village there was a sweet little old lady, Miss Polly Appleton who always decorated the baskets used for collection on Anniversary Day at the chapel with hundreds of pansies. The organist there was a Miss Dale who was renowned for her rock buns!'

OLD TIMES IN HOVINGHAM

'It is now over 80 years since I made my first visit to Hovingham and I have had a love affair with this village ever since I can remember.

My paternal grandparents came to Hovingham from the East Riding over 100 years ago and when they arrived (my grandmother told me) they had a Ploughing Day, which meant that the local farmers ploughed, and provided the horses and labour, and the incoming farmer gave the meat and drink – this kindly gesture continued up to 60 years ago.

There were the Hirings held at Malton and other market towns at Martinmas when the farmers and their wives sought new workpeople – the shepherd had a tuft of wool in his hat, or carried a crook, the carter held his whip. When the engagement was finally agreed a "festen penny" was paid. This could be a shilling, or even more; then – off to the fair to celebrate before starting the year's work. Some older residents, having spent their lives in farming, remember workmen who lived in and, not changing farms, being re-engaged from Martinmas each year.

An elderly resident told me about the Oddfellows Feast and Shepherd's Walk – this must have been an impressive sight when, with a band, and banners flying and sashes swinging, they toured the village, coming finally to the Worsley Arms, where ale was brewed and at this time given away free to all who took a jug for it.

On the top green, and down the village street, where our village hall now stands, booths and sideshows were set up – hurdy gurdies added to the festive atmosphere, and I was told that a certain Bessie Warwick used to come out from Malton with her stall on which the attraction was two-coloured toffee, which was produced by "pulling" this delectable sweet-meat until it became two shades of brown – light and dark.

As children we used to arrive at Hovingham Spa station on the four o'clock train. We were met by our Grandma and Bob Hill, and he would collect our big black shiny trunk and take it on wheels to the farm. Our tea was always laid ready on a snow white cloth, with home-made bread and butter and jam; home-cured ham and cheese-cakes – just scrumptious!

At one time Hovingham Spa station was a very busy place. Large consignments of limestone were despatched by rail from the quarry to Middlesbrough (Dorman Longs) until Dr Beeching used his axe and the last rolling stock came through in 1965 and the station closed.

There are still medicinal springs in the grounds of Spa House about one and a half miles from the village and at one time it was hoped to develop Hovingham as a spa, but this did not mature.

Hovingham was almost completely self-supporting when I came as a little girl, with tailor, cobbler, watch and clock repairer, saddler, registrar and at least four grocer's shops. In addition, a number of salesmen came round – Tommy Hurd, the old Scotch Draper, came out from York. It was so exciting when he unpacked his bags and cases, miniature Aladdin's caves with materials, haberdashery, inser-tion through which to pass a pretty ribbon and lace with which to trim your underwear and, joy of joys, broderie anglaise for your camisole or underskirt. Miss Wrangham and Freddie Marwood also came out from Malton and did a good trade, especially amongst the farmers' wives around. Mr Price came with his crockery and pots and pans; the fishman came and the carrier brought things from Malton.'

THE SQUIRE

'Sir Robert Walker was born in 1890 and succeeded to his father's title at the age of ten, in 1900. He lived in a beautiful hall at Sand Hutton and owned much of the surrounding countryside. During the First World War, Sir Robert joined the Coldstream Guards and was thought by many to be the wealthiest man in the army at that time. Following the war it is said that he never refused an ex-Coldstreamer a job on his estate.

One of York's horse-drawn trams in 1908, and the station road in 1913, showing the city walls.

He was a great collector of fire engines, originally horse-drawn, but later pulled by a Daimler lorry. These were widely used in and around Claxton. Men from the estate acted as firemen. Sir Robert's main interest was the light railway which he built round his garden and park, later extending this to Warthill and Claxton. The railway was used to carry timber and bricks made on the estate. Some open carriages with slatted seats were used for the village people, but there were armchairs for the more genteel. Sir Robert died in 1930, and his son, sold it to the Church Commissioners.'

YORK SHOPS AND SUNDAYS

'I was born in 1897 and remember as a child being taken for a ride into York on a horse-drawn tram which was pulled by two horses and had a driver and conductor. Behind the driver's seat were steps leading up to the open-topped upper deck. York's horse-drawn trams were discontinued in 1908 when electric trams were introduced. These went from York to Fulford, Dringhouses and Acomb and took workers to Rowntree's chocolate factory. It cost fourpence for a transfer ticket which enabled passengers to change trams and travel in any direction.

I worked in Brown's department store in York from 1913 until I married. The hours were long – weekdays 8 am to 7 pm and on Saturdays we worked from 8 am to 9 pm. We did not have to wear a uniform, but had to be neatly dressed and the junior assistants were in awe of the male shopwalkers who made sure they did their work properly. Woe betide them if the rolls of oilcloth were not carried out before 8 am, to be displayed by the entrance (oilcloth was a waterproof fabric, often prettily patterned, used to cover a kitchen table). My friend worked in the lingerie department and she had great trouble with the metal cylinders which travelled on overhead wires from the shop to the cashier, carrying money. She was too short to reach them so she was provided with a strong wooden box to stand on. All the shop assistants used to walk or cycle to work, sometimes many miles from the outlying villages.'

'Before the Second World War, York had shops of every description, each one a specialist. Most shopkeepers lived over the shop and I loved to visit my schoolfriend's home in lofty Georgian rooms above her father's furniture shop. The city was alive and families made communities round each of the many city churches.

When I was a little girl my mother used to take me to York market which was held in Parliament Street. We would go to Mr Cohen's stall where Mother sorted pieces from a huge basket of remnants and bought them for cutting up to make "clippie" rugs.

My neighbour told me how she and her sister used to set off from Poppleton at 6 am and walk four miles in to York, carrying their baskets of eggs, butter, jams, curds, cakes and chickens to sell at the market. They had to hitch their skirts up to keep them out of the mud as the roads were not very good. The farmers' wives would sit together to sell their wares and have a good gossip.

After shopping in York we travelled the four miles back to Poppleton by train or on foot. There was also a tram which took us part of the way. If we bought anything heavy or bulky, a carrier called Mr Armstrong would transport it home for us. He left his horse and cart in the White Swan Inn yard, and we had to label our goods and leave them on the cart. At about 8 pm the same night Mr Armstrong would deliver our goods and we paid him sixpence for the service.'

'The resident regiments stationed at Fulford Barracks, York used to have an annual parade through the city, ending with a service in the Minster. This was always a spectacular event which took place on a summer Sunday when huge crowds turned out to watch.

When I was a young girl in 1938, my mother took me to York to watch the parade. It was special to us as my 17 year old brother had joined the Territorials and was to play trombone in the band.

It was a beautiful, sunny day as we stood by the barracks gate and watched the Hussars, Royal Artillery and Cavalry, all in magnificent uniforms, glittering gold and red in the sunshine. I nearly burst with pride as I waved at my brother (much to his embarrassment!) as he marched past, resplendent in his red uniform.

The war came soon after and we never had a Military Sunday in York again and for a very long time never saw soldiers in anything but khaki. I will always remember that special day – but it has left me with a tendency to be tearful whenever I see a military band on the march.'

RESCUE TEAMS

'My father was a member of the Whitby area Rocket Rescue Team, with horses and waggons to carry their equipment and provide pulling power in a rescue. They were on call at all times to help ships which had gone aground near the shore, and anyone stranded on the high unscalable cliffs or inaccessible beaches. The team operated from the cliffs or the shore and would shoot a line onto a stricken vessel so that the crew could be brought ashore by breeches buoy.

In 1930 the team was called out to rescue a ship stranded off Kettleness Point. In appalling weather conditions the team struggled up and down the treacherous cliffs to perform a dangerous and heroic rescue.'

The Rocket Rescue Team in 1930, brave men relying on horsepower to get them over the rough coastal terrain.

'In the winter of 1950, all the fishing cobles of both Staithes and Runswick were at sea when a severe northeasterly gale sprang up, making it impossible for the boats to get back into the harbour.

The Runswick lifeboat, the *Robert Patton Always Ready*, was needed but the lifeboat crews were all out in the cobles. The lifeboat mechanic and only one other man crewed the boat and the women of Runswick hauled the ropes and managed to launch the lifeboat. It reached the fishing fleet, picked up its crew members and escorted all the cobles back into Runswick Bay. All were safe.

The women's efforts were rewarded by the magazine *Sea Breeze*, which presented each one of them with a brooch to commemorate the event.'

THE CIRCUS AT LITTLE OUSEBURN

'A farmer called Mr Barrett lived along the Thorpe Underwood road from Little Ouseburn. He was circus mad and trained animals in his barn. He had an elephant and there was a team of Canadian trick riders on horses who were called "The Yeldings". The team lived in a caravan in the winter and would sometimes ride the horses through the village without saddles and making "yippee" noises. We children were told not to be frightened as it was only a bit of fun and they meant no harm. One of the team, Freddy Yelding, fell from his horse in the ring and was killed.

The elephant keeper would walk his charge along the Little Ouseburn street until they reached the shop (this faced what we would refer to as the Police House). Here the lady of the shop would be waiting, and I remember she wore a cap with lace trimmings, and she would give the elephant a bun. Sometimes the elephant would be walked across the little bridge into Great Ouseburn.

We lived in a house facing the school and when my mother was widowed friends suggested that she set up a little shop in the front room of the house. Here she had sweet bottles in the window and stocked many small items which children could spend their pennies on. She also baked and sold her own bread. Once a week when the circus was at home I would take bread down to the farm in a large basket. I would have been about twelve then and was rather frightened as I thought the animals would be in the field and the elephant might try and get one of my new loaves with his trunk.'

LIFE AS A FISHERMAN'S WIFE AT STAITHES

'A fisherman's wife had a very hard life in the 1920s. Not only did she have to care for home and family, but she also worked very hard to help her husband.

It was the women who climbed the steep bank up to the railway station on the cliff top to collect the barrels of fish for bait brought by the train. They then carried the barrels on their heads, protected by a circle of twisted rope, back down the bank and through the cobbled streets to the harbour. This was heavy work in all weathers, but it did wonders for the women's posture!

Once the barrels were down on the quay side, the women would start baiting the lines, cutting and fastening small pieces of fish to the long ropes. In fine weather this was a pleasant job as they could exchange a joke and have a gossip. Bad weather, however, meant working alone in their cottages or in a cold fishing shed.

Fishermen's wives had the job of "skainen" (mending) the nets with large shuttle-like tools. The nets were draped over the fence and the shuttles woven across the holes – like tatting rather than darning.

My grandfather was a fisherman and he wore "ganzies" (thick jumpers) which were knitted by my Grandma. She also sewed the long-john trousers worn beneath his waterproofs. He needed lots of pairs because the waterproofs did not live up to their name and his long-johns were regularly wet through.

When my Grandma was confined to bed after having a baby, her sewing machine was taken to her bedside and she was able to sew Grandfather's long-johns. No time was ever wasted and when the daily tasks were finished the women would sit outside their cottage doors and get on with their knitting.

The fishermen's wives always helped to launch the fishing boats and when the boats returned from the sea, the women were waiting on the beach to pull them ashore. They would then unload the catch, gather up the lines and nets and sort them out for the next day's work.

My mother was a teacher at Ellerby, a hamlet near Runswick Bay. She read in the school log book dated around 1909 – "Runswick children absent today. Gone to the woods for heazels (hazels) to make pots."'

THAT WINTER – 1947

'Our son was born in October 1946, and until he was christened at Easter 1947, we endured the most horrendous winter in living memory.

It was an ordinary sort of winter until the end of January. A neighbour of ours, who had married a GI, left Forest Moor with her eight-month old daughter to join her husband in America. The night she left – 31st January – it was snowing heavens high. As we waved her goodbye huge snowflakes drifted down. That night was the beginning of a white world which persisted relentlessly until March.

The snow came down, often at night, and the severe frost froze it. It was impossible to keep paths and roads clear.

We lived in a rented Victorian semi, lit by gaslight, with an open coal range and an outside water lavatory. We had no electricity, no central heating, and when once the lavatory froze that was the way it stayed. Every time we used the loo we took a bucket of hot water to put in the overhead tank, so that it would flush. One morning I went up the yard and couldn't open the lavatory door – the guttering had fallen down with the weight of snow, and blocked the doorway.

Our baby son slept in a cot in the same large bedroom as us, facing north with no heat. I made him a sleeping bag out of a wool blanket, and before he went into his cot I put a hot water bottle in, and took it out as he went in. He wore a wool vest, cotton nightie, a nappie and a wool cardigan – and he survived the cold.

Fresh vegetables became very scarce, and we had to rely on tinned ones. It was just after the war and food in general wasn't plentiful, with some still rationed, so this was a further complication. After a few weeks of this severe weather, one of our neighbours who had a market garden was able to make a path to her garden and found a bed of cabbages. She cleaned off the snow and chopped off the cabbages with a small chopper. They were very frozen but made a lovely change from tinned peas.

So it went on, week after week of snow and frost; the roads were never clear, but the footpaths were sometimes just passable. It was no fun pushing a pram over frozen snow – more like corrugated iron.

At first everything came to a standstill; no mail, no coal deliveries, very few buses, which could not negotiate the hills, and shortages of all kinds. Eventually everyone found ways of coping. I remember our jovial postman delivering the mail on foot, feeling his way with the aid of a long staff.

Some mornings when the sun shone after a night of snow and frost, the sight was breathtaking, but we were too concerned with everyday living to appreciate it. The river Nidd at Knaresborough was frozen over to a considerable depth for several weeks and people were able to walk on it and skate and make slides – great fun. However, after many difficult weeks the thaw came. How gratifying it was to find that when the snow left the garden there were snow-drops in full bloom, and the grass looked so green. After the thaw came the floods, but that's another story.

The heating boiler in Knaresborough parish church had frozen up so all christenings had been postponed, but on Easter Sunday, 6th April, our son was christened, along with 13 other babies.'

'When I was 14 years old I used to make butter on our farm at Ugthorpe and go to Whitby market to sell it, many a time at one shilling a pound. By 1941 we had, however, given up making butter and had started to sell milk to the dairy at Whitby. In January 1947 we were completely cut off by snow for three months. When we were able to get our milk away it was taken by horse and sledge about four miles to a pick-up place. If you weren't there when the milk waggon dropped off your cans, someone else would be sure to have gone off with them. During that three months I had to go back to making butter, but all I could do was give it away to friends.'

'In the severe winter of 1947 West Burton was virtually cut off to all transport, because of the heavy snow and the high drifts. Each day the villagers dug narrow tracks through the snow but these would be covered overnight with further falls of heavy snow. Because of the high drifts, farmers had to walk on top of the walls to try to reach their animals. Many sheep were lost because they were blown over and quickly covered by snow. The snow had started to fall in January and could still be seen lying around in May.'

The winter of 1947 brought flooding to many areas of York as the snow melted.

'Holidaymakers coming to stay at Runswick Bay used to come by train to Hinderwell and walk the remaining distance, about a mile, to their destination. Luggage could be sent in advance by rail the previous day and was transported by horse and cart down the old Runswick Bank which was very steep and hazardous. Coals were delivered the same way and coffins too were brought out of the village by horse and cart.

In the winter of 1947 all roads out of Hinderwell were completely blocked for eight weeks, but we still had the railway line at that time. Bread, provisions and coal were brought in by rail and we had to fetch our own coal from the station on sledge. Workers were able to get to their jobs in Whitby, but only averaged a three day week. There were two tunnels on the line between Hinderwell and Whitby and they were blocked by blizzards every other night. Men would have to spend all the next day digging out. The going rate for snow cutting was one shilling an hour.'

'In March 1947 I was living in York in a house only 50 yards from the river Ouse. The whole of Yorkshire had been deep in snow for several weeks and when the thaw came the Ouse began to rise rapidly, swelled by the melting snow from the tributaries in the Dales. Soon large areas of the city were flooded and although my house was raised we began to take precautions.

Sandbags were piled round door steps, large items of furniture were put on bricks and smaller items were taken upstairs. Next morning my family went off to work – wading down the street in wellingtons – and I stayed at home. Gas and electricity were cut off so I started to cook the dinner in two saucepans on the open fire. After a while I heard a sizzling noise and to my horror I saw the water coming up through the fireplace – it put the fire out and soon covered the floor. The dinner was just about cooked, so we sat on the stairs to eat it.

We waded out of the house and onto the garden wall and 'tight-rope walked' to the shallow water higher up the street. There we were rescued by a coal cart, with the poor horse knee deep in water!

Four days later we were allowed back. The water in our rooms had been three feet nine inches deep and we had to wash the slime from the walls and floor with a hosepipe. We were allowed extra coal and kept our fire going continually to dry the house out, but things left in a cupboard next to the fire turned green overnight.'

CHURCH AND CHAPEL

Sundays were truly days of rest for most families, and attendance at church or chapel a regular part of life. For the children, Sunday school provided what for many was the only outing of the year, eagerly anticipated and well remembered.

SUNDAY AT WELBURN

'We lived in York but now and again our parents rented a small cottage for a short holiday in the village of Welburn near Castle Howard. This was in about 1914. How we loved it: so much to see and do during the week, but Sundays were different.

The village street was silent and deserted except for a woman's occasional visit to the pump for water, and the comfortable clucks of a broody hen, hunting food for her chicks, and the raucous call of her spouse the cockerel. The scent of woodsmoke filled the air, spiralling upwards from cottage chimneys as the preparation for Sunday dinner got under way.

Then, as the church bell began to toll for morning service, the children slowly emerged, the girls in best dresses and starched white pinafores, and boys in Sunday best attire. They were followed by the grown ups. Then down the road came marching a brass band followed by other boys, all in neat uniform and pillbox hats, marching from the nearby reformatory.'

AT CHAPEL

'Carperby had a Primitive Methodist chapel built in 1826, a Wesleyan chapel built in the 1890s, and a grand Quaker meeting house built in 1864.

In the chapel, each family claimed a pew, and if a visitor happened to sit in that pew he or she would be asked to find another seat. A lot of children in the village attended chapel Sunday school in the morning at the older building. Then in the afternoon they attended church Sunday school, walking the three quarters of a mile across the fields to Aysgarth. Sunday best was always worn and the children were expected to attend until they were 14 years old. The perk of going to Sunday school was the annual trip with their parents to Redcar. For many families this was the only day away together in the whole year.'

PREACHERS AND FESTIVALS

'I am 101 years old now and remember that in my youth magic lantern talks were very popular and given at Carlton by a minister named Davies who tapped a stick for the next frame. Mischievous boys were apt to join in by tapping at the wrong place and causing confusion!

Harvest festival was a great occasion when a table was set up below the pulpit for the meal in chapel for a one-off celebration. White moss was collected from a creek on Carlton Bank on which to lay the fruit to keep it fresh. The produce was given away to sick people in the village.

I attended chapel from an early age along with my brothers and sisters, my father driving the trap drawn by a "spanky" pony. Father had decreed the family should attend chapel since the church had been burned down. The journey was quite an adventure, especially in winter along a muddy unmetalled road. We were dressed appropriately for the weather, but always in Sunday best. Bicycles were used in summer. Services were held in the afternoon and evening. The chapel was heated by a cylindrical coke stove which needed stoking halfway through the service. Preachers normally took both services as they would walk, cycle, ride horseback or be dropped off there by the circuit trap. There was quite a competition to offer hospitality to the preacher – usually Sunday tea, or tea and supper. There were many preachers, I remember, including a schoolmaster from Ayton who always prefaced his sermons with "Now then..."'

'On Whit Sunday in the 1940s all the Sunday schools in Selby paraded round the town. Each school had a banner and some had decorated a lorry to sit on. The procession was led by the Salvation Army band and we would stop at different places to sing. This was an occasion for new clothes.'

MIDSUMMER FESTIVAL

'The Midsummer Festival in Gunnerside was always held on the first Sunday in July. For weeks before this event great house-cleaning took place, with walls scrubbed after being treated with soda. New rigouts were purchased. Large bakings were done for the tea, curd cheese cakes, white sugar biscuits and secret cakes etc.

The preacher and his wife were entertained by various families for the weekend. The children's service was at 2 pm followed by a love feast at 3 pm; and then at 6 pm there was community singing followed by a service at 6.30 pm. The choir along with a special singer led the service. The congregation always overflowed, because the families of old Gunnerside people who had left the Dale when the lead mines closed, came back for this reunion year after year, a tradition which still goes on. After the service the local people provided the supper in their own homes, and no one went without.

At 3 pm on the Monday following, the children of the village marched behind the Band of Hope banner through the village led by the Gunnerside band. After a short service in the centre of the village where music was provided on the chapel harmonium, usually played by Cissie Rutter, there were sports and the children were fed with spice buns and milk on Brow Top. At 7 pm the visiting minister gave a lecture in the chapel, which again attracted a good congregation.

The Shortest Day Festival (21st December) was a smaller version of that at Midsummer; tea and supper were provided in the chapel (always ham sandwiches), silver urns and copper kettles were the order of the day.'

SUNDAY SCHOOL DAYS

'When I was three years old I was sent off every week to Sunday school, half a mile away in Patrick Brompton, with my older sister and brothers. A local schoolteacher and her daughter took the classes. They lived in a house behind the church, and the children from Newton le Willows liked to get there early so that they could call for the teachers. We were always amused by the fact their cat slept in the oven at the side of the fire.

At Easter the teachers came to Sunday school with a basket of brightly coloured eggs, paste eggs, to give to the children. They were red, green, yellow, purple and orange. We never did find out how she achieved this. Our mother dyed them with flowers such as primroses, gorse flowers and onion skins, or wrapped in red flannel, tied up with cotton and then boiled. It had to be red flannel because that had the most dye in it. On Easter Monday we would go off to the nearest hill, armed with bread and butter, and a twist of paper with salt in, and we would spend hours rolling the eggs.

Once a month there was a family service taken by the vicar. On this day, if the font lid was up we knew there was going to be a christening. We never stayed to christenings, so this remained a mystery to us for many years.

On Mother's Day we were always thrilled if we could find purple violets on the way home from Sunday school, to take home for Mam; they had to be purple as the white ones were too common.

We had a Christmas party in the church school room on Boxing Day. We would set off at three o'clock with our bags of cakes for tea, and there was always a floor to ceiling Christmas tree, which was something we didn't have at home; we had to decorate a piece of holly branch. At the party we played "Pass the parcel", "Gathering nuts in May", "A-hunting we will go", "Postman's knock" and many more. Father Christmas came to give us presents, and books were awarded for attendance. These were very prized possessions. We ended up with indoor fireworks.

In summer we went to Redcar on a bus outing. This was a special occasion for us as it was the only time we went to the seaside. The beach in those days was covered in rows of beach huts, in which we children frequently got lost.

As we got older we joined the church choir, which meant attending morning service and evensong as well as Sunday school, and being at choir practice on Wednesday nights at the vicarage. In addition now we had the yearly choir trip to Scarborough.

Most of us continued at Sunday school until we left school at 15 years of age.'

THE OUTING

'I was the ninth child in a family of twelve at Claxton, and we all went to Sunday school. Once a year we had a picnic at Millington Springs. My father and other farmers yoked two horses to the rullies and everyone climbed on. There were poles at the back and front so if it rained we could put a stack sheet over us. The farmer's wife at Millington Heights boiled the water and tea was made in a bucket for our picnic by the side of the springs where we had been paddling.'

'One day a year in the 1920s all the Sunday schools in Easingwold, and most of the other people, went to Scarborough for a day's outing. This was the highlight of the year. We packed sandwiches, got our buckets and spades and off we went. We had a small railway in Easingwold which we called the "Coffee Pot", but it only went as far as Alne and then we were taken by another engine. When we all went on the outing there were far more carriages than on ordinary days, and it used to huff and puff so much we thought it would never make it.'

'Sunday school outings to Redcar were the highlight of the year for the children of Sowerby in the 1940s. Sometimes as many as 13 coaches would be used. The vicar would give every child a shilling on arrival in Redcar.'

'A good many of the local schoolchildren at Middleton St George were also Sunday school scholars. This was run by Mr and Mrs Carter; Mr Carter was the local joiner and undertaker. Each year we had a day's outing to Redcar. A special train was chartered at Dinsdale station to convey mums, children, babies in pushchairs, and picnic lunches. After swings and roundabouts, donkey rides and paddling, we bought a jug of tea from a stall on the sands. It cost one shilling and sixpence per jug and you got a sixpence refund when you returned the jug. One time, my young brother Edwin, aged two, tipped a spade full of sand into our jug of tea. Mother couldn't afford to buy another jug, so we just had to wait for the sand to settle!

Then paddling in the sea again, moving up the sands as the tide came in, and at 3.30 we children had to be along at Underwoods Cafe for our tea. Sandwiches, cakes, jelly and ice cream; we soon demolished the lot and then went back to the beach to look for our parents. After a last walk along the front and down the main street via the shops, it was back to the station to catch the train home at 6.30 pm, having had a marvellous day. We usually went home clutching a bag of candy rock. Then we could look forward to the Sunday school trip the next year.'

'Once there was a great day in Pocklington – the Sunday school treat. All the Sunday schools took part, a train was booked and virtually half the town boarded it, buckets and spades and sandwiches at the ready. We were off to Bridlington for the day. My husband tells me it was unbelievably quiet at home that day.'

THE ANNIVERSARY

'There being three chapels and one mission church in Staithes village, competition was fierce when it came to Sunday school Anniversaries, usually held in February or March. Weeks of preparation had been put in with the children learning the catechism, poems and songs for the events. All the girls wore white dresses and the boys white shirts.

The Anniversary commenced at 2 pm on the Sunday afternoon, the children being examined in the catechism by the Sunday school superintendent. Children "stood up" until 16 years old. After seven years' standing up they received their bible and hymn book. This service usually lasted one and a half hours then home for tea or if living on the "Bank Top" to one of your relatives for Anniversary tea. The Sunday evening events commenced at 6 pm but to get a good seat you had to be in chapel by just after 5 pm. The children sang and recited poems presided over by a visiting minister. During collection time, many times sweets were thrown from one side of the balcony to the other.

The events continued on the Monday with tea in the Sunday school; children were sent home from the village school early to get their tea and be ready for the evening. Grown ups followed in for tea after work. (In earlier days children had the whole day off school.) At 6 pm the evening commenced, again usually presided over by the resident minister. This time clapping was allowed so everyone received a loud ovation. About 9 pm weary children climbed down from the platform and were taken home to bed amid relief that no one had fallen off the platform and the "do you remembers" from older people and visitors. Chapel members were also eager to know how much money had been made.

One certain Anniversary a power cut occurred as the afternoon finished but the evening did go ahead in candlelight and the organ was pumped by hand.'

'The highlight of the year in the 1930s and 1940s at our Methodist church at Follifoot was the Sunday school anniversary. This was held in the middle of May, although preparations began long before.

Once the special hymn sheets arrived from the printers we began to practise. The hymns were good to sing, with rousing tunes and stirring words. The children were then given a poem or a song to learn, or a part to play, and I don't remember anyone opting out. This meant practising during the week with one of the Sunday school teachers after day school.

When the special weekend arrived the men of the church spent Saturday evening erecting the platform in front of the pulpit and over the altar rails. It had steps at one side and a rail around the edge. Sunday was very exciting with the Cubs, Brownies, Scouts and Guides parading with the band playing and flags flying. A visiting minister was usually invited to take the services, but the children were also involved in reading the lessons and taking the collection.

The main event was in the afternoon when the very young children sat on the platform. Mothers had been busy for weeks making new outfits. A frilly frock and a flower-decked bonnet was a must for the girls. These were proudly shown off as each child in turn sang their song or recited their poem. I was only three years old when I made my debut.

The evening service was conducted by the older children. We all looked forward to Monday after school when we met for the Anniversary tea, followed by a concert. Then the platform was taken down for another year.'

GETTING ABOUT

Most people got about by bicycle, by real horse-power, or by Shanks' pony in the early part of the century and the first cars were objects of some attention on Yorkshire's quiet roads. The country buses soon came to be part of our lives, and the steam railway has left many nostalgic memories.

THE ROADS

'My father who was born in 1908 tells how on the mile-long walk to school each day between Lilling and Sheriff Hutton, they would pass two old stone breakers wearing blue glasses who sat by the roadside chipping away at a heap of stones. These were brought from Flaxton station by horse-drawn waggon for the repair of the roads.

The broken stones were tipped onto the roads, soil was taken from the grass verges and scattered over the stones, then came the water cart to turn the soil to puddle. This was in turn pressed into the stones with a steam roller. When the depth of mud became too great, road scrapers drawn by men were dragged across the roads, the surplus mud removed and thrown back on the verges again.'

HEAVY TRAFFIC!

'I came to my present home at Fulford, on the outskirts of York in October 1935. We attended the St Lawrence primary school which was about two miles away and walked that distance four times a day unaccompanied. We thought nothing of having to walk. There were buses but we didn't see many on our daily journeys as the roads were almost deserted. The heavy traffic consisted of a greengrocer's horse and cart owned by Farmer Grey of nearby Heslington village, a horse-drawn coal cart owned by Percy Robshaw, and Mr Hollingsworth's pony and trap delivering milk from Fulford. These people were all local characters and known by all.

The tram lines to the Fulford Road tram depot were being removed at the end of 1935 and we were offered bags of tarred blocks for the fire at the princely sum of one shilling per brown paper carrier!'

33

'The only transport out of Bransdale was a big taxi which came every Wednesday to take people to the market in Kirkbymoorside, otherwise you had to cycle or go by pony and trap. It wasn't until after the war in the 1940s and 1950s that more people got their own cars. We used to cycle ten miles into Kirkbymoorside to the cinema or walk four miles over the moors to Farndale to domino and whist drives and dances.'

THE FIRST CARS

'When my grandfather got his car, in the early 1920s, roads were not always tarmacadamed in the Wharfe valley. It was mostly horse-drawn traffic, and all animals going to the cattle market were driven along the road. For this reason all private properties had gates which were kept constantly closed; and it was often possible to shovel up a little useful "muck" for the garden.

My brother and I had a favourite hobby in our school holidays in 1926; we would sit on the gatepost with pencil and paper and take down the numbers from the passing cars. I remember the excitement of dashing in to tell Mother when ten cars had gone by.

The numbers of cars soon increased. Motoring was so different; much slower of course, and less reliable than today. On steep hills such as Sutton Bank or Buckden Brow, we stopped to let the car cool down, and on occasion had to get out and push. In our car luggage was fastened with leather straps onto a folding grid at the back. The small back window had a drop blind, operated from the driver's seat with a cord; this was to cut out any bright light from a following car at night. All indications were done by hand, with the novel action for a left turn being to circulate your arm in an anticlockwise direction whilst making sure your passenger put his arm straight out on the left.'

'In 1912 when I was four years old, my father converted an old flour mill at Birstall into an engineering workshop. As soon as the war was over he made it into a garage and had the first Austin agency in the area. He also had a fleet of taxis. On my twelfth birthday I was allowed to work the petrol pump, which I did by winding a handle first one way and then the other while watching the orange-red petrol filling a glass cylinder. I learned to drive when I was 17 – no driving tests then – and would go with my father to drive the new cars back from the Austin works.'

'The year 1931 stands out in my memory, because that was when someone in the village acquired a car. On fine Sunday afternoons the farmer and his family would drive along the main street. The cry

A. Eyre & Co at Birstall had the first Austin agency in the area.

would go up that a car was approaching. Most people in the village had never seen a motor car before, as they were very few and far between and only the rich could afford them. As the cry went up, people would flock out to the unusual sight of a car going along at the rip-roaring speed of five miles an hour.'

ON THE BIKE

'In the 1920s when Dad worked in Darlington, he used to go on his pedal bike. In the hours of darkness he had a carbide lamp for the bike, a square lamp with a little door on the front with glass in it. Carbide was put inside and was lit with a match and this gave a very good glow. Dad had to clean it out every night ready for the next morning.'

'In 1950 I was living on a farm over a mile outside Snainton and I had to cycle into the village to catch a bus for work. It was getting near Christmas and very dark when I had to cycle my way home, but it was rare that I used my cycle lights as I knew the road with my eyes closed. One particular night I turned into our gateway and bang! I had ridden into something. When I collected my senses and looked to see what I had hit it was the local bobby, stood across the gateway leaning on his bike on "poultry duty" (looking out for poultry thieves). He had no lights on either. You can imagine the shock we both got, and I managed to get away without a warning.'

ERNIE THE MOTORBIKE

'It was a summer Sunday morning in 1933 and our father called to my twin sister and I to come and see "Ernie". We went towards the lean-to shed at the side of the house, and there he was – a big, old, secondhand motorbike. It was an Enfield and had big curved handlebars, to which was attached a carbide lamp which had to be topped up with water and lit by a match when lighting-up time came.

His sidecar was made of green wood and to get in, a door at the side opened. The seat and sides were padded in black. The horn had a big rubber ball fixed to it which was squeezed to make a honking sound to warn people we were coming. To our ten year old eyes he was a bit of a monster but he was going to give us lots of trips out so we were excited about him too. That summer saw us piling into the sidecar to go for picnics. Our mother sat in the seat, I perched on a box by her legs, and my sister had a tiny stool and sat right down at the front. She was most comfortable unless it rained, and then she got the backwash from the puddles. We all had to wear tinted goggles with fur to keep the grit out of our eyes. We must have looked like a load of beetles.

Father was a slightly built man and all the weight in the sidecar was a bit much for him at times. We didn't so much drive along, we wobbled, as he strove to keep the handlebars straight.

One evening it got dark, so Father pulled the bike onto some open land to start the lamp. It was dry. We watched as he strode away to a bush and came back with amber liquid in the empty milk bottle that Mother handed him. It was poured in the lamp and away we went. I wondered as we drove along if anybody could tell what we'd got in "Ernie's" lamp. We even caught fire one day when we were all overloaded but still came to no harm in him. He was a grand old bike.'

A WAY OF LIFE

'Crowes' bus was a way of life, now gone forever. It ran between Osmotherley and Stockton from 1926 and everything happened on that bus! A second-delivery mailbag was put on at Yarm for Hutton Rudby, chained to the seat, and the bus had to wait until someone came from the post office with the key. Doctors' prescriptions were sent to Swainby care of the driver. The daily papers for Potto were thrown out of the bus at the appropriate gateways. Wreaths and wedding bouquets were sent from Strikes at Stockton via the bus.

Goods were delivered to businesses in Stockton, shoes taken to be repaired and clothes to the cleaner's.

Nobody was ever left behind, though we were sometimes squashed in like sardines in a tin. Mrs Barker, the vicar's wife, was always running late and frequently sent a message to hold the bus as she was coming! One conductor helped scholars with their homework; he had a degree and should have had a career but had had a nervous breakdown and worked on the buses for many years.

When the Crowe brothers were haytiming their farm, the Crathorne blacksmith acted as relief driver. Harry Crowe's mother in law lived at Potto station and he often went in for a cup of tea, leaving his thirsty passengers waiting in the bus. The team of drivers seldom changed and they knew everybody. Those were the days.'

'Mr Appleby provided a bus service at Wass; on Monday it went to Thirsk and on Friday to Helmsley. The driver was called Billy and he was the most patient man I have ever known. He would carry and put on to the top of the bus all the crates containing rabbits, hens, ducks and eggs that were going to be sold at the poultry market. People in the village often stopped him to ask if he would shop for them. One farmer passenger was always late, ten to 15 minutes, and the driver just calmly waited until he came puffing along fastening his buttons and putting his tie on. A friend of our family was shopping one day in Helmsley and the bus left at the usual time. It had travelled half a mile or so when she suddenly shouted, "I've left the baby outside the newsagent!" Billy turned back and the baby was there, fast asleep.'

RAILWAY CHILDREN

'The station at Richmond was where the real railway children lived. Here our fathers worked for the London and North Eastern Railway company. We lived in the railway houses, and throughout our childhood the station and its surroundings were our playground.

The buildings, in stone, to a most attractive design, stretched along the platform. First the porter's room which smelt of Mr Jefferson's pipe, where oil lamps of various sizes sat on shelves in the gloom. Next door was the gents lavatory and then the parcels office. This was a favourite spot, harbouring all sorts of delights. Sometimes there would be day-old chicks cheeping away in their holey boxes, and we would poke our fingers through and feel their short, warm feathers, hoping to get a gentle peck. Better still, a black and white sheepdog from the Welsh hills waiting to be taken to a new home on a Swaledale farm. Friday night came the racing pigeons, with their iridescent plumage shining through gaps in the wicker baskets. There

Crossing the viaduct over the ravine leading down to Staithes in the 1930s. The cost of maintaining the tunnels and viaducts on this coastal line, and problems with erosion, led to the line's closure on 5th May 1957.

would be boxes and parcels of all shapes and sizes, and once a large trunk, destination India, with a label saying "not wanted on voyage".

Then came the booking office where passengers bought tickets at a little window at the far end. These were kept in serried ranks against the wall on each side, and as one was removed another dropped into its place. They were printed with destinations all over Britain, and it was quite a good lesson in geography to find out where they would be. In winter a blazing coal fire made the booking office a cosy place to be, and even better if we had been given a couple of potatoes from a waggon-load, and could roast them in the red embers.

Set into the platform, just by the waiting room was a weighing machine. Its cast iron floor moved when we bounced on it, and a long brass arm hovered gently before deciding how much we weighed, whenever we could persuade the porters to oblige.

The ladies room, at the far end, we definitely thought was for our exclusive use. It had a table and chairs and we could gather there on wet days. Over the fireplace was a mirror with the LNER legend on it, where we would check our hair. Most convenient of all it had three lavatories with "Please place penny in slot and slide catch" instructions on the doors. We always left one with the bolt forward to stop the door closing, so that we could spend a penny when necessary.

There was a WH Smith bookstall where we would stand and read the fronts of *Beano* and other comics, and if we had a penny to spare we could treat ourselves to a bar of Nestles chocolate or a Fry's Cream Bar from one of the slot machines. In the wall of the station two large bay windows were set, through which we could see the station-master's house. This enabled us to make ourselves scarce when he approached, though we were rarely chased away.

There were trolleys to ride on, and one of the pleasures for me was the coloured posters of various resorts at home and abroad, displayed on hoardings along the walls of the station. Above our heads as we played, geraniums, lobelia and other flowers cascaded from hanging baskets along the length of the covered platform.

Across the way from the passenger department lay the goods yard, where most winter evenings found us playing hide and seek. We could either hide in the half loaded box wagons, which were never locked, or better still crawl inside the meal warehouse. This building was secured by long tarpaulin blinds with wooden strips, fastened at each end with metal pins; very easy to undo. Inside, rows of sacks were stacked, three or four high, containing cattle cake, sheep nuts, calf meal, indian corn, kibbled maize and undecorticated ground-nut cake in large ribbed slabs, like Venetian blinds. We needed a torch to find our way about, and would fuss over the warehouse cat while we waited to be "found". Sometimes we would nibble at the various foods, and decided that animals did not have a bad diet.

The coal depot and yard were below the goods yard at the bottom of the hill, where we sledged in winter. In summer time it was our cricket pitch with stumps chalked on one of the thick walls which divided one bay from another. Fielding was quite a dirty job if the tennis ball we used was whacked up onto the coal heaps. Each bay had a name-board, giving the origin of the coal – Dawdon, Easington and Eden Hill colliery – the last being the coal my father favoured.

As Richmond was the end of the line, the engine had to disconnect from the carriages it had brought from Darlington, and move to the other end for the return journey. The highlight of the evening was to ride on the footplate for this trip. As soon as the driver was ready we were allowed to pull the whistle cord to alert the signalman to move the points to put the engine onto the other track. Once I pulled the cord so hard that the whistle stuck and tooted all the way round to the turntable, where we got out and pushed, and back to the tank to collect water, before being shunted back to the carriages.

One important event at which we felt we should have had front seats was the christening of the *Green Howards* engine, named after the Richmond based regiment. Everything was spick and span, with a carpet for the VIPs and rows of chairs. A bottle of champagne was crashed against the bright, shining, green paintwork, as we watched from the other side of the tracks, feeling excluded from our very own station. However, we did get a snippet of the green, white and gold ribbon, and a chance to climb all over the new engine, when the crowds had departed.

Catterick Camp, only three miles away, brought many troop trains, and the arrival of a new regiment was a red letter day. Hundreds of men would assemble in the station yard, after unloading all their equipment. This included the instruments of the band, which formed up at the head of the column, complete with mascot, perhaps a shetland pony or a billy goat, kitted out in magnificent regalia. Then the drums would roll and the whole army of men would swing out onto the camp road for the march to their barracks: alongside on the pavement we would keep time to the music, laughing and skipping until our legs began to tire. Then we would slow down, walking backwards, listening and watching until the last line of men disappeared from view.

Although still young children when the war started, we could no longer play as in the past. Now the station was geared up to cope with the huge increase in traffic, both goods and men. Hundreds and thousands of soldiers passed through, en route to the various theatres of war. Trains ran all night; sometimes I would awaken and hear voices, and from my window I would see a line of men sitting against our garden fence. All the station area was filled to overflowing, as the platform, despite its considerable length, could not accommodate them.

We had a new hobby – collecting regimental cap badges from boys only a few years older than ourselves. Before D-Day we watched the Canadian regiments, the Rocky Mountain Rangers and The Winnipeg Grenadiers depart. They brought the wonderful *Sir Nigel Gresley* engine to pull the train which took so many of them to die on the beaches of Normandy.'

HOUSE & HOME

THE WAY WE LIVED THEN

How different life was just a short while ago, when our houses had no mod cons and took all our time to keep clean. Every day had its own household routine too, and housekeeping was a full time job. Yet we remember our old homes with nostalgia and affection; maybe there were few roses round the door, but they were truly at the heart of the family.

LIFE IN THE FARMHOUSE

'In 1923, at the age of 15 I went to live with my aunt and uncle, who farmed a rented holding, part of the estate of Wigganthorpe Hall, near Hovingham.

I had to rise daily at 6 pm to set the breakfast table for Uncle and the two live-in workers (who ate at a separate table). They would eat after milking the herd. They brought the milk to the dairy, where I had to put it through a separator. After this I had to thoroughly wash all the parts and lay them out to dry. At the weekend the cream was put into a churn to make butter; this was patted into one-pound blocks and then taken, along with the eggs, to sell at Thirsk market every Monday.

The farm workers who lived in used a separate staircase to their bedrooms at the back of the farmhouse. They were rehired and paid annually on Michaelmas Day (September 29th). On that day in Malton there was a funfair, and the "hirings". This was where men looking for farm work would be approached by a farmer asking them what they could do, and how much they wanted to be paid for a year's work. Once agreed the farmer paid the "fest" (or "fast") – about £4, which secured the man's hiring. He would then be collected, along with his belongings in a tin trunk, and taken back to the farm in the pony and trap.

Food was good and plentiful on the farm. Though the butcher called every week, Uncle killed his own pigs. The stone floor of the dairy was covered in salt, the sides of bacon and the hams were then lain on it, and covered with more salt and saltpetre to cure. Later, when enough salt was absorbed into the hams and bacon, they were thoroughly washed and hung on hooks from the beams in the kitchen, often for months until needed.

Bread was made twice a week in the hot-air oven on the right of the fire oven range. A sack of flour was stored in a large bin in the corner. On the left of the range was a hinged, lidded water container, regularly topped up to provide all the hot water. Thursday was baking day for cakes, pies, custard pies, curd tarts, fruit pies etc. In season fruits were jammed and stored, and apples laid in trays in spare bedrooms to keep well. Oranges were a Christmas treat, bought at the market. Onions and red cabbage were pickled in large quantities and stored in the large pantry.

Every day the oil lamps had to be filled and the wicks trimmed; and coal came to Hovingham station from Bishop Auckland and was then brought by horse and cart to the farm.

In the herring season a man came to the village from Scarborough, with barrels of herring on his cart, and the housewives would take out a plate to buy 20 for a shilling.

We lived mostly in the big farm kitchen-cum-living room, the sitting room being used only for Christmas and Sunday tea. The "best room" – beautifully furnished – was never used, and seemed only to be a show piece.

News came daily with the *Yorkshire Post*, brought by the postman who crossed the fields from farm to farm.

Old clothes were kept, cut up, and on winter nights were turned into clip rugs, on hessian stretched on a wooden frame.'

NO CARPETS

'When I was a child in the 1940s there were no fitted carpets. We had a square carpet in the centre of the room and we would paint the floor round it with black paint. After one such painting my mother went shopping, leaving the floor to dry and on her return discovered that we had been burgled. However, the burglar was traced and caught by a trail of black footprints!'

SPARTAN DAYS

'We started off in our married life just after the war, in Starbeck, with a three piece suite, bought with my new husband's £100 savings, and purchased a secondhand red wool rug, a stork table and four chairs. We had an ancient black gas cooker, and an open fire with a tripod to put the kettle on. The sink was a low stone one, such as people put plants in nowadays, which had large brass taps. Our terrace house was rented to us by my brother, who wanted us out after a few months so that he could sell it.

He gave us £100 to move, and we were able to buy a three-storeyed terrace house from a neighbour for £1,100 with a mortgage. This was inconvenient and dark, but had the advantage of extra bedrooms, so that we were able to supplement our income by taking visitors and a lodger for a while. But we were troubled by cockroaches, so we sold it after two years and after much deliberation bought a very expensive semi-detached modern house with a large garden, for £1,950 – a sum we really felt we could not afford.

Our wage at this time was £10 per week, with some overtime, so we economised by doing our own decorating, and making our own bread and jam. We had no fridge or freezer and no washing machine. When we did buy a twin tub it lasted us 20 years.

During the time our children were little we had picnics and bonfires and walks in the country and up the Valley Gardens. We seldom took buses as we could not afford the fare, but we never felt deprived. The children often remember the "olden days" but they never mention the food. I was brought up on a diet of joint on Sunday, cold on Monday, shepherds pie on Tuesday, mince on Wednesday, rissoles on Thursday, sheep's head broth on Friday and sausage or savoury duck or fish on Saturday; so of course I followed a similar diet for my family, with the exception of sheep's head broth, which I loathed. The meals were always the same, followed by plum duff, jam roly poly, sago or rice.'

A FASCINATING HOUSE

'We moved to North Yorkshire in the 1950s, and started life in a fascinating house at Huttons Ambo. It was built in two completely different styles. It began life in 1600 as "The Cottage" – two up and two down with a two seater privy in the garden. This is still there but is now used as a store house for flower pots. Dung and straw were used for plaster on the kitchen walls, and daub and wattle internal dividing walls indicate the age of this part of the house. Sometime around 1800 a large addition was built providing two more bedrooms and two reception rooms. At what stage the bathroom was installed I do not know, but it was built in the passage between the two types of architecture, necessitating going in one door and out another – not very convenient as it contained the only "loo" to serve four bedrooms!

The kitchen was tiny, the larder huge and the scullery next door contained a "set pot" – an old fashioned copper with a fire underneath to boil the clothes. A hand-operated pump took the well water up to tanks in the roof to provide running water.

With three children it was vital for us to find ways to modernise this special house that we had fallen in love with. A further extension at the back enabled us to move the bathroom out of the passage, and have a downstairs cloakroom. By removing the tiny original staircase from the oldest part of the house, filling in the floor, and extracting

44

A fashionable wedding party at Knaresborough in 1928.

several ham-hooks from the ceiling, we also acquired a second bath-room.

The village builder told me how as a small boy he would listen for the previous owner to return in his pony and trap and rush to open the gate, which service earned him a penny! He also recalled all the boys climbing on the wall and pinching walnuts! The evidence of the days of the pony and trap is still there only nowadays the loose boxes are used to house motor cars and mowing machines.'

A SURPRISE

'In the 1940s I was asked to take care of an old lady for a short time. This entailed sleeping at her house while the lodger, who normally looked after her, was away. "Sleep where I sleep," said the lodger before he left.

My first night was quite a surprise. "Use the po because the lavatory is at the top of the garden," said the old lady, "and put your teeth in a cup." (I had all my own teeth!) The biggest surprise was when I asked where I was to sleep. "Get into bed with me," was the reply. I had expected the lodger to have his own room!'

THE COTTAGE

'One September in the early 1950s I was offered the use of a holiday cottage in Lealholm. I was told that it was remote, very basic, water from the well, heating and lighting oil and open fire, milk and eggs from the nearby farm. Food could be got from the butcher and the two shops in the village. With this information I packed a large blue suitcase with extra comforts, like towels, soap, spare warm clothes and non-perishable foods. This I sent by that now defunct excellent service "Passengers' Luggage in Advance", PLA on the label to await collection at Grosmont station.

Arriving at Grosmont in the early hours of the morning, having travelled overnight from the south coast, we (now two of us) were welcomed in the waiting room by a large fire, cups of tea, and the suitcase. At a more socially accepted hour the taxi came from Egton to take us up to the cottage on Oakley Walls. Once the cottage was spotted and a parking place found, bags, baggage case and sundry oddments were dumped at the roadside and the taxi sped away. We made a laborious way through the bracken as we were much encumbered. As we opened the garden gate a slight figure in a long navy blue raincoat with beret pulled down well, suddenly emerged from the side of the cottage, waited for us to reach her, then offered us the key and the inventory for checking, as we were complete strangers. It appeared that only the smaller items were to be checked as no doubt it was thought, correctly, that one would be unlikely to want to remove heavy furniture and carry it up the moor!

The kitchen was first entered. It was very low and contained a Valor cooking stove, one burner, a table on which there was a large basin, underneath a few cooking pots and dishes on a shelf. What caught the eye was an impressive row of galvanised buckets clearly labelled in white letters – "Drinking Water", "Washing Water", "Waste Water", "Coal", "Ashes", "Waste Tins etc" – all empty.

The sitting room seemed dark, the fireplace, part of an old range, black, the woodwork and curtains a dark green. It also seemed very overcrowded with a large roll top desk, two well filled bookcases, a wooden camp bed (ex army officer's of a bygone age), a teak table, four wooden chairs and a large, very rickety chest of drawers.

On the other hand the bedroom seemed quite roomy. A three foot bed, a much stronger chest of drawers, and a marble topped washstand, with various bedroom crockery. Having assured our guide that we had seen all we needed to see for the time being, and that we knew the use for which the buckets should be put, and how to use oil lamps, she left us as quietly as she appeared. We took a deep breath, and went outside to explore.'

OFF THE BEATEN TRACK

'As a new bride in 1946 I left my home in Letchworth, the first garden city in the country, to live on a small farm off the beaten track at Weeton. Facilities were basic in the extreme. I had to pump water from a well for all domestic use and, having learned to cook on a gas stove, I had to become skilled on a primus stove, a fire and a side oven. After cooking, out came the black lead! Toilet facilities were primitive – an earth closet with a wooden seat which needed scrubbing and eight-inch squares of the *Airedale and Wharfedale Observer* hanging on the door. When the birth of my son was imminent my husband had to cycle the two miles to the nearest telephone. Yet despite what today would be regarded as hardship, it was a very happy and satisfying life.'

'I had been used to all mod cons before I married a farmer in 1946, but I was really thrown in at the deep end when I found myself living on an isolated farm. Our nearest neighbours were one and a half miles away. There were no roads, only cart tracks, and I had six gates to open and close each time I went to the village to do the shopping on my bike. We had no phone, no mains water, no electricity and there were nine mouths to feed, including the farm hired lads living in.

We had a wireless that ran from an accumulator. This had to be used very sparingly, otherwise it would not last the week out before we could take it to the garage to be recharged. As all the men were cricket fanatics, I dared not use the wireless for *Music while you work*, as it would have been an unforgivable sin if the battery had run out when they wanted to listen to the cricket scores and the news at night.'

THE FARMER'S WIFE

'I was born on a farm in the days when farmers' wives worked very hard. As well as helping outside with the stock many, many hours were spent working in the house, with none of today's labour saving devices. Usually a maid was employed, who lived in, and she would also work hard all day for about ten shillings a week, and all her food of course.

Farm men often lived in the house and from having worked hard on the land all day they would have big appetites, so apart from looking after her own family the farmer's wife had lots of extra cooking to do. She would make big dinners, bake and make bread and teacakes, cakes and lots of pies, all in her coal oven. This often needed oven sticks, long pieces of wood, to create more heat than coal could give alone, and it needed to be cleaned out every week. Threshing, harvesting and haymaking were all busy times when the men worked long hours and a farmer's wife was kept busy providing the food. There was a lot of satisfaction in doing a worthwhile job, but now, as she switches on the light, puts on the electric kettle, toaster and oven, she may not be too nostalgic for the "good old days".'

A CHALLENGE

'In December 1945, my husband managed to find us rooms in Pocklington. They were in a dilapidated Georgian house which had seen past glories and had been overtaken by later development (it has since been demolished). The back of the house was now the entrance and we had two vast rooms on the first floor, in the front, which looked down a garden which we were assured "looked lovely in summer". Our kitchen was what had been the dressing room between the two rooms, and it sported a table, a washing up bowl and two gas rings! There was a lavatory with a cold tap on the half landing below, so cooking and getting washed was a challenge for an inexpert bride! Our landlady was kind and welcoming and always made us Yorkshire puddings on Sunday in the oven in her black range. The coal ration was a problem as we had to share hers and she would "go mad at it" when it arrived, leaving us very little with which to heat our vast rooms. I had no job at first, and took to going for healthy walks "stick gathering" so that we could have some sort of fire when my husband came home at night!

Came the great day when we found a house and put the few sticks of furniture we had managed to amass sparsely round it. It was a good solid little house in pale Pocklington brick, with two bedrooms, the third having been turned into a bathroom – but the flush toilet was in a back extension to the house.

The kitchen had a black range which didn't seem to have been used for years, a very antiquated black iron gas stove, and a set pot. "Ah," I thought, "I will show my husband how efficient I am." So I half filled the copper and lit the fire beneath it. It got going quite well, the water began to heat up nicely, and I put in the sheet. Disaster! What I didn't know was that the copper had rusted into a hole just above the original water line, and water and ash gushed out all over the kitchen floor – and it didn't do my precious sheet any good either!

The gas stove was also a challenge, at least not so much the stove as the town gas supply, which was adequate during the week but on a Sunday morning, when everybody put their Sunday joints in, everything was effectively at regulo 2. The solution I came up with was to get up at 7.30 am and with a bit of luck we got lunch at one o'clock.'

EVERY DAY OF THE WEEK

'Lady Cross, a new house built to replace an existing homestead, was erected at the end of the 19th century. According to family legend the old outbuildings, with the original farmhouse, were some several hundred years ago connected with Mount Grace Priory – hence the name "Lady Cross".

Although the house was "new" there was no bathroom and the toilet was an earth closet some 25 yards from the house! Unfortunately the farm was on the far side of the Whitby to Stockton railway line and mains water could not be brought across. A pump in the backyard provided all the drinking water, rain butts held water for washing and a pond provided water for the animals to drink. A very dry summer meant carting churns of water from a neighbouring farm across the railway to provide not only for our needs, but also for the animals. How we dreaded the limp action of the pump handle which indicated a droughty summer.

Each day of the week had its own importance. Monday – washday, Tuesday – ironing. The Rayburn (installed when water was eventually laid on) with its solid top certainly did a better job of heating the flat irons. Wonderful! No more black soot, that even the red embers of an open fire seemed to deposit. A good spit which jumped on the base of the iron indicated that it was hot enough to tackle the enormous clothes basket of neatly folded items, and provided that two or three hot irons were always ready to be exchanged for the first quickly cooling one, three to four hours would see the end of the task.

Wednesday – bedroom day. Having no electricity of course, every job was done by hand. Small mats were brought downstairs and banged against an outside wall "to get the dust out" while the large ones, and surrounding areas, were tackled with hand brush and dustpan. Dusting was done and areas washed, with particular attention being given to the jugs and bowls on the marble washstands and the under-bed pots. Everything was spring fresh and the windows were left open to give the bedrooms an air of moorland fragrance. The house faced south towards the Cleveland Hills.

Thursday – baking day. An after breakfast start with teacakes and bread to be put to rise in front of the kitchen fire. If the side oven was to be used in addition to the Rayburn, then the fire needed special attention to get the oven to the correct temperature – which simply had to be judged by experience. There were no temperature gauges or thermometers. Baking included scones, jam tarts, rock cakes, pies with apple, rhubarb or whatever was in season, plain cakes and fruit cakes. Baking was for the hungry farm workers and family. "No time for anything fancy," Mother would say. If a threshing day was due then baking took all day and perhaps a second day, as to feed 14 men was no mean feat, and the dairy and pantry were hard pressed to hold this harvest of the kitchen.

Friday – cleaning downstairs day. The kitchen was the family living room and was furnished with a long wood table which seated ten, or twelve with a crush, and which needed to be scrubbed. The coconut matting and rag rug were taken up and the floor brushed and scrubbed, the settee, chairs and grandfather clock were polished and the windows cleaned. The back-kitchen, with similar wood table and matting, was given the same treatment, and the pantry and dairy tidied and cleaned. The sitting room, with carpet and easy chairs, settee and piano was given the careful attention befitting the special occasion room, and when it was all finished the house smelt cleanly disinfected and the finishing touches were given to the door steps with a sanding block. The last Friday job was scrubbing the wooded seat of the closet after my father had emptied the "ash pan" and this and the floor were then strongly disinfected.

Friday, too, was bath night and all the menfolk vanished as female members of the family brought in the tin bath, filled it with hot water from the fireside boiler and, in front of a blazing fire, bathed in turn, starting with the youngest. Mother always gave the children a weekly dose of syrup of figs while in the bath! The females, having taken themselves off to bed, it was now the men's turn!'

I TOOK OVER

'My mother died when I was six years old and we had a succession of housekeepers until I was 16. Then just as I was thinking about applying to go to college I was brought in to take over. Usually in those days the only career you expected to follow was farming, so with few regrets I just got on with it; and I found that I got a deep sense of satisfaction from my work.

We lived in an old, damp, cold farmhouse with no electricity, so it needed a mammoth springclean every year. Feather beds out to air, carpets to beat and pantries to be lime-washed; the latter was an awful job for the lime burnt and dried your hands and stung your eyes. On the next washday there were the great number of blankets to wash, which were needed to keep the family warm in those near arctic winters.

One task I remember well was taking the food to the workers in the hay fields. Besides ourselves and the four men, there were people from the village and also the "visitors". These were the genteel people with second homes in the village who liked to help when they were there. I think we hoped some of the gentility would rub off on us. I never knew just how much food would be needed and was always glad to see that I had provided enough. When they had eaten I would help a while before collecting my basket and strolling home in the cool of the evening along the side of the Swale.'

TEA LEAVES

'Fridays were always clearing out days when everything had to be scrubbed. The farmhouse kitchen at Easingwold had long lengths of coconut matting on the floor that were always taken up and brushed outside. Tea leaves were kept for Fridays, as they were used to keep the dust down under the matting. When the tea pot was emptied we saved the leaves, and when we took the matting up we sprinkled them onto the floor before sweeping up, after which the floor was scrubbed on hands and knees.'

COVERING THE LEGS

'Victorian customs did not die with Queen Victoria, and as late as the 1920s my aunt was using covers on the legs of furniture. She said it was to prevent them from getting scratched, though originally it is said that legs were covered from a sense of modesty! The covers were of a linen material called holland. My aunt also protected her stair carpet by covering it with a strip of white material called drugget, which had a red stripe down each side.'

'ANGEL GUESTS'

'Swainby vicarage was literally "open house" in the 1920s, not only to parishioners but also to tramps. There were special marks on the telegraph poles from the entrance of the village right up to the vicarage as a code for fellow tramps. Mrs Barker, the vicar's wife, called them "angel guests" and gave them food and money, washed their dirty socks and gave them a clean pair to go away with. If their boots needed mending the vicar would send them down to the cobbler with a note saying he would pay the bill. Apparently, the tramps were expected to do a few jobs at the vicarage before they were given money, like weeding the drive.'

'In the 1920s and 1930s there were still many workhouses in use, where temporary accommodation was given to tramps. There was one at Otley and another at Wetherby, and these poor people regularly walked from one to the other, because the authorities kept them on the move. We got quite accustomed to them calling at our house during the day, asking for food and drink. My mother was very generous, often pouring tea into their tin cans and giving them teacake. They then left a message in the hedge bottom, and more would call to beg from her. Some were frightening to us children, as they were dressed in rags and often diseased, but mostly we just accepted them as normal.'

LIGHT, HEAT AND WATER

The things that we take for granted today were unheard of luxuries for most people a few decades ago. Everything had to be worked for, from gathering peat for the fire to fetching water from the well. No running water meant no indoor sanitation. Washday was perhaps the hardest task of all, taking all day and involving a great deal of heavy work for the women of the house.

COAL FIRES

'My father worked at the colliery and so part of his wage was a delivery of coal. Because it was "home coal" it didn't come in sacks but was tipped out of the lorry in a pile at the end of the row of houses where we lived at Brandsby, and we had to carry it in buckets round the back to throw into the coalhouse. It was a back-breaking job, and it always seemed to rain before we had finished. It was then time for a bath, which meant bringing the tin bath out from the cellar onto the hearthrug and filling it from the Ascot gas heater over the sink with the "lading can". The clothes horse, draped with the tablecloth, was the only means of privacy but it meant no one missed out on *Take it from here* or *ITMA* on the radio.'

'Like many others in the neighbourhood, my childhood home at Alne was heated by coal fires and each room had a fireplace as its focal point. When we were ill it was most comforting to have a fire in the bedroom on cold winter days, the crackling twigs and flickering flames providing company. We enjoyed looking for pictures in the fire, sometimes with a tingle of excited fear as we imagined monsters and even the horned devil. At the side of the fire in the kitchen was an oven and at bedtime the shelves were taken out, wrapped in blankets and placed between the sheets to warm the bed.'

PEATING

'In the earlier part of this century, and for generations before, the main source of fuel in most farmhouses in the upper reaches of the Dales was peat. This is a fossil fuel, derived from the remains of plants and trees which grew thousands of years ago, and is the main element of the soil on the higher moors.

The process of obtaining the fuel was begun in early June, considered optimistically to be a good month for drying! The peat was cut from a peat "pot", which was a long mound with a suitable edge, characteristic of the moorland environment, enabling blocks of the soil to be dug out. Each farmstead had its own peat pot near at hand. The blocks were cut out with a suitably shaped peat spade, laid out and sliced, and then spread out to dry. Hard work and rather messy. After a fortnight or so, dependent on the weather, the pieces were set up in threes and left to dry again for a similar time.

The fuel was brought down from the moor on horse-drawn peat carts. Most farms had a peat house in which to store it. It was very satisfactory to see this building filled to capacity as winter approached, and very comfortable to sit beside a peat fire, which if well stoked up threw out a great deal of heat. The only disadvantage was that it needed frequent replenishment or you found yourself sitting in front of a pile of ashes. The scent of peat smoke is unforgettable, a lovely smell compared with that of our modern heating boilers.

By the end of the Second World War, as other fuels took over, the gathering and burning of peat declined, until now it is a nostalgic memory with no part in today's farming.'

THE CHIMNEY SWEEP

'In the 1940s we had coal fires in our house at Batley, so each spring the chimney had to be swept. My mother always booked the chimney sweep to come very early, at 7 am, so the room had to be prepared for him the night before. The carpet was rolled up, all the furniture was pushed together and draped in dust sheets, the curtains and light shade were taken down and we all went to bed early, hoping for fine weather in the morning.

A sparse breakfast was eaten at 6 am, my father left (thankfully!) for work and we waited. We children were always in awe of the sweep and watched his arrival from the safety of dust sheet-draped furniture.

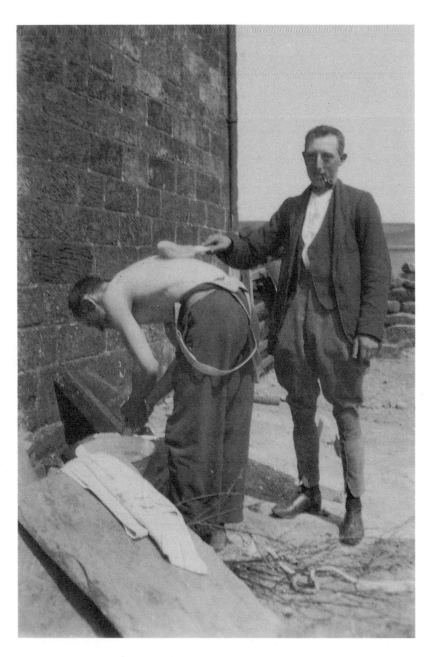

With no running water, washing meant a bowl of cold water outside after a day's work in 1933 at Cropton.

However early the sweep arrived, he always had a sooty face and hands, and wore a dirty, shapeless suit, a shirt with no collar and a flat cap on his head. The rods were tied in a bundle with the round brush sticking out and he carried sacks and a bag for the soot.

His first job was to push his brush into the chimney and put a piece of sacking over the fireplace with the brush handle sticking through a hole. He then screwed a rod onto the handle and pushed it up the chimney. Rod after rod was screwed on and pushed upwards while the smell of soot became stronger. At last came the moment we had all been waiting for. 'Run outside and watch for the brush," the sweep instructed us. Out we rushed and gazed roofwards at the chimney. Suddenly a cloud of soot shot out followed by the round brush. "We can see it!" we yelled to the sweep, and then we watched as the brush twisted round and disappeared back into the chimney. We had to keep well out of the way while the sweep shovelled the soot into his sack and cleaned up the mess!

Mother then gave him a cup of tea (in an old cup!), paid him, and off he went to his next house – face and hands blacker than ever.

Then began the cleaning up. The carpet was put out on the clothes line and beaten, dust sheets were shaken, the walls cleaned, and everything was polished. It took nearly all day and although everything looked bright and clean the smell of soot lingered for days. Thank goodness that it was only once a year.

Later on the sweep acquired a large vacuum cleaner to suck up the soot as he pushed the brush up the chimney. This meant that there was not so much mess and clearing up, and everything was back in place by lunchtime. The trouble was that the service cost more. On one occasion when there was a further price rise we were told that this was because the cost of electricity had gone up. He had left for his next job before we realized that it was *our* electricity he used!'

'Years ago when a chimney needed cleaning you either set it on fire or else you got someone in the village who owned brushes to come and sweep it for you.

My neighbour was asked to sweep a chimney which was completely blocked and the fire could not be lit. First of all he tried to use the brushes, but they would not go up. Not to be outdone he got an old hen, tied its legs together with rope and then climbed onto the roof and lowered the hen down the chimney. The terrified bird flapped and struggled so violently that she loosened the blockage which fell down the chimney. The hen was hauled back onto the roof, taken down to the ground and cut loose (according to the owner, no worse for the ordeal, only dirty and annoyed).

Close examination of the fibrous mass which had blocked the chimney revealed a football-sized tangle of hair. It seemed that the lady of the house was known for her long hair, which she brushed a hundred times each night. She put the hair from her brush onto the fire but the draught pulled it up until eventually the chimney was completely blocked.'

BEFORE THE ELECTRICITY CAME

'My husband had an uncle who in his youth, around 1916, set up his own supply of electricity. He fashioned a water wheel with empty tin cans attached to fill and turn it, driving a dynamo. This was near their house by the river Derwent.

An elderly lady told me that when she was in her teens, 1914 to 1920, she was given 20 or so hens to look after. Housed in an old building, they stopped laying eggs in October, but her inventive brother concocted a light to switch on every evening for a few hours. Realising that light also coming on in the early hours of the morning would further raise egg production, her idea was to modify an alarm clock so that string pulled by the turning alarm key would turn on the light. Her timeswitch, I was told, very rarely failed.'

'I remember the day my grandmother had a new invention when we went to stay. Electricity! My sister and I were so amazed we ran all over the house putting switches up and down, and if we moved a switch in the hall the light on the landing came on, and this could also be switched on or off on the landing. That was real magic!'

THE MILL COTTAGE

'My grandparents came to live in Salterforth in the early 1900s from Airton and Bolton Abbey, for work in the cotton mills. The only alternative was farming for the boys and going into service for the girls. At that time life revolved round one cotton mill owned by Mr Anthony Brown, and later by the Slater family. The mill owners also owned many of the cottages, so if work was found at the mill, the family could apply for a rented cottage.

Life in the mill was hard, working from 7 am to 5.30 pm and 7 am to 10.30 am Saturday morning. Many people were out of work and they would queue up at the mill door at 6.30 am. The manager would stand outside with pocket watch in hand and anyone arriving at one minute past seven would find a "sick weaver" on their looms.

My early recollections are of living in a two up and two down cottage rented from the mill at four shillings and twopence a week. The living room had a big iron fireplace with oven and side boiler which heated our water. This was filled and emptied with a ladling can. The fireplace was blackleaded every week and the brass rod (where we warmed our socks) polished. There was a big square table in the centre of the room covered by a velveteen cloth, beneath which we used to play and hide. The stone flagged floor was covered in matting – what a great day when we got our first carpet!

The kitchen was large with a slop-stone sink, a black gas cooker and a tin bath hanging on the wall. Friday night was bathnight, the bath placed in front of the fire, and filled from the side boiler. We were bathed and had our hair washed and wrapped in lovely warm towels. What luxury it seemed.

When my mother worked in the afternoons I was cared for by my Granny. She had white hair and wore a long black dress covered by a coloured apron in the mornings. After lunch she washed and changed and put on a snowy white apron. She let down her hair, brushed it and then coiled it into a bun, fastened by tortoiseshell slide and hairpins.

Monday was her washday, with dolly tub, scrubbing board and big wooden mangle. Tuesday ironing and Wednesday baking day. The smell of the bread baking in the oven are wonderful memories.

OUTDOOR TOILETS

'When I was about five and living in Escrick, our toilet was an earth closet across the yard. I was frightened to go when it was dark so my mother came with me and waited outside with a lamp. I would ask, "Are you still there?" every few seconds.

Emptying the closet was a weekly job for my father, who had to

An earth closet at Tholthorpe with three seats, one lower and smaller for children.

dig a hole each time somewhere in the garden. We had beautiful roses, but it wasn't a pleasant chore. Mother would say, "Don't do it now, Joe, there's someone waiting for the bus." '

'We had a two-holer toilet, and my sister and I used to go together and sit and chatter. The older sisters had to take the seat off every week and scrub it well. All the ashes from the fires were put on the waste from the let-down back. Every so often the whole lot had to be shovelled out, right down to the concrete floor, on to a cart to be taken away and buried, or spread.'

'The outside earth closet was reached by a path through bushes of lilac, holly and ivy. When it was dark a lantern was carried, and often the trip to the privy was a family affair as the wooden box had three seats – two full size ones and one lower and smaller. The walls were plastered and then rudded with red oxide wash.'

'When my sister married her nightmare was the lavatory outside called a "tippler". A wooden seat covered a nine foot deep pipe. This had a bowl at the bottom which tippled when full. All waste water from the house flowed into this, and the joke was to run the tap and tipple the loo when someone was sat on it. A horrible experience.

This was near Skipton. At Cawood some toilets were built over a very deep dyke, the water underneath varying according to the tide (the Ouse being tidal).'

'When my husband and I were engaged we used to visit his brother who had a farm. It was in a beautiful area, but the farmhouse was quite primitive. There was just one tap, on the kitchen sink, no hot water and no bathroom. The toilet was in the garden and was a three-hole earth closet – two large holes for adults and a smaller one for a child. Each week the waste was removed by council workmen, who opened the back and shovelled it into their lorry.

On one memorable occasion, my sister in law had gone to "spend a penny" and rushed out screaming. The men had been to empty it, but had forgotten to replace the back, and the farm dog had wandered in. When my sister in law sat down the dog pushed its cold nose up through the hole...!

The waste from my grandparents' sink and bathroom went into a septic tank, which was emptied each week by a large tanker which sucked out the contents. It was a malodorous event and everyone named the tanker "The Scent Bottle". Neighbours with a large family often used more water than the septic tank would hold and it would overflow for a few days before it was emptied. Not very pleasant on a hot summer's day!'

GETTING THE WATER

'In the late 1920s I lived on an isolated Wolds farm with no water supply. Several times a week a large barrelled cart, drawn by a horse, was taken down to the village of Warter (aptly named!) by one of the farm hands to be filled at the village pump. The water brought up from the village was strictly for drinking. Rainwater was collected in butts for washing.'

'Until mains water came there were water pumps sited throughout the village at Dishforth, and it is said that when the mains water did eventually come some of the villagers ignored the convenience of having taps in their houses. They still came to use the pumps because they said the water tasted better. The only reminder is Pump Yard.'

'The houses at the top of the bank at Harmby were supplied from a tank situated by the side of the main road – the water reached this with the aid of a "ram" which pumped the water into the tank. The rest of the village was supplied from a spring above the quarry, which also fed the three taps in the village up to the 1950s. The supply then came from Sowden beck on East Witton Fell.'

'Piped water and mains sewerage came to Poppleton in 1939 but each house had its own pump, the cottages shared, and everyone collected rainwater in either butts or a tank. This soft water was used for bathing, washing hair and special woollens like blankets. It was full of water beetles and mosquito larvae so it had to be drained through an old blanket before being put into the copper to heat up.

The village pump is an artesian well and never runs dry, and it is the most beautiful water to drink. Many folk collected a bucketful each morning for drinking, as often their own well was not so pure. The water was kept so good by the effort of old Mr Summerton, the "cowherd". Every morning after milking the farmers would send their cows on to the village green and the cowherd would pump gallons of water into the front trough which then ran through a pipe into the outer trough. The cows would drink and then they all ambled, munching the grass, up the village into the lanes where Mr Summerton sat on his stool and ate his lunch. Then he turned the cattle round and they all ambled back to the pump at 4pm where he pumped and they drank before dividing out to go to their own farm. The farmers paid the parish council a certain sum known as "cow gaits" to cover the costs – but it kept the green short and the water pure.'

WASHDAY

'The stone cottages in Well village look attractive, but earlier this century there were no mod cons. Carrying water was heavy work if you were far from the pumps in Church Street, by the almshouses, or halfway up the Bank. The water in the beck, which comes down from Holly Hill and runs the length of Church Street, was used for washing clothes.

Either a cauldron on the range-fire heated the water, and boiled the clothes, or some had a copper boiler built in an outhouse. A fire was lit underneath, and gradually the soapy water with the whites was brought to the boil and simmered for about 20 minutes. The boiling hot clothes were lifted out on sticks or wooden tongs, allowed to drain on a ladder-like frame, and then dropped into cold rinsing water. After wringing by hand they had another two rinses if possible, the last in blue (a dolly-blue block had been stirred in the water of the final rinse, and this helped to keep the whites white). Coarse soap was used for household jobs and extra washing soda was added to hard water. The soap was roughly cut into small pieces or grated to melt more easily, and a lump was rubbed onto dirty places. Stained clothes were soaked overnight to make washing easier. Table linen, linen mats and some petticoats were stiffened with a starch solution. This was made by crushing lump starch in cold water until smooth and pouring on boiling water till it thickened, and was then diluted according to need.

A mangle was used to get as much water out as possible – hence the need for linen (non-breakable) buttons on underwear – and the clothes were hung out to dry if at all possible. It was usual to have a creel hanging from the ceiling for drying or airing clothes. Flat irons were heated by the fire, and there was a constant fear of getting smuts on the clothes – particularly Father's Sunday collar, or a blouse front. The other hazard was scorching, as the methods of testing by putting the hot iron near the cheek, or listening to spit sizzling, were hardly scientific temperature gauges.

The hot soapy water was not wasted, but used suitably cooled for the coloureds, then for woollens; there was finally some left for scrubbing the floor, frequently flagstones, downstairs in the kitchen/scullery and washhouse.

A regular chore was cleaning the grate. Ashes had to be taken out each morning to an ash pit, and the fire alight early, as that was the only way to heat the water for tea and cook the breakfast. Tea had to be made for the bottle and 'lowance (food for his break) packed up, and all this done before the man left to walk to work by 7 am. Later the grate might have a quick brush to keep it presentable, but a regular clean ready for the weekend involved using blacklead such as "Zebra", applied with a rag or brush, and another brush to polish it, and any steel parts burnished with newspaper. Fire irons of steel or brass were cleaned and might be put away till Sunday, when they were brought out along with the Sunday hearthrug.

It was useful for housewives to have a set order for their work, but whatever else was done dinner had to be ready on the table when the man came home at noon, particularly if he had a long walk back to one of the outlying fields.'

'The washdays I remember are the days we washed the blankets. My mother brought extra dolly tubs in from the shed. It seemed to be never ending, washing them through all these tubs and the last one had to have ammonia in to keep the wool soft. We could not put them through the wringer as this would have flattened the pile, we could only squeeze them and let them drip dry. The clothes horse was called a "winterhedge".'

'As you can appreciate, washday took literally all day, as when the washing was dry the big heavy flat irons had to be heated up in the fire for ironing. Yet my mother always had a hug for me when I came home from school, no matter how tired she must have been after her busy day. We always had bubble and squeak for tea with

61

cold meat, and for afters a home-made rice pudding, done in the oven heated by the fire.'

'Nothing was wasted. When the washing was finished and hung out to dry, the hot water was used to wash the pavement outside the house. Then Mum would colour the steps with an orangey-brown stone which was called a donkey stone. Then everything was neat and tidy again and the next thing on the agenda was the evening meal. On Monday tea was always a large meat and potato pie, made from the leftover Sunday joint and lots of vegetables. A large onion was used to hold up the crust.'

'My grandmother at Wolsingham was only five feet tall and when Granny got possing, the tub used to dance round the yard!'

'I helped my Mum when I was a little girl but when I tried to use the peggy stick I hadn't quite got the knack and I remember my Grandma saying, "Nay lass, thoo daisn't use your behind to peggy – give it us here" and she took the peggy stick and showed me how to do it.'

FOOD AND SHOPPING

The kitchen was the heart of the household and every Yorkshire-woman worth her salt could fill it with the aroma of baking day. We may have had less choice in our food in the past, but it was wonderful family food, and many of us could turn our hand to making butter or cheese, or cope with the inevitable workload that killing the pig provided. Most shops delivered in those days, and tradesmen became familiar figures at the door.

COOKERS I HAVE KNOWN

'The first cooker I remember was a gigantic black range that presided over the kitchen of my childhood home. It was blackleaded with great vim and vigour every Friday and the hollow beneath the actual fire was actually whitewashed at the same time! It positively ate coal, two whole bucketfuls were needed to bring the fire up above the top bar. There was a sliding bar that came down from its upper innards, upon which would be hung the griddle when required. It had sundry trivets that could be swung over the fire and upon which stood the enormous black iron pans with hollow handles used for simmering broth and boiling vegetables. The oven, however, was decidedly temperamental, it depended very much on which way the wind was blowing as to whether we had an apple pie or an egg custard for tea. Not only that, but it smoked, so badly in fact did this occur that towards the end of its life it was pensioned off altogether except for Christmas Day.

The cooker upon which I first actually did any cooking by myself was the gas successor to the blackleaded monster and, oddly enough, I seem to remember more about its maintenance too than its performance. All its innards were removed en bloc every Friday morning (Fridays were traditionally dirty job days) and put into the big stone sink. A few handfuls of washing soda were added and a kettleful of boiling water poured over. There they steeped for an hour or so before being given a good scour and put back in time to cook the dinner. Often gas jets got blocked up in those days and had to be blown out. Oven blowbacks were common enough too, and lucky indeed was the housewife who hadn't lost her eyebrows at least once during the course of her career.'

'If you were going to do some baking and wanted the oven quite hot, you had first to make a good fire, and if you were in a hurry poke thick sticks under it. All the cooking had to be done with that fire. In the morning it had to be lit long before we wanted breakfast because it had to be burnt up long enough for the coals to be red, so that the kettle could be boiled on them, the bacon and eggs fried over them and the toast made near them. For making toast the bread was held on a special kind of fork with a long handle, so that you could hold the bread near the red embers without getting your hands burnt. There was no thermometer on the oven. You had to put your hand into it and feel if you thought it was the right heat.'

FISH OVER THE FIRE

'Many coastal recipes used fish, of course, and these were cooked over an open fire on "speets and racks". Two metal racks hung on the grate at the front of the fire and metal tongs or speets held the fish and were then hooked onto the racks to be cooked.'

TO THE BAKERY

'When our family lived in Price's Street, York, my mother would make up bread dough and put it into tins. Then my brother and I took it to the bakery in Nunnery Lane to be baked. We would transport it in a wicker clothes basket with a cloth over it and collect the cooked loaves later.'

BAKING DAY

'I may have been only seven or eight years old but I knew which day to visit Granny – baking day! This was held at least once a week and on that day I would run down the few hundred yards between our house and Granny's at Wigginton.

As it was after school time, the gas griddle on its stand would already be at the end of the table. The same gas connection also fitted the irons when the blanket piece was spread and the kitchen table became an ironing board, but on baking day the baking board was at the ready. It was a large board with three edges to keep the flow at bay, and the open side was large enough to allow the wooden rolling pin to work. I was tied into my pinnie, and given a metal scoop to get the flour. This was kept in a large sack, alongside one of wheat-meal, in a cupboard by the chimney piece. The soda farls were made first, a scoop of flour, a pinch of salt and soda and a splash of butter-milk in the well made in the middle. Scales were not amongst my Granny's possessions, but the dough was always perfect – rolled and coaxed into a round and cut across into quarters, then each laid care-fully on the floured griddle.

A round of wheaten or treacle farls was soon ready to follow, but before they were laid on the griddle I was allowed to sweep the now browned flour off the griddle with the goose wing which was kept for that purpose. I managed to sweep the flour into a neat pile at the edge of the griddle, but not always to catch it in the cup of my hand, like Granny could, and deposit it in the pig bucket.

There were still two uncles and two aunts left at home, so a lot of bread was needed and always included potato farls using up any left over mash. No family liked to be without its "tatty baps", but I was always impatient for the next part.

After the farls were set upright against each other to air off, the kettle was put on, the kitchen table was wiped, the griddle left to cool and a slab of home-made butter was brought out from under its net. There was no fridge, but the scullery always seemed to have a cool spot for such items.

I suppose that it was a blessing in some ways that my Granny died early in 1939 and was never to know margarine or the strictures of rationing. Her memory will always conjure up the smell of warm bread and butter.'

EVERYTHING FOR THE WEEK

'Wednesday was always baking day at our house at Salterforth, when everything required for the following week was made. We had a fire oven, that is a large black range with an oven on one side and a boiler on the other. Apart from one small gas jet, we had no other means of cooking, so on Wednesday the oven was in use for the whole of the day. One of the side irons was removed so that the heat from the fire could circulate under the oven and the day's mixing began.

The pastry was usually the first to be made for jam pasties, Eccles cakes and a fruit pie, to be followed by biscuits which varied each week, sometimes ginger, Shrewsbury and Anzak. Plenty of things had to be mixed ready because the heat of the oven varied, no regulo of course, but my mother was a master at judging the heat, putting her hand in the oven or if in doubt, a scattering of flour before deciding the next item to be baked. All these operations were carried out on the table top which covered the wooden mangle.

While all this was proceeding, preparations were made for the bread. Ten pounds of flour and a handful of salt were put to warm in a large baking bowl in front of the fire. The barm (yeast) which had been bought the same morning, was put in a basin with sugar and milk to warm on the "top bar" until it started to work. This was then poured with more warm milk, water and lard into the baking bowl, and the kneading began. The table was too high for the kneading so our mother used to put the bowl on a buffet, and we children used to watch for the dough coming from the sides of the bowl, when it would be turned over, and we could all (three of us) give it a good smack. It was then covered with a cloth and put to rise on a chair near the fire, it hadn't to be in a draught. When ready it was weighed out and put into greased tins to rise again before it went into the oven. When the bread was nearly ready, a loaf was eased out of the tin and tapped, if the sound was hollow the bread was cooked. The loaves were then put on a clean cloth, each standing on its end to cool, and were not put away in the bread crock until the following day. Sometimes if there was any spare dough it was rolled out into an oven bottom cake and put in the oven on a baking sheet. This tasted delicious when warm and spread with butter.

The last lap on baking day was the mixing of the cakes eaten for Sunday tea or when visitors came, queen cakes, Russian sandwich or perhaps a currant loaf, which was really what we now call Dundee cake. Finally came the wiping out of the cake tins which had been airing, lining them with greaseproof paper and putting all the baking away in the pantry, and not forgetting the washing up. It's not surprising that during the hot weather in summer, the heat in the kitchen became overpowering and when we came home from school for our dinner (no school meals then) the table was laid in the backyard where it was cooler.

Thursday was the day when we went to the Co-op for the "shop stuff" for the following week's baking and everything began all over again.'

BUTTER AND CHEESE

'In the 1940s I made butter every week, helping out a neighbour at Kirby Sigston. The milk was brought in every morning and evening after milking and put into large vessels made of wood for the cream to rise, then it was skimmed off by hand with a round tin sieve. The cream was put into a large bowl to wait for the next day's milking. The separated milk was fed to the pigs. After a week's collection of cream, it was put into a large wooden butter churn and rotated by hand until it became very hard to turn and the butter was formed. The buttermilk was then run out and the butter was washed and salted. It was turned out onto a cold stone slab to weigh into one pound pieces and be patted into shape with wooden pats. I used to make about 40 to 50 pounds every week. It was taken down to the Wednesday market to sell by the roadside. Dealers were always waiting to buy.'

'My earliest recollections of butter and cheese making are in the 1920s. On leaving school at 14, being a farmer's daughter I was expected to stay at home and help on the farm at Gunnerside. This entailed working on the farm, helping in the house and with the dairy products.

We milked twelve cows in the summer and eight in the winter. We made both cheese and butter in the summer, but only butter in the winter. The first task in cheesemaking was to warm the milk and put it in a large container called a cheese kettle. After adding rennet, it was stirred thoroughly, then covered with a clean cloth and left to stand for about an hour. We then mixed it up with a flat wire mesh until it was properly broken down. It was again covered and left for another hour. The whey was drained off by a tap at the bottom of the cheese kettle.

The cheese curd was then transferred to a shallow lead bowl, which also had a hole in the middle for drainage. After the curd was firm it was cut into squares and thoroughly mixed by hand, put into cheese vats and taken outside at the back of the house, where there were two cheese presses. By turning a handle the cheeses were pressed down and left until solid. Once taken out of the presses the cheeses were bandaged and taken to the cheese room upstairs, where they were put on wooden shelves to dry. They were turned every day for four weeks, when they were ready to take to market.'

'Most Sundays in summer we went to my grandparents on their smallholding at Scalby Nabs. Grandma was a wonderful cook and she also made her own butter, which I helped to churn. The cows sometimes ate garlic plants which gave the butter a strong flavour.'

RABBITS

'Saturday afternoons in winter in the late 1940s, I used to go catching rabbits with my father and brother. We went to Salmon House Farm at Snape, taking nets, two ferrets and my father's gun. We blocked up all the burrow holes with our nets and put the ferrets down. My brother and I used to empty the nets and my father would shoot any rabbits that ran out before we got the nets back over the holes. The netted rabbits sold better than the ones that were shot. The rabbits were then legged together in pairs and hung from a pole that my brother and I carried between us. The land there flooded in winter and the rabbits would be sat in the bushes and trees and we used to walk into the water in our waders and pick the rabbits out of the trees. The man who collected eggs from the local farms purchased the rabbits from my father, paying two shillings and sixpence to four shillings. We used to catch between twelve and 20 most weeks.'

KILLING THE PIG

'My husband was born in a village near Scarborough, one of a family of seven. He was born in 1917 and he can remember pig-keeping and killing when he was a child.

His father and eldest brother would fetch a piglet home in a sack, bought from a local farmer sometime in February. It was housed in a small sty at the end of the garden and was fed on scraps, pig meals and pig potatoes that his mother boiled up in the copper she washed in – the sort you lit a fire under.

In November a local chap came to slaughter the fattened pig. A couple of men would hold it and he would drive a metal spike into its head and stun it. Then it was laid on a creel, a kind of bench with rollers, and its throat was cut. My husband's mother would catch the blood in a bowl and make black puddings with it. The pig's body was then scalded and its bristles scraped off before being gutted and hung up by its forelegs in the kitchen until it stiffened.

The butcher then came and cut it up for the payment of about a quarter of the pig. The prime cuts of the remainder of the pig were sold, and the money used to pay the rates. The family used the rest of it, and what they didn't use straight away was salted down, with salt broken from a big block that the grocer had delivered. The meat was then hung up in the kitchen to dry and stayed there until it was all used up and it was time to go for another piglet.

Nothing was wasted of the pig. Its head, trotters and scraps of meat were boiled up to make brawn. The offal was fried for tasty dinners and its fat rendered down for lard. Little pieces of crisp fat that were left after the rendering, called "chittlings", were eaten salted for tea. The bladder was blown up and my husband played football with it.'

'Pig killing day at Cropton was looked forward to with a mixture of excitement and dread. It was all drama, from the moment Mr Bowes arrived with his bag of tools and the poor pig was dragged, shrieking horribly, from the dark sty. Grandma came from Pickering to help cut up the fat to be rendered over the fire into lard, which was put into pancheons and stored away for future baking days. Scrappings with salt for tea that day, and for several days after! Also liver and onions with dumplings in the roasting tin to look forward to, and brawn, and making up parcels to be shared among friends and neighbours. Grandad salted the sides and hams, then much later they were hung from hooks in the granary. The salt came in a big rectangular block which had to be broken up with knives and rolling pins.'

'The only thing I didn't like about Sunday tea in the 1940s was the huge slices of fat bacon which were served up. These were about half an inch thick and had just a small streak of lean bacon running through. I used to struggle to eat it, but my mother in law's chutney helped it down.'

ICE CREAM AND MUSSELS

'The dairy farm at Escrick made ice cream and we would go with a basin for some for Sunday tea. The Eldorado ice cream man would sometimes call as well. He had a bike with a box on it which said "Stop me and buy one". The herring man was another visitor at a certain time of the year and we would be served from a barrel at the back of the van.'

'When the muffin man came round North Duffield we would buy pikelets, which were thin and cheap, and toast them in front of the fire. Sometimes the mussel man would come and ladle mussels into our pan for fourpence a measure. These we cooked in their shells over the fire and ate with bread and margarine. I didn't like the slimy texture but there wasn't any choice. Occasionally we would have half a kipper for tea.'

SHOPS AND SHOPPING

'We had a shop at Ugthorpe which sold groceries and sweets. The butcher came round with his pony and cart every Friday, and Mr Readman came each week with his pony and flat cart selling fruit and vegetables. Bananas were seven for sixpence. He also bought fresh eggs from some cottagers who kept a few hens. He always sat on the side of his cart and always had a cigarette dangling from his mouth.'

'In the 1930s we would go shopping in the open market at Barnsley, which had an atmosphere of its own. You could buy anything there, and when it got towards nine o'clock on a Saturday night every stall-holder was shouting his wares and saying how cheap they were. Not much could be saved till Monday because there were no fridges or freezers then. So if you wanted to do your shopping then you could get some good bargains and everybody seemed to enjoy the banter of the stallholders which brought smiles to people's faces.'

'In York in the 1930s milk was brought in a can and "Mr Ernest" would ladle it into jugs or basins which were then covered with little cloths with beaded edges to keep out flies. Even during the war our grocery order was written in a book and left at the shop (F.A. Stone-house in Colliergate) each week when the previous bill was settled. The order was delivered on Friday afternoon and I enjoyed watching the checking off. Sugar was packed in deep blue, stiff paper bags, and when dried fruit was available it came wrapped in clover pink or deep golden coloured paper, always very neatly done up. Shops used to smell good: after the war I looked forward to buying in Bor-der's in Coney Street or Rowntree's or Collinson's in Pavement – they always seemed to be roasting coffee!'

'Standing at the check-out at the supermarket the other day, the cus-tomer in front of me lifted her bag of sugar on to the conveyor belt and the bottom dropped out and literally sugared up the works. "Paper isn't worth a toss these days," she said and I was reminded of when I started work at a wholesale grocery in Whitby in 1947.
 I was engaged as a "Point account slip clerk" and it was my job to allocate to each shop the amounts of rationed foods. Tinned fish,

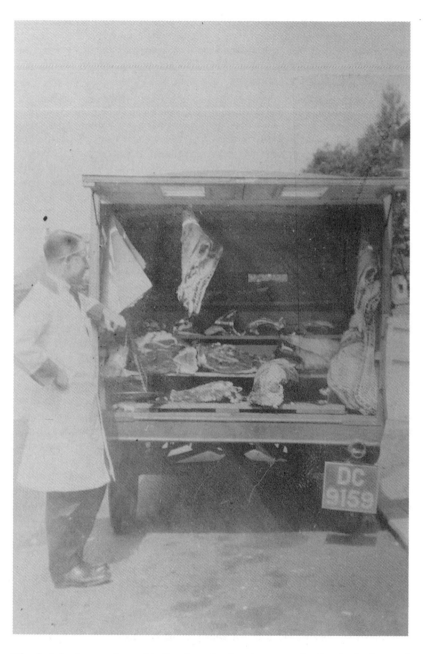

The butcher's van brought the shop to the customer in the Stokesley and Osmotherley area in the 1940s.

tinned fruit, tinned meat, butter, sugar and all dried fruits were still in short supply and each shop was given a number of points, according to the number of customers per month. Many a row I had with customers who wanted "just a few more, luv". The business only received about half the amount that they ordered and it was very difficult to be fair to everyone.

There were 20 staff in the warehouse and six of us in the office. The three directors travelled each day getting the orders. The area covered was quite extensive, especially in wintertime in the snow. They travelled to Stokesley, Kirkbymoorside, Bridlington, Scarbrough and all villages in between.

All the dried fruit came to the warehouse in large wooden crates, sugar in hundredweight sacks, and everything had to be weighed and packed into small sellable amounts. Half-pound, one-pound and two-pound packets were the most popular. The men were very adept at packing these commodities, folding the tops of the little blue paper bags swiftly and securely. I never saw a grain of sugar or a currant escape from a bag the whole time I worked there. Large sheets of brown paper were used to wrap small orders in and fastened with string. No plastic bags or sticky tape in those days.

Waggons were out delivering the orders every day. At that time there were at least 40 small grocery shops in Whitby and every customer was known and valued.

OTHER CALLERS TO THE DOOR

'The muffin man came round every Sunday afternoon at Fylingthorpe, ringing his bell. He carried the muffins on his head in a wooden tray covered by a cloth. In summer the Walls ice cream man came on his tricycle. We had to put a card with a big "W" on it in the window and he would come to the door.'

'One of the most vivid memories of my childhood is the visit of the tea man. I lived on a farm and we had all our goods delivered by van but the tea man came in his own motor car, which was a rare sight in the 1940s. He was from another world, always dressed in what we would class as Sunday best. He was a tall, handsome man with well groomed grey hair and he wore a smart overcoat and smelled different (of cologne, I now realise). We would hear the car arrive and run out to meet him and help carry his bags. These were large, hide leather Gladstone bags and he would open them up to display the containers of tea. After my mother had decided which tea to buy, she would make afternoon tea, after which the tea man smoked a cigarette, which we thought was the height of sophistication.'

'My mother in law, who came from Great Ayton and was born in 1888, used to tell of the dressmaker's yearly visit. This would be in the early part of the 20th century. She would arrive in time for breakfast having walked some five or six miles from a neighbouring village. The sewing machine was provided by the household, and a costume or dress would be made for mother in law and her sister in the day. The dressmaker's wage was three shillings and sixpence including all meals.'

'All through my childhood the "Order Man" used to come to our house in Thirsk from the local Co-op on a Monday or Tuesday and sit in the kitchen drinking tea while we went through the cupboards to see what we wanted. He would write it in his book (blue carbon paper and all) while chatting about local news, interspersed with suggestions for the order – "this is good this week". The order would be delivered on the Friday and paid for on delivery or at the store. I remember our number was 48227, and we had a cash "divi" at the end of the year. What service!'

EATING OUT

'Compared with today, it could be said that between the wars eating out hardly occurred at all. As the reasonable prosperity of the 1920s was followed by the poverty and austerity of the 1930s, country outings were usually supported by home-made sandwiches and a flask of tea, bar lunches being quite unknown. The country inn and indeed its brother in the town, was largely concerned with the selling of beer, five to seven pennies for the pint, and little in the way of food could be expected.

On the other hand, "hiking" (that awful word with its associated picture of knobbly knees and shorts) had just become popular. Can you remember its theme tune *I'm happy when I'm hiking*? One could knock on any farmhouse door in the Dales with the confidence of a welcome, and a substantial egg, or better still ham-and-egg tea, for anything between a shilling and a half-crown.

I well remember a long day's walk from Ilkley up the Washburn, which found me in the late afternoon at the Hey Slack end of Pock-stones Moor. I took a line on Rocking Hall, then over the watershed the top of Kex Beck, to be rewarded by a two-egg tea, with lashings of bread and jam and cake, washed down with buckets of tea. It cost me one shilling and threepence, and helped me make light work of the three or four miles down to Bolton Bridge, and the bus back to Ilkley.'

FROM THE CRADLE TO THE GRAVE

We were far more likely to be born, to suffer our illnesses and to die in our own homes in the past. Most villages had a local woman who would attend births and come to lay out the dead, and since the doctor had to be paid for we relied to a great extent on home remedies, handed down through families. When hospitalisation was essential, for the dreaded scarlet fever perhaps, the treatment received seems positively Dickensian!

NO NEED TO CALL THE DOCTOR

'One of the things that afflicted both adults and children was boils, said to be caused by "bad blood". One cure was to fill a bottle with hot water, empty this out and clap the neck of the bottle over the boil. As the glass cooled so the boil was drawn. One man recalls having five on his bottom, which required a jam jar!'

'Grandmother was a firm believer in salt as a cure for most ailments. Cuts were bathed in salt and water, sore throats gargled it, and a blocked up nose was relieved by sniffing up lukewarm water with a pinch of salt in it from a saucer. If anyone had a bad chest, and there were workmen around with a heated tar barrel, she would recommend that the afflicted one should be lifted up and held over the barrel to inhale the fumes. I saw lots of children having that done to them and many of them were quite frightened.'

'Sixty years ago, when I was a boy in Ripon, high cholesterol levels and the present concern about saturated fats were unheard of; the medical "fad" in those days was the need to be "regular". An aid to this desired state of affairs was a weekly dose of liquorice powder, a mixture which smelled awful and tasted worse! Daily doses of cod liver oil were a normal thing during the winter months, or perhaps cod liver oil and malt, a much more pleasant substance.

If you did catch a cold there were several remedies available. A dish of onions boiled in milk was the first line of defence, eaten at bedtime; hopefully this would sweat the cold out before it got any worse. Inhaling the steam from a bowl of boiling water to which a few drops of eucalyptus oil had been added was helpful in the case of blocked sinuses. A heavy chest cold called for special treatment; a mixture of goose grease and camphorated oil would be rubbed into the chest and covered with a linseed poultice.

Poultices were also used to reduce the inflammation of such things as boils and abscesses. Iodine was much in use as an antiseptic, and I have personal experience as to the effectiveness of this. At the age of twelve or so I managed to slice the end off the third finger of my left hand. Mother, realising what I had done, thrust my hand under the kitchen tap and made me hold it there in the running water while she searched for and found the finger end, washed this under the tap, smothered both finger and end with iodine and bound the end firmly back into place. In due course it healed completely, although I still have scar to this day.

Spring was the time for that popular blood purifier brimstone and treacle; can't say that it ever did much for me, I still came out in spots.

In those days, many medicines were home-made from herbs or even garden plants. I must have had my share of coughs for those that I remember best were cough medicines. An excellent expectorant was made from the herb coltsfoot, known locally as "Cough Wort". Sage, which grew in every garden, produced an effective remedy for laryngitis, tonsillitis and sore throats. Thyme was well known as a natural antiseptic and really did relieve throat and bronchial irritation. A certain cure for headaches of the migraine type was a couple of leaves of feverfew eaten in a sandwich. Simple remedies perhaps, but they did work.'

'Senna tea every spring – I can visualise the pale yellow liquid, with sultanas drowned at the bottom of the glass and a revolting taste! Marshmallow leaves applied to bruises, and bicarbonate of soda mixed to a paste with water or milk and applied to ease sunburn or bee stings. Mother ground Epsom salts into lard or boracic ointment to make a painful poultice for any septic cuts, and flowers of sulphur were blown down our throats if ever we dared complain of any soreness. I remember, too, "Worm Cakes". I could never eat the similar looking liquorice allsort!'

NEEDING OUTSIDE HELP

'If you were lucky, and I was, an older member of the family, usually a grandmother, always seemed to know good simple remedies for most childhood illnesses. It was only on rare occasions outside help was needed. I remember my mother paying fivepence a week to something called "Medical Aid" and when a doctor was considered to be required a message was sent to a surgery in York. This usually meant a visit to a local telephone kiosk.

After the outbreak of the Second World War, during the second blackout when I was 16, I fell on some rough pavement sustaining a badly cut face. My mother was on war work at the sugar beet factory and I was told to go to a surgery in Clifford Street for treatment. I can remember like yesterday, everything was dark, dark passage with brown paint up to dado height, dark green lino and the waiting room was the same apart from rows of dark wooden chairs along each wall and a spluttering gas fire. The surgery was no better, only the furnishings – glass front cupboard containing numerous, not too clean, instruments and the desk covered in papers. The doctor himself seemed to me to be very, very old, and no doubt he was, probably recruited when young doctors were required elsewhere. No nice white coat but a short bald headed man in an old tweed suit, the lapels curling and his fingers with nicotine stains. However, as I remember it the bruise and gravel rash was cleaned with something or other and I seemed to suffer no ill effects. I think it is the darkness which I shall remember forever.'

'In the early 1930s there was no electricity and no telephones in Lealholm, except for one in the post office. My brother had been to the dentist in Whitby and had teeth removed and the gums would not stop bleeding, so at about two o'clock in the morning I had to go in haste from Lealholmside to Lealholm village to rouse Mr Briggs the postmaster to phone for the doctor. He lived at Grosmont, six miles away. Unfortunately, the resident doctor was away and a locum was in charge who had never been to Lealholm before so I had to wait by the roadside to show him the way. There were few cars in those days so I had no difficulty in recognising the doctor's car – the first lights to appear. The operation to stop the bleeding was a success, even though the doctor had to work by candlelight.'

'My sister and I had our tonsils and adenoids removed on the kitchen table in our home near Skipton. She was 18 and I was seven. An open coal fire was the only means of hot water. My mother had a nice bar of toilet soap ready for the doctor but he asked for carbolic soap.'

'There was no official home help when my mother in law's neighbour was taken ill in the 1930s. The old man lived alone, so when the doctor arrived he immediately asked her to help him. "We need to get rid of this fluid," the doctor told her, "so hang on this and no matter how much he shouts, swears or cries, don't let go." Horrified, she obeyed instructions and so much water came out that it filled a bucket. The doctor called two or three times after that day, but Mother hid under the kitchen table and wouldn't answer the door.'

IN THE FEVER HOSPITAL

'I vividly recall the year 1918 when my brother and I were struck down by scarlet fever. I was five years old and he was only three. We were not allowed to stay at home, but were collected by horse-drawn carriage and taken to Selby isolation hospital on Selby Common. During the three weeks that I was there, my parents could not enter my room, only look through a window. Our house had to be fumigated to get rid of any infection.

By 1954, when my own daughter contracted scarlet fever, the option was given of keeping the patient at home provided that "barrier nursing" was employed. A sheet wet with disinfectant had to be hung over my daughter's bedroom door, and I had to put on an overall to go in and nurse her. Fathers were not admitted though.'

'When my sister was in the fever hospital at Yearsley Bridge in 1936, we had to check her progress from the daily bulletins in the local evening paper. No telephones, and no visiting.'

'My memories of scarlet fever in 1934 are not too pleasant. My family were farmers living on an out of the way farm. My mother employed a female worker to help with the household chores and the home of the current worker 60 years ago was in Middlesbrough. One weekend this girl went home for a few days and returned with a very bad cold and sore throat. Some days later I started with a cold – or so we thought! Mine turned into a fever with a rash and very red skin condition, terrible head pains and pain in all my joints. I was in agony. The doctor was called and diagnosed scarlet fever, a dreaded disease for which there was very little cure. No antibiotics, penicillin or modern drugs in those days – just quinine and bathing the rash with bicarbonate of soda to keep it cool. The local doctor was on holiday and so a locum came and sat with me for three days until there was a slight change in my condition. He dare not leave me as I was semi-conscious most of the time and my fever was so high.

There was an isolation hospital in Northallerton, and when I reached the turning point of being slightly better it was decided to move me there. My mother, who had nursed me, also started with the flu-like symptoms so she and I were wrapped in blankets and taken to hospital – not by ambulance or car, but in a horse-drawn hansom cab belonging to a blacksmith in Northallerton. How well I remember that terrible six mile ride! Jogging and rocking from one side to another in my semi-conscious state could not have improved my health. On arrival at hospital we were each put in a room of our own, and before morning all the lights had fused and we were in total darkness. I screamed, and was so afraid that my temperature soared and I was much worse for some time.

Following the severe head pains I had a three week period of total deafness. I could not hear a word and as visitors were only allowed to stand outside and speak through glass windows and doors there was not much point in anyone coming. No one was allowed into the room except Matron and Sister. They were the kindest people and I kept in touch with them until they died. Matron made some delicious lemon barley water and porridge which I well remember. It was lovely, and I must have drunk gallons of the barley water. I had waist long hair when I went into hospital but this was cut off as it was felt that it was taking the strength away from me.

One of our male workers also contracted the disease and was brought into hospital so there were three of us occupying different wards. We were kept isolated at all times.

At home the house was fumigated with sulphur candles. These were wax candles with added sulphur and were in round yellow tins about six inches in diameter. The wicks were lit and these huge candles burnt for weeks and smelt for years! Twenty years on the wardrobe in my bedroom still smelt of sulphur! All our clothes had to be burnt and it was very traumatic. Scarlet fever was very infectious, and supposedly started in dirty conditions and for some time we were looked down upon by some members of the community. Inspectors came to test the milk we produced and examine the outside toilets. If only there had been newspapers and means of communication for country people we would have heard of the scarlet fever epidemic in Middlesbrough, and that young lady need not have gone home and brought back the deadly fever.

Life might have been so different for me as after this terrible illness I developed agoraphobia and therefore all my life have been afraid of the wide open spaces. Not much fun for a person living on isolated farms! But – I am lucky to be alive, as many thousands of people died from scarlet fever.'

MARRIAGE CUSTOMS

'An old custom at Ugthorpe, which seems to have died out, was that as the bride and bridegroom came out of the church a friend of the family would fire a shot from somewhere behind the church. It always startled the guests!'

'When there was a wedding at Lealholm the bridegroom was expected to throw a handful of coins to the waiting children as he came through the church gates. This was known as a "scramble". On a fine evening sometime after the wedding, races would be run for the men and these were held in the field behind the joiner's shop and were known as "ribbons".'

'In the 1930s it was expected that farmers' sons would marry farmers' daughters. When my father announced he was going to marry a schoolteacher, it caused some doubt, an old farming neighbour saying: "Nay lad, you'll get nowt but bowt bread and fish 'n' chips!"'

'One family in Hovingham had seven girls and kept the custom of giving bride and groom, as they returned from church and before entering the house, a plate with a small piece of cake. They both ate a small piece and then threw the rest, plate and all, over their heads.

One elderly lady still remembers the races run at weddings, when the prize for the men was a silk handkerchief and a kiss from the bride, and for the women a quarter of tea.'

INTO THE WORLD

'Lucky were those babies born with a "caul" about them, they would never want or drown. I once saw a caul. The owner had kept this wrinkled, precious object in a little box. Babies wore head shawls and little boys wore dresses until the age of four, so that it was hard to tell boys from girls (this continued until about 1910).'

'Births were usually at home at Settle. The mothers would have new bed valances with deep, white crocheting, all prepared for the "lying in" after the birth. Neighbours were very supportive and would knock on each other's walls to attract attention.'

'During the First World War, Dr Greenwood, our Poppleton doctor, set up a maternity nursing home at the Hall, Nether Poppleton, where he allowed the village mothers to have their babies. He gave them a new pain relief process to ease the agony of childbirth. I think that this was the forerunner of the modern "gas and air". The young mothers were delighted to have the treatment and subsequent nursing all free of charge.

The treatment proved safe and popular and Dr Greenwood left Poppleton to set up an expensive maternity home in Harrogate, using the "Twilight Sleep" process.'

'A new mother at Moulton, even in the 1930s, was not welcome in another house until she had been churched, which was a short service from the Prayer Book to give thanks for a safe delivery. It

Contestants in the baby show at Thornton Watless in 1928.

was considered bad luck, not only for the mother but to any house she might enter. Often the ceremony coincided with the baptism at six weeks, so new mothers did not venture from home for quite long periods.'

THE LAST JOURNEY

'The Second World War possibly put an end to those long periods of mourning following a death in the family and that dreadful ritual of black – black-edged handkerchiefs, black armbands, black-edged paper and envelopes, mourners sitting like crows in complete black mourning dress and smelling of the preserving mothballs. It all added to the solemnity and gloom of the funeral service.

Nowadays we may think a little patronisingly of funeral teas, with lavish helpings of ham, spice loaf and even funeral biscuits, but it should be borne in mind that many relatives had not met together since the last wedding or funeral and may have come a long way by pony and trap, so they could not be sent home with just a cup of tea and a biscuit. Shame on those poor relations who actually economised on the funeral tea by seeing off the dear departed with *brawn*!

Quaint beliefs are still held by some members of the community. I can remember when there had been two deaths close together at

Telephone—Crosshills 92.
Day or Night.

Established 1872.

CONONLEY, Sept. 24 1937.
Near Keighley.

Funeral of the late Frank Third.

Dr. to James Laycock & Sons

(Partners—Jonas Laycock & Frank Laycock)

Joiners and Merchants,

Terms—Monthly. Nett.
Contracts due on Completion.
5 per cent. Interest charged on overdue accounts.

FUNERALS COMPLETELY FURNISHED.
DISTANCE NO OBJECT.

		£	s	d
Sept. 16	To Oak coffin casket fittings & Undertaking	10	·	·
	Grave and. Vicars fees as paid. herewith	2	2	6
	Hearse and fetching from Skipton		17	6.
	30 Memorial cards.		10	6.
	Boards. to protect the coffin.		6	·
		£ 13	16	6

Received with thanks
Sept. 1937.
James Laycock & Sons.

A 1937 bill for funeral expenses, including the traditional memorial cards.

Hovingham, and the last had been "laid" over the Sunday. An elderly gentleman said to me: "There'll be a thud, there'll be a thud. It might be me and it might be thee, but there'll be a thud." I found this a very sobering thought.'

'Mrs Gaines was the local midwife at Harmby until after the war when most confinements were at The Mount, Northallerton. She also laid out the dead for the princely sum of one shilling.'

'There was an old custom at Staithes that when a person died a "bidder" visited all the houses and invited people to the funeral. Time, church and interment were all announced. The lady was usually dressed in black complete with black bonnet and apron. The last known "bidder" was Annie Crispin. This custom has now died out.

Village funerals were also the place for "waiters". These were women friends or neighbours of the deceased's family, usually four in number, who walked behind the coffin and in front of the family, wearing white lace shawls round their shoulders (many families still have these in their possession). While the funeral party visited the cemetery, the "waiters" prepared the funeral tea. Bearers wore dark suits or jerseys and had a white ribbon tied in their buttonhole.'

THE WAY OF DEATH

'Death and funerals have always been a source of terror to me. My first memory of death was in January 1924 when my aunt with whom I lived, died. It was a heartbreaking experience in those days. My mother sobbed and sobbed for days, and as a three year old fear just gripped me. Living on an isolated farm with no papers, phone or motor cars, one of the family was sent to the village to inform the undertaker, a local joiner, and also to tell friends and relations of my aunt's death. The undertaker would inform the vicar and the sexton would ring the "passing bell" – a much dreaded sound in country areas. Local people wondered which friend had passed away.

The undertaker and his lady assistant were brought to the farm in a horse and trap and the assistant, the lady who helped at all births and deaths, laid out the corpse of my aunt, washing her and laying a very elaborate sheet on the bed – all drawn thread work, ribbon and much lace. My aunt's nightdress was also pintucked and embroidered. Some people had very rich purple bedcovering, but they were usually white. Due to my age at the time I did not know, but was told later, that my mother, in her grief, gave the undertaker and some relatives a drink to warm them, only to realise later that she had proffered vinegar instead of whiskey! The relatives drank, but the undertaker had no intention of being the next victim and left his drink.

The undertaker went round the houses "bidding" people to come to the funeral. A visit was made to Thirsk to choose and order "Death Cards". These were ornate little cards, white with black edges, and the envelopes also had a black edge. (Another dreadful moment was when one of these arrived in the post.) My aunt's cards had snowdrops on the front, being January. The details of the funeral, the name, and age of the deceased were printed on these cards.

Black hats were always worn, and Mother bought a new black dress for the funeral and black button boots. The boots had buttons from toe to knee, needing a button-hook to fasten them each time. Wreaths were either made at home or very plain ones could be bought from a nursery. Many wreaths were sent as a token of great love.

The table waitresses, usually friends, were each given a new white fancy apron to wear at the funeral tea. These aprons were much thought of and were kept for years. The bearers or coffin carriers were each bought a new pair of kid gloves.

On the morning of the funeral the undertaker and bearers arrived with the horse-drawn hearse. Black horses were always used on these occasions, and the hearse was very elaborate with stained-glass sides, silver furnishings and all held together by wrought iron fittings. The ladies of the house were not to be seen until the coffin was brought downstairs and loaded into the hearse. Lots of friends and relations arrived at the house and then followed the hearse over the rutty road to the village either in traps or on foot, all upset and crying. A very sombre occasion. Hymns chosen for the service at church were heart-rending, usually *Rock of Ages*, *Abide with Me*, and *Sun of My Soul*.

After the funeral service, relations, friends and all concerned made their way back to the farm where the huge funeral tea was served. It was very plain food (no iced cakes) but masses of it, which had all been home-baked following the death. Ham, home-fed and delicious, was always served in the farmhouses. An old Yorkshire saying was that "Orr 'So & So' was alus put away wi' 'am". I well remember being plied with "funeral biscuits" to console me whilst the others were at the funeral. These were dry finger biscuits which were always served at funerals.

My mother must have been very upset and frightened as she was 20 years younger than my aunt, who had always been the head of everything. The thought of coping without the older person must have been very traumatic. It was many years before Mother laughed and joked as before. Following the funeral black clothes were worn for three years in respect of the dead. My mother had worn black outfits for school for nine years, having lost her mother, father and grandmother in succession.

I wonder what the young of today would think of these traditions, but that was the way of death 70 years ago.'

Yvonne Bennett
Thornton Le Dale. N

CHILDHOOD &
SCHOOLDAYS

GROWING UP IN NORTH YORKSHIRE

Our childhood days are fresh in our memories, whether of town or country. They were for most of us days of freedom, of a kind sadly denied to today's children.

HALFPENNY DELIGHT

'We lost Dad in 1919, when I was eight months old and my brother two years and at that time we lived in Pickering. My grandparents helped to look after us while Mum worked in Grandfather's butcher's shop.

When I was about three I went with Mum to the shop to her work. Next door was a saddler's shop where horse collars and harnesses were repaired. My cousin and I used to sit outside the two shops wearing horse collars. As we got older, Grandad gave us one penny to deliver a brace of rabbits. When we acquired twopence we could go to the pictures on a Saturday afternoon where we sat on wooden benches. If threepence was ours, we could afford to sit on the plush seats, and if we had fourpence we bought a pomegranate and ate it with a pin in the cinema.

Sunday breakfast at my grandparents' was always a kind of "mixed pot" – a large black iron pan, hanging from a "reckon" over the open fire, filled with cowheels, pig's trotters, and tripe all bubbling hot. My Grandma always got up at 5 am and milked six cows before breakfast. She did this every day until she died, aged 73.

Later, Mother went to work on a farm at Salton – a tiny remote village near Kirkbymoorside. She cooked for six men, all on coal fires. Pig killing day was a real occasion. There was fat rendering for lard, bacon was hung from hooks in the kitchen ceiling and joints of fat bacon boiled for breakfasts. Bowls of beetroot helped to get the fat down!

The coal strike came in 1921. I was toddling around then, so Mum gave me the job of collecting kindling (in my wooden cart) for lighting the fire. The farm men chopped wood and logs as we had no coal for a year.

One day Mum lost me – I was found fast asleep in a nest box in the hen house. Covered in fleas I had to be stripped outdoors and

Prams were made to last in 1927! When baby Robert and his cat had grown out of it, the pram would still be used for carrying heavy items and the wheels would be sought after as a base for a child's box cart.

washed in the pond before being taken indoors for a bath.

I started Salton school at four years of age. My big brother attended Pickering school. One day the hounds met in the village and all 14 children absconded leaving only me at school with our one and only teacher, Mrs Martin.

Our transport in those days was ponies and traps and bicycles. Mother rode her bicycle with me in a basket on the front and my brother on a carrier seat on the back. When my brother learned to ride his small bike, I was promoted to the carrier seat.

When I was eight Mum left Salton to nurse a sick aunt at Bramham, near Wetherby. We never went back. Later Mum started a sweet and tobacco shop and imagine our excitement on taking 8s 4d on our first day. This shop developed into a thriving business in later years. The most exciting thing I remember was Mum's halfpenny tray for kids – school being just over the road. It held custard cornets, snowballs, kali suckers, marshmallow sandwiches, assorted liquorice sticks, gobstoppers and loads more. Even now elderly Bramham people still reminisce about Mum's famous halfpenny tray!'

THE GAMEKEEPER'S DAUGHTER

'My earliest memory is of my father's khaki greatcoat hanging behind the door of our house at Blenheim, where he was a game-keeper. I had a terror of that coat, as he had been in the Great War for all of my first three years and I had seen little of him. My grand-mother once took me to Blenheim Palace and I recall being allowed to hold the enormous gold key to the unique lock on the huge front doors. My first schooldays were spent in Bladon school, and then in 1924, we moved to the Princess Royal's estate at Goldsborough.

As there were then three children and another imminent, no house large enough was available, and we lived temporarily in a small cottage adjacent to the railway at Allerton Mauleverer. During the General Strike of 1926, compassionate engine drivers often arranged that huge lumps of coal would fall from the tender of the engine, which was a great help in keeping our home fires burning. We soon moved to a large newly built house on the outskirts of Gold-sborough. School was now much nearer; we appreciated not having to walk in all weathers through fields and woods from Allerton.

We often saw the late Princess Royal who brought her two sons walking around the woods and lanes. She had a small dog-cart pulled by a Shetland pony, and later, after a visit to Ireland, two large Irish wolfhounds. The park was used for brood bloodstock and contained a pond with a shed for a fire engine – in case of fire at Goldsborough Hall. We loved the foals which accompanied their mothers, all the horses were very gentle – I recall that one mare was called "Canary Seed". The Princess Royal was very concerned and interested in all the estate staff, and her memory of events in their lives was remarkable. Christmas time brought surplus toys from the Hall nursery – these were disguised by my parents and said to have "fallen from an aeroplane". Each tenant and employee on the estate had a Christmas gift geared to their circumstances. I still have a French clock in working order which was one of these.

Although we lived outside the village, we were never short of occupation. My brothers had great interest in my father's job as head gamekeeper. They had a pet fox-cub – christened "Charlie" – which he had rescued. This pet was once taken on a bus to a pet show at Oatlands school – now St Aidan's school, but then a private estab-lishment which moved to Goldsborough Hall during the Second World War. The fox escaped and caused panic until we caught it again. Eventually my father sent it by rail to a friend in Kent so that it could re-establish itself in the wild.'

A PALACE CHILDHOOD

'In 1928 my father was an unemployed cotton mill worker in Preston, Lancashire. He had, due to the slump, been out of work for several years. But he had learnt to drive and was a sergeant in the Church Lads Brigade. When Bishop William Temple was to be translated to York he required a chauffeur. He approached the Church Lads Brigade and my father had an interview and got the post. He and my mother were married in the January and travelled to York. There they had a flat over the garages at the Palace Bishopthorpe.

In 1935 on Silver Jubilee Day, 6th May, I was born at the flat and duly baptised in the Palace chapel by Archbishop Temple. At that time it was still very much an upstairs/downstairs situation at the Palace, but my sister, five years older, myself and my cousin, two years older, had a very happy childhood.

We roamed in the Palace grounds as long as we were not seen from the house. We went to the kitchen gardens to collect the vegetables for my mother on Saturdays, the milk was delivered by churn from the Home Farm. The flat had a very large kitchen cum living room and in it was a Yorkshire range. Mother used to make bread in it, and still nothing beats the taste and smell of fresh bread rolls. Monday was washday. It was always cold meat and chips on Monday.

On Christmas Eve Mrs Temple and Miss Sinker, her companion and my godmother, came with presents to be opened after lunch on Christmas Day. My Aunt Phyllis in the village always made new dresses for my sister and I for the staff party to be held at the Palace. They were white organdie and had blue sashes, I still remember how the sleeves scratched. These were worn after church on Christmas morning ready for the party. After lunch we went over to the Palace and entered by the front door. In the entrance was a huge Christmas tree which reached the ceiling and hung on it were the presents for all the staff.

After a huge tea which was laid out on the long formal dining table, we had games and I have a vivid memory of dancing Sir Roger de Coverley with the Archbishop. At the end of the afternoon we all received presents from the tree.'

PEARS SOAP AND GRANDMA

'Pears transparent soap personifies a beautiful lady! To this day the aroma of this toiletry brings back the happiest memories of my childhood, days spent in the company of a caring gentle person – my Grandma.

Grandma Sleightholme was a reserved and respected lady with an abundance of warmth for her family and friends. She was widowed at 36 and left with five children, my mother being the eldest. Although her life was a struggle Grandma's wisdom and calm gave those around her the security needed in a child's life.

On a small table beside her work basket (with the intriguing darning mushroom) stood a jar of pot-pourri and her bible. She rarely missed evensong at the local church. I think her belief in God gave her the envied strength and endurance. Prayers were said kneeling at the bedside.

During the cold weather, our bodies fresh and fragrant after a bath (using the luxurious Pears soap) were wrapped in a shawl. I would tumble into the huge bed, already thawed with a stone bottle, and sink into a feather mattress surrounded by feather pillows. Pulling the eiderdown over my head, the lingering perfume of Pears transparent soap exuded from my glowing body. Could I win the "Miss Pears" competition as a beautiful lady? Childish dreams! Grandma's words of wisdom: "Handsome is as handsome does".

The treadle sewing machine, habitually used, stood discreetly in an alcove of the sitting room. My check gingham dresses, with knickers to match, were one product of this appliance. In comparison, majestically prominent, was an organ. The sing-alongs featured at family gatherings were memorable. A great attraction too for the grandchildren, was pulling out the stops and pressing the pedals! Received from these grandchildren, proudly displayed on a whatnot's shelves, were mementoes and gifts for all occasions and holiday souvenirs. Treasures for Grandma!

I can picture the fire burning in the grate and the fender with a slipper box on one side, and the box on the other side containing cleaning materials. A clipped rug representing hours of work lay in front, where I knelt on a winter's evening toasting bread. Toast never tasted so good! From a very tender age Grandma educated me with books, music and games. As the years passed, we visited the library together, and listened to the plays on the radio. She introduced me to the classics, and I discovered the meaning of words as we read aloud paragraphs from Trollope, Dickens and Thackeray. I was fascinated by Walter De La Mare's poetry. We played halma and patience and charades. The lyrics and music of Gilbert and Sullivan were prominent in our leisure hours. Was there more breathing space in those days?

Never without a hat or gloves, her shoes always polished, and carrying her beaded bag, Grandma lived with dignity. Children were not allowed on the ward where Grandma was ill. Just before she died my mother was at her bedside as I held my six month old daughter at the window. Grandma looked at my daughter: "She's a Miss Pears winner!" she said smilingly.'

AN ISOLATED LIFE

'In the 1930s my father rented a farm of 20 acres from Commander Vyner of Studley Royal with Fountains Abbey. It was a very remote place, being three fields and a lane away from the road, and I had a further walk up the road when I went to school at Galphay, five miles from Ripon. Transport was by horse and cart or trap.

It was an isolated life. My brother and I had to rely on each other for almost ten years, our parents always being occupied with the running of the farm. There were other farms a few fields away but they mainly had boys, and I lived in a very male-dominated society. Boys were important to farmers.

I know we had a wireless run from an accumulator and we also had a wind-up gramophone with a large horn and old 78 rpm records of Sandy Powell. I had piano lessons from a lady who lived two fields away. But it was visits away to grandparents or aunts and uncles that gave me the chance to see another way of life, and these windows on the world allowed me to dream about what to do with my life.'

A CAREFREE TOMBOY

'I was fortunate to live in a house with an extremely large garden at Ingleby Arncliffe, which at one time had been a small dairy farm. My father kept a smallholding, so we were surrounded by animals and pets. We, and our friends, were given great freedom to play, and we took full advantage of it. The outbuildings of stables, hen houses and pig sties made excellent hiding places. The roofs became vantage points when playing cowboys and indians, and we could leap easily from one roof to another. My father built a swing for us under the lowest limb of our enormous Jargonelle pear tree and we used the swing to climb up into the branches, which became tree houses and my refuge in times of trouble.

Friday night was Amami night, when we washed our hair. I enjoyed mixing the powder to a paste – henna for my dark-haired sister and myself, and camomile for my fair-haired sister. But the tooth comb followed. This was a metal comb with the teeth very close together and was meant to remove nits. The shrieks as the steel comb was dragged through our hair must have frightened the neighbours.

I had a wonderful childhood, ended by my commencement as a scholarship girl at high school. I could no longer be the carefree tomboy.'

LIVING ON THE MOOR

'We loved the long summer days at our home on Farnhill Moor. My mother made jugs of tea to sell to picnickers, who came up from local villages and towns to enjoy the fresh moorland air, pick bilberries and cranberries in July, blackberries in September and walk up to the Pinnacle to see the panoramic views of Airedale.

One summer evening in 1936, my father rushed in to tell us to come outside and see the Zeppelin, which was making steady progress southwards down the valley. What a splendid sight! We learned next day it was the German "Hindenburg". In the uneasy years before the Second World War, there was much speculation as to whether it was on a spying mission. It did in fact come low over Keighley to drop some flowers and a cross with a request that these be placed on the grave of a German prisoner of war who had died at a local hospital in the First World War. I like to think this was the only reason for its trip down Airedale.

In the winter evenings we hugged the fire, read books by the soft light of the Aladdin lamp and listened to the crackling sound of our "wireless". I was most enamoured of the wireless as I was often called on to take the glass accumulator (a wet battery containing lead plates and a weak acid solution) to be recharged and also to carry it back up the hill.

We had many shops supplying the twin villages of Kildwick and Farnhill. There were two grocer's shops, a Co-op, sweets and drapery, butcher's, barber's, fish and chips and a boot and shoe shop where shoes and clogs were repaired. The post office was in Kildwick, across the "dangerous" Kildwick Corner, round which passed the occasional motor car or bus. There were also ladies in the village who baked bread, teacakes and confectionery for sale in their own homes.

Living on the moor I was given the option of wearing boots or clogs. I chose clogs as I thought these were the lesser evil. They were very comfortable and kept the feet dry and warm. Most boys wore clogs and so did some of the girls.

The Church of England school at Kildwick provided an excellent basic education in the three Rs. We were also taught scripture and now and again there was an examination in this subject. I remember feeling very anxious when Canon Watson was to come and question us. I need not have worried, as this kind gentleman with pleading eyes and a sense of humour soon put us at our ease. He came in the morning and we had a holiday in the afternoon, making the ordeal well worthwhile.

We had a well-polished chest of drawers in my parents' bedroom, the big top drawer containing sheets and pillowcases. Beneath these was a white linen nightdress, embroidered in white and crocheted.

A concert in the Methodist chapel schoolroom at Kildwick was eagerly anticipated.

My mother told me she would be "laid out" in it when she died. I don't know what happened to it but it was not there when she died over 50 years later. I think this custom was a relic of Victorian times.

Our social life centred round church, chapel and the village institute, where children showed their talents in singing, dancing, playing the piano and reciting poetry. The village institute held "at homes", every year, when there would be teas, concerts and dances.'

RINGLETS

' "Oh dear! I shall have to use the tongs." A night in very uncomfortable rags had failed to produce the desired ringlets, and it was the day of the school photograph. Mum lit one of the rings on the gas cooker and set the long-handled tongs into the flame. They were tested on newspaper to see if the requisite shade of brown scorch had been achieved, and then, unless the paper actually blazed, they were clamped over the ends of a hank of hair and twisted up towards the roots – this was when I held my breath and sat very still as the warmth of the tongs neared my neck: hold for a few seconds, then unwind the tongs and on to the next ringlet. Poor Mum, her first born had fine straight hair and ringlets were in fashion!

The worst of the winter was over so I had been allowed to cast my night-time tabard of brown paper soaked in goose grease (I had always been "chesty") and today, in honour of the occasion, I was allowed to put aside vest and liberty bodice, but Mum's courage failed her at the last minute and I was put into a thick woolly jumper before my dress was popped smoothly over the top.

There I sit, frozen forever on the school photo, with rapidly unravelling ringlets and one thick woolly sleeve creeping out from beneath a fine silky one!'

VISITS TO MY AUNT

'In the late 1930s I used to stay with my aunt and uncle on their farm north of York. We made our own fun. When Auntie did a bake larger than her usual weekly one I knew there was going to be a family get-together. It was not unusual for well over a dozen to sit down to a home-cured ham supper followed by sherry trifle and mountains of cakes. Then we'd gather round the fire and "reminisce". The same old stories would be trotted out as if new and the old jokes were never stale. Or we would have a singsong round the piano.

On special occasions there would be party games. I remember being sent out of the room, blindfolded and bid enter. Someone took my hand and stroked it over someone's head. A ghostly voice said, "Feel the Mummy's hair." Then, "Feel the Mummy's face. Now deep, deep down into the Mummy's eye." My finger was thrust into an orange. Ugh.

Mindful of early morning milking, Uncle would go to bed about 9 pm. When our fun grew too noisy he'd bang on the bedroom floor with his walking stick, we'd pull faces and quieten down.

Next day Auntie would clean the sitting room, which was only used on special occasions. It had a carpet square with a surround of lino. She would start in the middle of the carpet and brush the dirt outwards onto the lino where it was swept up and the lino washed. At springcleaning time she took up the carpet, put it on the clothes line and beat it. Then she and a helper each took one of the four corners and dragged the carpet along the grass face downwards.

Sunday afternoons were boring. After a huge lunch Auntie would go to bed for a rest and everybody else seemed to doze off, even the dogs and cats. The only kitchen sounds were snores, the tick of the grandfather clock and the settling of the fire in the range. About 4 pm they would stir. Auntie filled the kettle at the pump in the scullery and settled it on the fire which warmed the oven on the right and the hot water boiler on the left. After a cup of tea the men went out to "fodder up" and Auntie made the tea.

At harvest time we had to take the 'lowance to the fields. Scones or cakes and sandwiches in a basket and tea in a can. Uncle's orders were: "Not so cold they'll grumble and not so hot they'll sit around waiting for it to cool."'

FIRST JOB

'In 1933 I was attending secondary school having passed the school exam. Unfortunately, I hated school and was allowed to leave when I was 14.

My mother bought me a long blue coat with an artificial fox fur collar, and a grey felt hat, which made me look at least 20 years old, and I wore these to an interview for a job. I could see all the machinists staring at me during the interview in the factory office. Imagine the stir when I turned up for work in my navy blue gymslip and black stockings. It was a long time before the girls realised that it was the same person.

I must say that I grew up quicker working in the factory than I would have done if I had stayed on at school until I was 16.'

GAMES AND TREATS

When there was little traffic on the roads, we played in the street (and sometimes in more dangerous places) and our games came round in their own seasons. We had little play equipment apart from what we made ourselves but we made the most of our own imaginations and a day out or a picnic was a treat.

LIBRARY NIGHTS

'Friday night was library night throughout most of my childhood. Until I was eleven I was not considered old or responsible enough to actually have a ticket, but my mother was allowed three and one of these she gave to me.

The library at Knaresborough smelled of leather and musty paper. I can smell that special blend still in my senses. Its lights were a welcoming eight as we trudged along in the winter evenings after dark. Whatever the weather we always set off after tea, with last week's books in my mother's basket. The same people were always in the library. It may well be that it was only open on Fridays. My mother built up a network of library friends whom I do not think she shared any other occasions with. They exchanged books with each other and recommended a "good read". All this done in whispers for the library lady was of a stern, not to say formidable appearance and wore pince-nez glasses and a serious expression. She stamped the books with great determination and I held her in some awe, whilst envying her her job. I imagined she would be able to read all the books in the library if she so desired.

The children's section was small and all the books were covered with uniform bindings in plain, dark colours of brown, dark red, blue or dark green – no bright dust jackets, and most were without illustration apart from black and white prints. Nevertheless the library introduced me to the "William" books which I adored because he did all the naughty daring things I secretly longed to do had I the courage. The school stories of Angela Brazil and Maisie Grieg made me long to go to a boarding school. *What Katy Did* and all the *Anne of Green Gables* books were later favourites. Sometimes I would be more adventurous and take home Rudyard Kipling's *Jungle Book* or his *Just So Stories* but the language was pedantic and I soon returned to my old favourites.

When we had chosen our books we then repaired to the warm, brightly lit reading room. Here were copies of the *Strand Magazine*, *London Illustrated News* and *Punch*. I can remember reading carefully all the captions underneath the cartoons in *Punch*, probably not understanding that they were meant to make one laugh.

I was an early and also an avid reader and can still recall the feeling of Friday library night with Saturday next day to enjoy my new book.'

PLAYGROUND GAMES

'It was not a particularly well made place – our school playground, when I was five. It sloped quite steeply downhill and the asphalt surface, I recall, was very rough and stony – I have a scar on my knee to this day to prove it! At the bottom of the slope was a covered area which housed some wooden benches and was open to the elements at one side rather like a large bus shelter. It was here that we all gathered on wet playtimes – no indoors for us 60 years ago.

We girls shared our play area with the infants without interference from the more boisterous activities of the boys who could be glimpsed through the high iron gates which separated us. Who decided it was skipping time? or whip and top season? or marbles? or scraps? Probably the shopkeepers who suddenly displayed skipping ropes with shiny wooden handles or whips and tops and packets of coloured chalks. Whatever it was, all these activities seemed to appear around Easter time. We would spend hours chalking elaborate patterns on the tops and then perfecting our whipping techniques so as to keep the tops whizzing round and round in a kaleidoscope of colour. The skipping ropes seemed to come next. We skipped forwards and backwards or in twos and then someone would produce a larger rope begged from an old clothes line so that five or six or more could join in.

Marbles were more popular with the boys and though we collected them they were more for their colourful appeal than for the competitive use the boys found for them.

Perhaps my favourite activity was scraps. These were brightly coloured sheets of shiny pictures which one could buy. One sheet broke down into perhaps a dozen small pictures, some of pretty children, or posies of flowers, or small animals, all painted in what we would now see as gaudy colours. We kept them in toffee tins and the great joy was the swapping that took place as we traded with each other for a coveted picture. I can also recall putting some amongst the pages of book and allowing friends to see them. One scrap I recall I would never exchange; it was considerably older, almost Victorian in design, and must have been acquired as a "swap" at some stage.

At other times we played singing games: "Poor Mary sits a-weeping", "The farmer's in his den", "Lucy Locket", "In and out the windows", "Here we come gathering nuts in May". Thirty years later I was teaching them to a new generation of children who did not learn them, as I had, from their peers in the playground.

Our playground was surrounded on three sides with high walls and these were put to good use. The boys used theirs as goal posts or cricket stumps. We used them for our "exercises". These were different ways in which one could throw a small rubber ball – forwards, backwards, twisted from behind, bounced and patted – the variations were endless. Who had originated these sequences which were universally followed?

Most of our activities involved small groups of perhaps half a dozen children, all good friends. I cannot recall any adult being present as supervisor though someone must have kept a watchful eye. I do not remember any occasion when there was discord or quarrelling, though there must have been that too. Were we all more obedient and law-abiding? Our headmaster was liberal in his use of the cane and all his teachers used corporal punishment of one sort or another, so some of us must have misbehaved! We were good at amusing ourselves though, the adults seemed too busy to involve themselves in our play – and a good thing too!'

SKIPPING RHYMES

'One of the rhymes we used went like this:

I am a Girl Guide dressed in blue
These are the actions I must do
Salute to the King, curtsy to the Queen
Turn your back on the village green.

A variation on this at the time of the First World War was for the last line to be:

And turn your back on Kaiser Bill.'

WINTER WARMERS

'We had a sheltered childhood but indulged in some surprisingly hazardous occupations – climbing a huge sycamore tree near our home in York, and making winter warmers. These were balls of rolled up newspaper with firewood, set alight inside a treacle tin with holes punched in it, with a string handle and we whirled it around to get it glowing hot. We never had an accident that I remember!'

BOOLERS AND BALLS

'The children of Lealholm played together, different ball games including French cricket. The girls enjoyed skipping and the boys had boolers and hooks (iron hoops), and we all played marbles. Before Lady Ley allowed us to use her hard court and form a tennis club, a grass court was laid out in one of the fields at Lealholm Hall Farm.'

IT COULD NEVER HAPPEN TODAY

'My home was situated in close proximity to the mill in Pool in Wharfedale in the 1920s. As small children our playground was the mill yard and the factory floor. Factory inspectors must have been few. Our friends were the workmen manning the dangerous machines in the paper mill. Our survival now seems surprising. Deep water courses were important to the making of paper, including the use of a water wheel and turbines.

There were filter beds, unprotected settlement tanks, and a boiler house partly under ground in the yard; swirling beaters, rollers, guillotines, dramatic ten foot polishing arms, driers and engineering workshops. There were miniature trains of trolleys carrying pulp on and off the main road, and much horse-drawn transport continually in use. For me to help the boiler firemen stoke the boiler was a treat. To speed, on our solid wheeled tricycles, between machines was normal. In 1929 when an overhead crane was installed I was allowed to try to drive it.

It could never happen today.'

LAMBS' TAILS AND MINNOWS

'We were lucky to have a farm very near us at Skipton and this was our chief place to go, helping cut the cow cake which used to come in large blocks. We were allowed to ride the cart horses back into the fields at night during haytime. When it was time to cut the lambs' tails off we collected some and took them to the beck near and with a bit of soap washed them over and over again until they were beautifully clean. Then a piece of string was tied on the end of the tail and it was hung up to dry, and then combed until it shone and curled. A black one was a real bonus as they were lovely when washed. The beck also gave us hundreds of hours' pleasure. It was fished in for minnows and dammed to paddle in and used as a jumping game, sometimes resulting in a fall into the water, when we took our socks off and battered them on a stone to get them dry.

We played in the road at football and cricket, as only a steam-driven waggon came past once a day filled with coal for the cotton mill in our village. We called it "Puffing Billy" and waited for it eagerly each day.'

FROM MARBLES TO CONKERS

'Games at Moulton came round each year in their season, but hoops or boolers as they were called were used all year. They were a rim of a bicycle wheel, with a stick in the groove to propel it, and were chased for miles.

Marbles often started the season in the spring to be succeeded by tops and whips, with chalk patterns drawn on the heads of the tops. When these were put away for the following year it was the turn of skipping ropes and then yo-yos. We made our own yo-yos by stitching two large buttons loosely together. High summer brought out the chalk to mark hopscotch squares, and also cricket stumps and rounders bats. Larwood and Bradman were every boy's heroes. There was a season for ball games played against a wall with chanting of what to do, and in autumn conkers were collected from the chestnut trees and various treatments used on them to make them hard and potential winners. The most favoured treatment was to soak in vinegar and dry in the oven.

Ropes of threaded chestnuts yards long were used to decorate the chapel pulpit at Harvest Festival. Cowboys and indians was an all season game, and the making of necklaces from hips and haws and ash keys for the indian costumes was done in autumn. May 29th was Oak Apple Day to commemorate the time King Charles hid in an oak tree. The rhyme chanted by schoolchildren was: "29th May, Oak Apple Day, if you don't give us holiday, we'll all run away." It was a half day holiday from school, and if the girls didn't wear a sprig of oak leaf on their jackets the boys would thrash their legs with nettles, though what connection that had with King Charles I do not know.

A favourite game in fine weather was to sail wooden "boats" decorated with mud and flowers along the beck. Father used to dam the beck in summer to make a swimming area for the ducks and geese in case of drought. He placed a plank of wood across the water, which soon become dirty and feather strewn, to give access to the other side. This wood was bendable and we used to jump up and down on it. I'll never forget the laughter when Maureen fell off into the dirty water, which didn't do her fancy dress any good at all.'

LONG SUMMER EVENINGS

'Whenever I visit Northallerton, I am reminded of the long summer evenings before the Second World War, when we played rounders at the junction of East Road and Crosby Road, using the prison walls as one of our bases. We were seldom interrupted and felt quite safe though we were embarrassed and even somewhat frightened if one of our teachers went past on a bicycle. We also played hopscotch in the road, including a form of hopscotch that spiralled outwards like a snail – this took a long time to draw and we were mortified if it rained. I also remember the fascination of treading orange peel in a puddle and producing rainbows. When I pass the prison now the walls are twice as high and there is so much traffic that traffic lights are necessary at "our" corner.'

THE FIELD

'In the mid to late 1940s, after the Second World War, I recall a period of quite frenzied activity in the field next to our house at Anlaby. The word "field" is perhaps a misnomer, a little too grand. It was in fact a large unused area of very rough, tussocky grass, bounded on one side by a deep ditch and a hawthorn hedge, and on another by our house fence. The remaining two sides were a con-

Farms were a natural playground for children, here watching the ricks being thatched at Tholthorpe in 1910.

creted road and a concreted "ten-foot", ie a rear approach to the house.

The road, built in the 1930s, was on a higher level than the grassy waste. Much of the road base was a chalky rubble, abounding in the Wolds to the west. These small chunks of chalk provided us with an endless supply of drawing material for the hopscotch frames which we scrawled onto the concrete road surface. There we played at hopscotch for hours on end, in an almost traffic-free environment. At other times our entertainment ranged through a great variety of catch and chase games, and marbles, especially marbles! Our forté was the "holey" version, the aim being to claim our companions' marbles. Thereby we built up fine collections of the beautiful glass balls with their myriad of swirling colours within. Never did anyone seem to buy these beauties; they simply kept on appearing as if from nowhere, as they circulated repeatedly round the children.

Though the road carried few cars it was used by the coal delivery men and the rag and bone men, each with a horse and cart. One day my father expressed his opinion that the inevitable piles of manure left behind on the road would be excellent for enriching our garden soil. The still-effective wartime maxim of "waste not, want not" sent me scurrying out with a bucket and spade to gather up this horse-gold at the next opportunity. The ensuing hoots of derision from playmates on all sides ensured that this early effort at recycling was never attempted again.

But I have digressed, and must return forthwith to the story of the "field". Whether we had a subconscious urge to reinstate the wartime air raid shelters in our gardens, or an early teenage desire to create our own "homes" gripped us, I do not know. All at once den-building completely took over our energies, and filled our waking hours. We dug hole after hole through the following months. We moved all around the field; after spending time and effort perfecting and using one den we moved on to the next. The holes were three to four feet deep with an adjacent, shallow fire-hole attached. Every available scrap of timber, and discarded corrugated metal sheet, was collected. From these we constructed flat roofs over the holes. Hours were spent down-under, wreathed, and frequently choking, in wood smoke while potatoes baked in the fires, skins getting ever thicker and blacker. They did taste good!

As time passed, we children left home. Years later my mother related a recent conversation with a very puzzled builder, just then developing the wasteland into a site of post-war homes. While clearing the area, he said, he had encountered numerous holes in the ground, which he found completely baffling. Had doodle-bugs fallen there perhaps?'

A KEEN ROLLER SKATER

'As a child in 1951 I lived in South Bank and I was a very keen roller skater. When I was eleven years old my cousin, a friend and I would go every Saturday to Albert Park in Middlesborough and hire roller skates. Then the great day came, when for my birthday I was given my very own skates. My Mum gave me one shilling for the fee to skate, which included fourpence for the bus fare each way, a two mile journey. Then we had to walk from the bus stop to Albert Park.

These were the long hot summers that we used to have. Many times we travelled on the train to North Ormsby, which only cost twopence, and skated the rest of the way so that we could buy an iced lolly with the twopence saved! We then became very clever and a few times we actually skated all the way from Pym Street to Albert Park, skated at the rink for an hour and skated all the way home again – all for the sake of those delicious ice lollies. Those were the days!

GAMES AND HALLOWE'EN

'Singing games were very common in our schools and Brownie packs both during and after the war; for example "Do you know the muffin man?" and "The farmer wants a wife". The children danced round in a circle with the chosen child or children in the middle.

"The Grand Old Duke of York" was very popular, the words and actions having a historical significance. For this game the children stood in two rows facing each other. They skipped up and down with their partners singing and clapping.

The children today are so much more sophisticated but the pleasures were very simple years ago.

Hallowe'en was such fun pre-war, but later it developed rather into begging. Where I lived in Sheriff Hutton we had a large kitchen and friends were asked round for the evening, usually dressed up, quite simply. There was a large tub of water on the floor with apples floating in it. We began the fun by kneeling on a chair, one at a time, and attempting to drop a fork, which we held in our mouths, so that it stuck in an apple. We also "ducked" for the apples – putting on a bathing cap we tried to bite an apple in the water. A bit of mess added to the fun! Sometimes the apples were hung up on strings and with hands behind our backs we had to try to take a bite out of one. There were always plenty of nuts and fruit to eat. Hallowe'en was never frightening, just fun.

Other games played throughout the year were "Blind man's buff", "Spin the plate", "Put a tail on the donkey" and "Flip the kipper".'

SATURDAY

'Saturday was *the* day. They went to Northallerton on Atkinson's bus. It was thrilling to go the "back" way, by Bog Hole watersplash, past the cricket field and the reading room at Thimbleby – who reads in a reading room, Mum? – through Jeator Houses where Mrs Page sheltered a jail-breaker, and Kirby Sigston where the kids lived in trees and never went to school.

Even more people thronged the market than packed the field for the Swainby village show, and Danny Hoare shouted the price of his apples – but the real treat was the return journey. Richard squashed onto the back seat among the men coming home from their Saturday morning work. They let him match his puny arms and baby-smooth hands against the knotted rope of their blue-veined muscles.

In the afternoon the lads dashed, somebody hugging the precious "casey", down Cowley, over Cod Beck's tin bridges to the football field. A mill race – these days it's the orchard of a highly desirable country cottage – ran behind one goal, and the fable went that unpopular referees finished their match with a ducking. The hope now was for a good kick-about on the men's pitch before they turned up – with their studded boots and their coloured socks and their striped jerseys. Most wonderful of all, they hung a net on the goal and Richard's hero, the village goalie in his peaked cap, was unbeatable in front of it. On a really good day, while the red-faced players panted their half-time argument, the lads sneaked the match ball and sent it swishing into that magnificent net.

Then darkness was falling; the match was over and they were running up Cowley. There were end-of-the-day quarrels, fisticuffs in the high-hedged shadows that used to be that lane. It seemed a long way home. One shocking time a teddy boy from a rumoured world settled his scores with a knuckle-duster.

Yet the picture is clear: Saturday ended in a fever of anticipation in the flickering firelight of Mrs Pybus's blackleaded range, with her wireless conjuring the magic of Sports Report ... Eammon Andrews, John Webster, the football results. Has Mrs P come up on the Pools? And, to make it a truly great day, who has won the match for the Boro?'

ELECTION TIME

'At elections we children formed ourselves into groups, gangs really, each with a tightly rolled up newspaper tied with string, swinging it as a weapon. One gang hunted the others, chanting: "Vote, vote, vote for Mr ..., you can't vote for a better man. Mr ... is the man, and we'll have him if we can, and we'll push old ... (the other candidate) up the flue." To my knowledge we never struck a blow.'

OPENING THE GATES

'The road going through the dale was gated. Not much traffic passed through during the week, but Sundays there was quite a thriving business among the local children "opening the gates". One was not allowed to poach a gate but my cousin had one so I got a turn. All the motorists were generous and seemed to have a good supply of coppers for us.'

PLAYING IN THE MEADOWS

'I remember the long warm summers of my childhood in York; even the smell of those summers remains vivid in my memory. The smell of the hot pavements while playing with top and whip; the pungent smell of the gutters as we played at marbles, while trying to avoid losing our marbles down the drain.

My mother would make up large bottles of lemonade, from lemonade crystals, for my sisters and me. Armed with these and a packet of sandwiches each, we would spend the whole day playing in the meadows and streams and we would amuse ourselves by making daisy chains. Buttercups grew in confusion when I was a child, and we would pick large bunches of them to take home. We swam in the river year after year; water rats would swim past us to scuttle into their holes by the river bank. One day we watched a cow being pulled from the river; it was quite common to see the dead carcase of an animal in the river. Our parents warned us of the dangers of drowning, but dead carcases and water rats didn't appear to worry either them or us!'

SCHOOLDAYS – THE BEST YEARS OF OUR LIVES?

Long walks to school, wet clothes steaming on the stove, all-age schools and frequent use of the cane – memories shared by generations of Yorkshire men and women. Yet our teachers often gave us a good education despite the lack of facilities and basic mod cons, and many are remembered with respect.

SCHOOLDAYS AT SNAPE

'The village school at Snape opened in 1880 and in 1900 had 72 pupils on its register with only two teachers. Pupils came from the village and neighbouring farms, including the hamlet of Firby and Thorpe Perrow estate. On more than one winter the school had to be closed because of snowstorms, for even the floors were wet and damp, and the weather was often bad for a number of weeks.

There were regular visits from the school inspectors, as well as the county council drill inspector. The vicar as a school manager never failed to call each week. Another caller was the school nurse.

Every year the school used to be closed for a day for the annual Wesleyan Sunday school trip. Coronation celebrations for Edward VII and later for George V and Queen Mary gave the children another day's holiday. Many people remember the hay and corn harvest and "tatie" picking were important, and consequently saw a drop in attendance for the children were needed to help, as so much was done by hand on the farms. Children awarded a scholarship were transferred to Bedale grammar school, but very few were

A precious memento of schooldays at Snape in 1904, showing the school-master Mr Ward and the youngest pupil, Fred Hullah.

able to use this opportunity as education was not seen to be so important.

Perhaps it was because I'd been threatened when I'd been naughty – as so many others were – with "wait until you go to school", that I wasn't in 1919 so very keen to go. However, off I went to our small village school where we had a qualified headmaster (though there were periods when it was a headmistress) and uncertified assistant (these latter, in my opinion, were very often superb teachers).

Outwardly, from the village street, the small stone-built school, with its slate-tiled roof and its fenced tiny border of a garden appears today as it did years ago, but there has been a lot of modernisation inside. An all-age school, it had two classrooms, the smaller one for the infants and the other for the juniors and seniors. A glass door was set into the wall which separated them and there was also a fireplace at the end of each room. I can remember the big fires burning there, surrounded by strong iron guards. These were really essential as many children had miles to walk to school, some over boggy fields, arriving very wet and cold, so the welcoming fires helped to warm them and dry their clothes. They would bring a packed lunch and something to drink.

Outside there were two playgrounds with a dividing wall and a gate set into the wall. The bigger one for the junior and senior boys and the smaller for the girls and infants. The ground was very rough and stony (and pools of water stood in the winter) and many were the cut and bruised knees! The toilets (earth closets) were at the far end of the big yard.

Inside the classrooms there were long wooden desks with inkwells and shelves underneath, with a long bench seat for four to six pupils. Maps and botanical pictures hung on the walls. The wooden floor had many knots and nails in it and when it was swept, clouds of dust rose from the joins.

At that time, though water was laid on, there was no electricity (oil lamps were there, but I don't ever remember their being used). We worked on slates – often sharp edged – using slate pencils (their squeak would set my nerves on edge!).'

ADDERS AND STICKS

'I only had about one mile to walk to school when I was five but in summer we had to be very careful where we walked as there were a lot of "hag worms" (adders) about. This was in 1909 and we lived on the moors of Rudland near Kirkbymoorside. It was a very small school with about 18 pupils and only one teacher, who liked to use a "stack prod" (stick) to hit us with. I often got it. Once I didn't want to sit next to a boy because he didn't smell very nice so I got a good whack across my hand. I said "Thank you" so I got it again. The desks at school were long and about seven children sat in a row at one desk. I left school when I was 13.'

WALKING TO SCHOOL

'At the age of four I walked a mile to the village school with my six year old sister. We met other children and if we were early we put a stone on the gate post to say we had gone and if a stone was already there we hurried to catch up with the others. When we got bicycles, to share them we would "ride and tie", which meant riding on ahead, dropping your bike for another child to ride and setting off to walk. The next person repeated the procedure so we got to school more quickly.'

NOT USED TO BOBBING

'Way back in 1927 I was in the infants class at Sutton church school and at Christmas we were ushered into the big room for prizegiving. (I got a Bonzo book: remember the pup with one black eye?) The local manufacturer gave away the prizes but the highlight was when his spinster sister appeared.

I can see her now, wearing a black ankle-length dress with a high boned collar, leg o' mutton sleeves and a huge hat trimmed with ribbon and veiling. Even then it was old-fashioned as this was the Roaring Twenties. She stood flanked by orange crates and graciously handed us three oranges each as we came up two by two. The girls had to curtsey and the boys to touch their forelock. We had been well rehearsed beforehand amid a lot of giggling, for being junior Yorkshire tykes we were not used to bobbing.

At the end of the little ceremony we were requested to sing Miss C's favourite carol which was "We, three kings". Across the years, even across an ocean, that carol triggered my memory and how I had learnt what it was to touch the forelock!'

EXCITEMENT IN GOLDSBOROUGH

'I was five years old in 1920 and started school at Goldsborough a year or two before King George V's daughter Princess Mary married Lord Lascelles, son and heir of the Earl of Harewood, and came to live in Goldsborough Hall, causing much excitement and great upheaval in our quiet little village. The schoolchildren were lined up on the roadside to wave flags and welcome them in, but were more interested in the big black shining car as there were not many about then.

One day the Princess, always accompanied by her lady-in-waiting, brought a huge box of chocolates to the school for us. Our teacher was the only person in the village who tied a yellow (Liberal) ribbon on her dog on voting day when the only colour was *blue*, and who did not favour royalty, so I think the Princess was not encouraged though she gave us a lovely Christmas party and personally bought gifts for every child at Woolworths in Harrogate and presented us with them after tea, sometimes in her hunting outfit after a day's hunting. The cottages were improved and the church collections benefited by crowds of people who came to see the King's daughter.

I met children from Coneythorpe and Flaxby. We walked to school and back home together, we were a happy lot and our teacher was kind and caring. When two "poor" girls' mother died she made them warm winter dresses. Some children passed "The Exam" and went to Knaresborough grammar school. We learned early that everything must be paid for and "three of the best" on each hand was a small price to pay for all the fun we'd had following the hunt which had met at the Hall, and gathering forbidden walnuts returning to school with brown stained fingers.

Our teachers organised a school concert in winter to raise money to take us for a trip to Scarborough by train from Goldsborough station, the highlight of summer to us. We would gather on the station platform in our best clothes and compare spending money and buckets and spades. What excitement when the train came into sight, what a good time we had, all meeting at Boyes store for dinner.

Sometimes on a sunny day our two teachers took us on a nature walk by the river, and in autumn to gather blackberries in the big wood. In winter the big blackleaded stove would sometimes get red hot and make comforting noises when you were doing hard sums.

I was eleven when my uncle brought us a wireless. After he had gone a soprano singer nearly drove us crazy as we did not know how to turn her off. We were just going for the big hammer when Father found the switch.

In the holidays I loved going to Knaresborough market with my parents in our horse and trap. There were all kinds of things to buy on the stalls, Bob Morrison's pots and the herbalist who kept popping into the pub. I always bought a gas filled balloon.

Then suddenly the Earl of Harewood died and the new Earl, the Princess (later to become the Princess Royal), and their two sons went to live in Harewood House and the bubble burst for Goldsborough village which gradually became as it was before.'

JUST A WORD

'A walk to school and back for lunch and back again to afternoon classes was the norm in the 1920s. There were no buses. Some had much longer treks. For me it was about one mile. I first went to Pool school in 1925 with my elder brother aged eight.

The school was the typical design of stone building. Inside was one small separate room near the entrance and a remaining high ceilinged hall divided by a glass windowed partition, which ran along raised metal tracks in the floor. This made two classrooms, which could be opened up for assembly and for the many village functions – plays, lectures, whist drives and dances. I well remember the hazard of tripping over the ridge on the floor when dancing.

Off this room was a cement floored cloakroom with pot sinks, hooks around the wall for coats and wood benches below. The toilets were down the yard. Boys and girls well apart of course. It was horribly cold to go out in winter to these stone-built almost open air "conveniences", dry closets with torn newspaper for toilet tissue.

All school work was conducted on small blackboards with chalk. There were a few ragged books and no other equipment except beaded counting frames and a large blackboard for the teacher's use.

We moved to the little room at about seven years old. The headmaster's wife taught us and sewing was her pet subject. We learnt the four basic stitches – tacking, hemming, seaming and back stitch. All in white cotton to make a fully hand-stitched pillowcase. Did I say white! It was far from that as we progressed.

The three Rs took priority – reading, writing and arithmetic. At ten we learnt geography from a large wallmap of the world and a globe.

A district nurse was a regular visitor to inspect our heads. Nits were often found. But the horror of the year was the visit by a dentist. His drilling machine was foot operated. He whipped out teeth without anaesthetic. Lining up for our turn was so frightening.

Swear words were unheard of in our strict Methodist household. So when one of the boys led me off the straight and narrow there was mayhem. "Just tell ye' father he's a bugger! It's just a word." So I tried it out. The impact of that way of addressing him is a story told in our family to this day.'

DEDICATION

'At the Church of England village school in Kilburn in 1926 there was a "big" room and a "little" room. Each had its own porch where round the walls were symmetrically placed black iron coat and hat pegs. The walls were dark green and in the corner was a porcelain sink with a cold water supply suitable for drinking or hand washing.

Young pupils at Knaresborough Wesleyan Methodist school in 1905.

There were two concrete-surfaced playgrounds, one for the girls and the other for the boys. These were divided by a long low stone shelter with entrances on either side to the girls' and boys' toilets. The building was heated by two rows of six inch diameter cast iron pipes, carrying hot water from the coke boiler housed down several steps in the backyard of the school house.

Children walked to school, often long distances of two miles or more from the outlying farms. Those who could not get home for dinner brought sandwiches which they ate in the classroom. Some brought dry cocoa and sugar and their own mug to have a hot drink made, but sometimes the cocoa and sugar mixture had been eaten at playtime and they had to drink water from the tap.

Classes one and two had lessons in the "little room" under the supervision of the infants teacher; classes three, four, five and six had lessons in the "big room" from the headmistress. The headmistress had no office to which to retreat. She supervised her classes from a raised platform halfway down the side of the classroom where she had a bird's eye view of the pupils' behaviour.

We had a dedicated board of governors who paid regular visits to check on the progress and discipline of the school, and the vicar came in regularly to teach scripture. We were taught to recite the collects, catechism and commandments. One period a week was devoted to "Citizenship", and the local doctor lectured on hygiene.

We walked to church in a crocodile for services on Ascension Day and saints' day. Long nature walks were the norm and we played netball and cricket in the fields adjoining the school.

The headmistress never married, she devoted her whole life to her pupils and ageing parents with whom she lived in the school house. We all loved her. She taught us about life and how it should be lived as well as preparing some of us for further education. Some twelve years ago a handful of us attended her funeral and as we sat on the seat together outside the church we were able to remember and give thanks for her dedication; so simple – yet so real and lasting.'

OFF TO THE MEET

'Pupils at Spennithorne school in the late 1920s recall one pupil who locked all the children and teachers in and went off to follow the local foxhounds, taking the key with him. Each year the Bedale Hunt would meet at Spennithorne Hall and the schoolchildren would be taken down to the churchyard where they sat on the church wall for a grandstand view of the meet.'

GARDENING AND COOKING

'The school at Topcliffe comprised an infants room and a very large room with a stage at one end and a glass partition across the middle which divided the room into two classrooms, but which, when folded back, gave space for concerts. There was one coal fire in each room so the lucky few were kept warm but those towards the back felt very little heat. Each fire was surrounded by a high fireguard. There were between 90 and 98 pupils, but never 100 which would have entitled them to another teacher.

Most of us felt fortunate to have a school garden at the other end of the village because that meant we escaped from the classroom for gardening lessons in spring, summer and early autumn. We learnt about rotation of crops and how to sow vegetables and flower seeds and then look after the crops. There were regular customers for the produce which was sold cheaply but provided funds for the following year's seeds and manure. An outside building in the schoolyard was made into a woodwork "room" so the older boys could learn woodwork while the girls had needlework.

The older girls looked forward to the coming of the cookery van because they had lessons in it for three weeks, covering cooking, cleaning and household management. The cookery van went to the villages on a rota basis, the teacher moving round also and taking rooms in the village. The van arrived drawn by two horses and was wound out like an old extending table to twice the size. A bag or two of coal was put underneath the van ready to light the cooking range, girls taking it in turn to clean up, blacklead and lay and light the fire each morning.

As was usual at that time, children left the village school at the age of 14 and were then considered able to earn a living. The majority of boys went as farmhands and the girls as maids, but the lucky few got work in a shop where they had more time off. If it was possible to find a living-in job that was a bonus as there would be one less to feed at home and also food would be more plentiful at the place of employment. I shall never forget the shock of being sent one dinner-time with a note to one of the cottages and seeing, when the door was opened, a kitchen table with no cloth and two forms pulled up to it seating five or six children and dinner was on the table – a loaf of bread and a packet of margarine. I had just had stew and dumplings and those children, or the older ones, were at school with me.'

ALL CANED

'I did not like school. Our schoolmistress at Claxton was always using the cane for no reason. If there was even a hint of mischief and no one would own to doing it, everyone, boys and girls alike, was caned hard.'

WHAT WE WORE

'At five years old I went to school during winter in a Chilprufe vest and combinations, a liberty bodice, a kilt and jumper, fleecy lined knickers with a loose cotton lining, knee length socks and, worst of all, soft leather leggings with innumerable metal buttons up the side. On top of these I wore a coat, hat and gloves. It is a wonder I could move at all!

After the month of May we "cast off" the combinations, liberty bodice and thick knickers and wore a cotton underslip, gingham dress with knickers to match, ankle socks and a cardigan – bliss.'

'When I went to boarding school in 1938, aged twelve, I went with one enormous handicap – combinations! To make matters worse, I was the only girl in the school to be encased in them. Made of cream coloured wool material, they had short sleeves, baggy legs and some strategic openings. Undressing on my first night in a large dormitory was all right until I saw what every other girl was wearing and they all saw what I had on; disbelief was followed by unsuccessful

111

attempts not to laugh. They were not unkind, and I soon enjoyed my fame and would heave up my clothes to show anyone who wanted a look.

As well as the dreaded combinations I wore a liberty bodice with lovely soft flat buttons, knicker linings and black "over knickers", and black stockings, all this topped by a Vyella blouse, tunic and cardigan. The black knickers had one vital piece of equipment – a pocket. Gristle or chunks of turnip were whisked under the table and stuffed into it to be prised out later on to feed the house mice we cherished in the basement.

As we were in a large country house with virtually no heating all this equipment was very necessary. We had jugs and basins on tables by our beds and it was not in the least uncommon to have to break the ice prior to washing – as far as I was concerned as skimpily as possible. When spring arrived Matron would announce that our liberty bodices were to be abandoned – everyone in a vest, except me, and with summer knickers my combination legs were too bulky to be stuffed in. I could not wait for half-term when I announced to my mother that I refused to wear "them" anymore. Summer vests were produced and my "combs" made marvellous polishers. I quite wish I still had a pair.'

CLOGS

'Our village of Salterforth is on the Yorkshire–Lancashire border and when I was a child we had a cotton weaving mill in the village. Clogs were the customary wear in a weaving shed where the weaver stood on a flagged floor that was cold and often damp. The clog irons lifted the wood base off the wet floor.

Our village had a clogger's shop where clogs were hand-made to the customer's feet. The alderwood sole was attached to the black leather top with brass tacks, and irons were put on the soles and heels. Inside the clogger's wooden hut was a bench where we sat whilst instant repairs were carried out to replace broken or worn out clog irons. It was a right "kalling" shop where men went to gossip and put the world to right. We children went to listen and were fascinated by our clogger Jesse Peel, who made and mended a wide variety of clogs: men's heavy working clogs fastened by leather laces, women's clogs less substantial and fastened with a strap and button, clogs for children and clogs for babies just walking.

In the 1930s most children went to school in clogs and kept them on all day – just imagine the noise made by the clog irons as we moved around the classrooms. The clogs were wonderful to wear, warm and dry in all weathers. The clog irons were used to make sparks and to slide down the playground. On snowy days thick pads of snow and ice formed on the bottom of the clogs and we would see who had the highest pads on arrival at school. Before entering, the pads were knocked off into a pile near the door.

I remember as a child of about eight, going with my friend Kathleen to a rather posh wedding in the village chapel. We clattered down the aisle in our clogs and sat on the front row "to get a good view". My friend's mother along with other villagers had not realised who it was "clacking" down the aisle until it was too late to reach us. We were none too popular when we came out after the ceremony but the bride and groom did not seem to mind.'

FULL CIRCLE

'I went to school at Settle when I was only three years old, taken in early because my mother needed to go out to work. I was a keen learner. We had spelling lessons and early on we wrote compositions, usually describing pictures given to us, and we had the usual sums. Once you had finished your tasks you could go to the corner and get a library book from the shelf, but these books were never allowed home. I was "bright" and always finished first, and was allowed to point the spellings for the rest of the class, on the blackboard with a pointer.

In the junior school we sat in long desks and had writing lessons, and arithmetic. I can't ever remember drawing lessons or acting; there were singing lessons, but looking back it was all very austere. We never had an outing – not even a school walk. We all had to have our clean hankies on display first thing in the morning; some boys who didn't always have theirs used to ask to leave the room and tear a bit of their coat lining off to serve as a hanky.

It was a messy job being the ink monitor and filling those tiny inkwells. There was little pupil–teacher relationship, and no parent–teacher meetings of any sort. The headmaster had no office and we all enjoyed the visits from irate parents who burst into school, and in front of us confronted him because he had refused to let pupils off to take their father's dinners to them. The big boys used to do the headmaster's garden in school hours.

Being a Church of England school we had a day of scripture examinations, when a clergyman came to test us. We had prayers every morning, but the Catholics were exempt. There were visits to the school dentist in another building, and free cod liver oil and biscuits were dished out in school for the delicate. My younger sister, who was never too well, qualified for this but I did not.

Some days a man with goldfish used to stand outside school, collecting old rags. My mother was of course at work, and we took some clothes and got a goldfish. When she got home poor Mum had to take the goldfish back and try to rescue the things we had given him. He stayed outside school for more than one day from time to time.

At eleven years we could be entered for the Scholarship to the local high school or the boys' grammar school. We were kept after school for extra lessons, and I passed and went to the high school. I remember the thrill of the uniform with my name tapes on it – with the local authority grant I could have new clothes. School dinners were then a gracious affair, with tablecloths and flowers on the table. I loved the work and revelled in doing my homework; we had outings and walks in the lovely countryside. There were gymnastics, not in a fully equipped gym, but there was apparatus. I liked the competitive spirit in games and in work. I was in the teams and travelled to different schools. The teachers seemed more human and friendly, and interested in people. There were lovely Christmas parties.

I left when I was 18 years old to go to college. After college, which was the years 1937 to 1939, I was appointed to a school in Maltby near Sheffield. I never taught for the first three weeks but we all helped to make sand bags. My salary was £12 per month, and I remember spreading my first wage out on my bed and wondering at the fact that I had been paid without doing one bit of teaching. Out of this pay I had "digs" to pay for and something to pay each month to repay a college loan. I sent £1 home to my mother and I had £1 left for my personal use.

In 1950 I moved to Skegness grammar school, a mixed school where I found the children were not ambitious, their parents making money fast in the hotel business. The pupils used to sleep in garden huts in the summer, to make more room for the visitors, and they used to wait on table. But they were very pleasant people. I was there during the dreadful floods.

I moved again in 1954 to Carlisle but found the climate did not suit me, and so after one year I returned to my old school – Settle high, where I stayed until I retired as Deputy Head. Here I was teaching the children of my own primary school friends, in a way so different from that when I was at school.'

THE SCHOOL BUS

'It was early in January 1936 when I started to attend the infants school and I remember the long journey and in particular the school bus. We lived in a remote part of a Dales village and my older brothers and I had to walk about a mile and a half across fields to reach the road which ran down the opposite side of the dale, to the school, a further three miles.

This lovely old stone-built school was perched on the top of a hill about a mile from the village. I suppose it was fairly centrally situated for both the dales and the village children.

The school bus was in fact a covered waggon with four iron-shod wheels, which rattled and trundled its way up and down the dale every weekday. This waggon was intended to carry the "little ones" to school. At least that was the theory but in fact it was much more exciting to run alongside, in front, behind, or just sit on the steps at the back (if you were really tired) – only softies sat inside. Sometimes the local policeman would ride up on his bike, so of course we all sat inside on the two wooden seats, at least until he was out of sight.

This waggon was drawn by an old grey horse and the owner sat at the front on the shafts, except when he had to jump off and put a wooden chock on the wheels to stop the waggon running away down the steep hills, of which there were several. He was a kindly old man named Aaron (I must admit that at five years old I was sure he was brother to Moses, and I once had a fight with a girl because she said he was not). There were at that time about 40 children of school age who travelled to school under the kindly care of Aaron, in all weathers, twice a day, an hour's journey each way in the school bus.'

TEA BOXES

'I went to school at Grafton, near Skipton. When we were old enough we took it in turns to make the tea at lunchtime. We used to take tea boxes to school – these opened at both ends. In one end you had your tea leaves and in the other your sugar.'

ON HIS OWN

'My husband remembers that it was a walk of over two miles to his school. His mother went with him for the first two weeks and thereafter he went on his own. Only five years old and the road was an A road – something we would not dream of letting children do today.'

THE KID CATCHER

'The Attendance Officer visited Escrick school regularly and if any of the children had been absent for any length of time without a good reason, he visited their homes for an explanation. His visit was dreaded by some people as the children were probably working on the farm for much needed cash. He was known as the "Kid Catcher".'

A MAGNET

'School at Salterforth was only a short distance from home and the noise of the children at playtime was like a magnet to a little girl of two and a half years. When Granny was busy in the kitchen I would slip out through the front door (always open in the summer) and run away to school. The school door had a shiny brass sneck, but it was too high for me to reach. So I would sit on the step until someone came out to go to the toilets in the yard, and sneak in. My sister recalls seeing the little hand knocking on the window of her classroom door, and no doubt the annoyance of having her little sister share her desk until Granny came to claim me. By the time I was three they allowed me to stay.

There were two classes, with an age range of three to 14 years. Mr Smith was a wonderful headmaster. We had little bottles of milk every day for which we paid twopence halfpenny a week. Mr Smith would order extra bottles to give as prizes for "special achievement" but they always went to the poor children whose parents could not afford to pay.'

SCHOOLDAYS IN THE 1940s AND 1950s

Little changed in schools over the next generation, though war brought strangers to our classes and the danger of air raids.

INTO THE COUNTRY

'We had many air raids on Teesside, living within a five mile radius of ICI. After one dreadful night in 1940 my father decided that my mother, older sister and myself should go into the country. We rented half a farmhouse just outside the village of Rosedale Abbey in the old North Riding. I was ten years old and attended the local village school, in t' Abbey as the locals called it. Living there in the country was an entirely different life from the one I had become used

116

to; no more broken nights' sleep and wailing sirens; no more rushing down to the icy-damp cold in the air raid shelter. All was quiet and peaceful.

I walked to school from the farm down a country lane, through a wheat field following the old stone flagstones, over a stile, across a bridge, into another field (where I often ran as two over-friendly cart horses were often there); then through a tiny passage into the school yard. It was the late summer of 1940, and the weather was glorious.

After about two months we moved into a rented cottage in the village. Father came over most weekends, sharing transport with another man whose young family had "evacuated" themselves. Petrol was scarce so they pooled their precious coupons. Father sometimes took us into the nearest town – Pickering – ten miles away, where Mother would stock up at the local market. At other times Father and the other man went out shooting rabbits, to help our meat shortage.

In September 1940 I started at Lady Lumley's grammar school in Pickering. Both my elder sister and I got there at first by taxi, then by school bus, which stopped all along the way picking up children from farms. During one very snowy spell the driver told us we must get out and push, at the bottom of Cropton Bank. With about 15 of us pushing, the deep snow was still too much; so much to our delight we didn't get into school that day. Our headmaster was Mr F. Austin-Hyde, a very highly esteemed person and a great authority on Yorkshire dialect. He always referred to our bus as the "Rosedale Charabanc".

Sometimes at weekends we climbed up onto the moors to gather bilberries or brambles from the hedges. Mother made pies or just stewed the fruit, as fruit was hard to come by. Other days I visited my school friends who were all farmers' daughters, and we played in the fields and often gathered mushrooms. Our cottage was next door to Mrs Readman's sweet shop, but sweets were rationed, so we did not have much of an advantage there.

Our biology teacher, Mrs Pearson, took us out into the school grounds, where we had to dig up the turf and plant potatoes, and later other vegetables. I still have my gardening book in which I noted down "The growing of brassieres" instead of "brassicas"!

KEPT APART

'Our school at Horbury was a church establishment with mixed infants and then separate boys and girls primary departments, and never the twain should meet. When I was in the top infants, the infants teachers made tea at breaktime for themselves and also the men's staff in the boys' school. A chosen few of we infants used to help by carrying individual cups of tea in to them, so I got a look at this forbidden territory at an early age. But once I reached the girls' department, never again.

The older girls, who were still at the school until 14 if they did not pass the eleven plus, used to let their eyes turn fondly in the direction of the boys' playground at breaktime. Although the two schools were joined, the playgrounds were separated by a six foot high wall. They would write notes to the boys and secrete them in a slit in a tennis ball, and throw it over the wall. The trick was to retrieve the reply lobbed back, without the women staff on duty noticing. We tiddlers stood in awe of the daring of our elders.

We didn't have playing fields, just the concrete yard; and oh, the joy of landing on sand after your high or long jump, or running on yielding grass when you were fortunate enough to represent your school at the inter-school sports. A friend and I were a whizz at the three-legged race (a novelty); she, being much smaller than me, fitted with her shoulder under my armpit, and when we linked arms and had our middle legs tied together we were unbeatable, and always scored three points for our school on every occasion that we ran.

During the war we knitted for refugees, those of us who joined the Red Cross. Later on in the war small parcels of toiletries were sent by the Americans to British schools, and our headmistress gave them out first of all to the girls who had been doing the knitting. Lovely soap, talc, flannel and toothbrush, but the only disappointment was the flavour of the Ipana toothpaste which stayed with you all day.'

SCHOLARSHIP DAY

'I was one of a small, excited but rather anxious group of ten year olds, who travelled from Oatlands to Grove Road school, at the other side of Harrogate, in the spring of 1943 to "sit the scholarship".

Grove Road school was built in 1896 as a Board school, and is a forbidding three-storey stone building. As we neared the gates, our chatter subsided and we parted – the boys going in one yard and we girls in the other, to stand in small groups, looking round nervously.

Soon a bell was rung and everyone clattered up the stone stairs and shuffled timidly into a huge hall, filled with row upon row of desks. On each desk was a small card with a name and number, a pen, pencil, ruler and a piece of blotting paper, and a full inkwell in the right-hand corner.

"Find your place quickly," a strange but kind voice ordered, and when everyone was seated the first papers were distributed. It was a mental arithmetic test, similar to those that we had at school each week. That completed, we had a short break to go to the lavatories at the far end of the yard, and then back to work. Next was an arithmetic paper, with problems which required more careful thought. In spite of our initial nervousness, once we started work the morning passed quickly and it was dinner time. This was the first time any of our group had had school dinners, so we enjoyed the novelty. Afterwards we made new friends with girls from various schools in the borough of Harrogate.

Too soon the bell rang for our next sessions. I think that we were more relaxed during the afternoon; we exchanged smiles with other children around us and did not feel so lonely. We had become used to the silence in the hall, broken only by the scratching of pens and the rustle of paper.

During the afternoon we completed an English comprehension test and wrote an essay. The choice of subjects was similar to those with which we were familiar so we were not really troubled.

It was a tired but rather self satisfied group who returned to Oatlands that afternoon – we had "sat the scholarship"!'

INFANTS SCHOOL

'Every morning a monitor from the "big school" brought us a crate of milk. Each of us was given a small bottle and a straw. The milk bottle tops were cardboard with a small scored circle in the centre which was pushed out with a finger to make a hole for the straw to go in.

Each afternoon we had to have a rest and little camp beds were put up for us to lie on, covered with a rough grey blanket.

The milk bottle tops were washed and saved, as they had many uses. Two put together were wound, round and round through the hole in the middle, with wool until the hole was almost closed up. Then we would cut the wool all round the edge, separate the two discs and tie very tightly round the middle of the wool between the discs. When the two discs were removed we had a pom-pom.

We made shopping bags by wrapping the discs with raffia and then sewing them together. The bag handles were made of plaited raffia strands, and the bag was lined with material. Raffia-covered discs were also sewn together to make table mats.'

JAM JARS AND DRIED MILK

'School at Whenby consisted of one large room divided into two classes by a folding screen. One open fire, with a good fireguard, served the two classes. Each morning the little class used to recite a jingle to teach us our ABC: the letter B ran, "Boys' big boots go bump, bump, bump." The next day we would move on to another letter. Morning milk was reconstituted National Dried Milk, as it was

The school at Whenby, showing the separate entrances and playgrounds for girls and boys.

wartime. I disliked it, having been used to fresh cows' milk, but somehow it went down.

School dinners were cooked in a room off the chapel next door and eaten in the chapel, but after a short while our school closed and we went temporarily to Terrington village school. There, containers of milk were brought across and we had to use jam jars to drink from.'

WHAT A RELIEF!

'During the war Askham Bryan school had a relief teacher. She lived 40 miles away in Huddersfield and travelled to us by bus each Monday morning. Two boys met her off the bus with a bicycle which she rode to school, leaving the boys to walk the mile there carrying her case.

Every lunch time she went to the village public house, telling us she had to give the landlord's dog some medicine. We wondered why the bicycle was rather wobbly when she returned. We children were very happy, but we didn't learn very much!'

RED APPLES

'Just after the war, about 1947 or 1948, big boxes of red apples arrived at our school for distribution amongst the pupils. I think they were sent from Canada. Also, chocolate powder was sent to the school. We were told to take jam jars from home and they were filled with the lovely sweet powder. Probably only half the powder reached home, the rest was eaten on the way.'

STILL PICKING ROSEHIPS

'When we came to Swainby in 1956, my husband as headmaster of the village school, the "rose hip collection" started in wartime was still in force. The schoolchildren went out after school and at weekends to gather as many hips as they could find, bringing them to school to be weighed and being paid a penny a pound. Some children brought large quantities, some only a few ounces. The "rose hip lady" from the WVS at Northallerton collected them when we had a sufficient quantity.'

THE WORLD OF WORK

ON THE LAND

Farming has been a way of life for generations of Yorkshire people, and many of us can remember the days when horses provided the power on the land. Work had its seasons and there were high spots in the year, from threshing day to clipping day, that we look back on with nostalgia. It was, and still is, a hard life, but whole communities depended on the land and its people.

FARMING LIFE BEFORE THE WAR

'Leaning on a gate watching a combine harvester the other day brought back long forgotten nostalgic memories of life before the war when I was on my father's farm near Lockton, which is on the edge of the moors, about six miles from Pickering on the road to Whitby.

I was 17 years old when Father moved there after farming for some 45 to 50 years near Durham city. My elder brother Ralph was 18 and my two younger brothers, Jim and John, were three and five years younger than me. The farm, Mount Pleasant, was about 225 acres when Father took it on and I remember he paid a rent of £120 a year. The only drinking water, in fact all water, was collected from the roofs when it rained, into two huge underground tanks and had to be hand-pumped for use. No rain, no water unless it was collected from the stopcock at Lockton in a home-made, horse-drawn water carrier. Quite a job as Lockton was about a mile from the farm and shire horses do not walk very fast.

Lighting at night was by paraffin. Hurricane lamps which had to be filled and cleaned during the day were used for all work outside the house. In the house we first used the Aladdin lamp and later on the new fangled Tilley pressure lamp which hissed and hissed so much that it was often a relief to turn it off and just use the ubiquitous candle.

Mother was completely responsible for everything which happened in the house. Father ruled everything outside as only a Victorian autocrat could, but indoors, which in many ways was the heart of the farm, he bowed to the wishes of his wife. Six days a week Father used to take Mother a cup of tea every morning soon after he got up at about 6.30 am. This situation was reversed on Sundays when he had a lie in and Mother would take him tea at about 8 am.

Father would see to the killing of the bacon pigs, also the salting

John Turner from Tholthorpe wearing typical working clothes, including gaiters and a sack tied round the waist.

and hanging of the sides of bacon and hams in the attic. He would also select which sides of bacon or hams to eat, and slice off the thick rashers, which, together with fresh farm eggs and thick slices of fried home-made bread, made a breakfast worthy of the name, especially after an hour or so in the stable or the cow byre before eating. There was no Milk Marketing Board in those days, just the hand-operated separator which, by the use of centrifugal force, separated the cream from the milk providing skimmed milk, which was used to fatten the pigs, and huge bowls of lovely thick golden cream which was hand-churned to produce the most heavenly butter ever known. This butter, and all the eggs produced on the farm were Mother's perks. What was not eaten was sold locally, or exchanged with the butcher or whoever, for meat or whatever. Mother made sure that whichever way eggs and butter were disposed of, or otherwise used, she came out of the transaction the winner.

We looked forward to threshing days when adjoining farmers and their men used to turn up to help, as ten or twelve men were normally classed as a threshing gang. It was, as well as being a change from the lonely routine of ploughing etc, a means of earning some money for ourselves as Father allowed us to keep any money we made at threshing. Five and sixpence for half a day's threshing when our weekly pocket money was only five shillings was an added bonus and too good to be sneezed at! Edgar Dowson, who lived at Lockton, owned the traction engine and threshing machine, and providing coal was provided by the farmer – I think he must have been paid as well, although this did not interest me in those days – would raise steam in the early morning and threshing would commence promptly at 8 am.

Because Father wanted to choose his own threshing days and not have to rely on Edgar Dowson, and also because he was forward looking and always saw the suitability of the tractor on the farm, he soon bought a very old, standard Fordson tractor complete with removable side pulley. This was strong enough to drive a threshing machine as well as to pull a two furrow plough. Then, for the "huge" price of £35, he bought a secondhand Clayton and Shuttleworth threshing machine.

Ralph, my elder brother, was the tractor man and also carried out all the machinery maintenance on the farm as he'd had training in electrical engineering. My job was horseman. This pleased me greatly even if it was probably the most demanding job on the farm. Horses, especially working farm horses, take up a lot of one's time if attended to properly. Out in the stable at 6.30 am every working morning, 7 am on Sundays, to feed, water and muck out. The horses had to have at least one good hour's eating time before going out to work, and Father made sure that they were out of the stable, fully harnessed, by eight o'clock. Then back from the field soon after noon, fed, watered and allowed another hour to eat before starting work again. Leave the field normally at 5 pm. Feed and water before attending to one's own needs. From 6.30 to 8 pm was taken up by thoroughly grooming the horses, letting them out to the pond for another drink, bedding down with clean straw while they were at the pond and then a final feed of corn and hay to see them through the night. But I enjoyed it all and it kept me away from cows and milking which I hated.

Edgar Dowson from Lockton, as well as owning the threshing machine, kept the local stallion. His was the only one in the area and he used to travel this magnificent shire round the various farms in the district, serving those mares which were in season. Normally he would go off with the horse on a Monday morning, stay overnight at farms out in the wilds and be back in Lockton on the Saturday to serve those mares which were close enough to walk to the village. Sunday was a day of rest both for him and the stallion! If he ended his weekday travels at Goathland or in that area on a Friday evening, he and his horse would catch the local train, disembark at Levisham Halt and walk back to Lockton from there.

Mr Smith owned both the local bull and the local boar. No artificial insemination in those days, just good old fashioned servicing, much more appreciated, I am sure, by the recipients.

Father's farm, being on the edge of the moors, had a fatal attraction for the "jock" sheep which had grazing rights on the moorland. Most of these rights in our area were owned by the "Maclay Clan" as we fondly referred to them. Old Bill, who lived in the Hole of Horcum, was a great character as was his brother Dave who farmed, somewhat loosely, under Blakey Toppin. Dave was a bachelor who, not having a hair on his head never removed his cap, and who, whatever the weather, wore numerous jackets, pullovers and overcoats. We always knew when spring was near as Dave would leave off one of his overcoats.

Apart from his sheep his main hobby was bees. Once I went with my brother to cut his hay. To reach the hayfield we had to go through an orchard where Dave had about 40 to 50 hives of bees. It was a hot summer's day and we were very dubious about either going through the orchard or mowing in the adjacent field. There were bees by the thousand all over the place! However, after voicing these fears to Dave he said, "Hod on a bit" and walked ahead of us into the orchard. He wandered about muttering to himself for a while then came back to where we were waiting and said, "Tha'll be allreet noo. A've telt them tha's goin' through and they'll not touch thee now." He was right. We worked amongst the bees all day and not once did they come within yards of us.

Dave was a canny Yorkshireman. He would never use two cartridges if one could do the same thing and he'd sit outside his house in the evening, looking over the grassy meadow which bordered the steep heathery slope where rabbits lived in their hundreds. Although he was right-handed he used a left-handed twelve bore shotgun (mainly I think because it was the only one he had – I think he said once that he'd picked it up cheap somewhere) and he'd quietly and patiently wait there until a number of rabbits were eating close together. Then and only then, he'd shoot, more often than not killing three or four with one cartridge. His proud boast was that during his whole life he'd never killed less than two with one shot.

Life on the farm in those days was so different from today. No TVs or videos, just a small wireless set operated by an accumulator which had to be recharged in the village every week or so when the power ran down. There were compensations however. There was no North Yorkshire Moors National Parks in those days and we wandered where we wished without let or hindrance, more often than not carrying a twelve bore shotgun, either after rabbits, hares or the occasional pheasant or grouse. The area north of our farm was all heather then. It has since been ploughed up and laid down to grass. All the rabbit warrens where we used to go ferreting have now gone as well as all the hares, pheasants, grouse and partridge.

The village of Lockton was self supporting in those days. Every year we went to the local village tailor to be measured for and equipped with a new set of cord breeches. Sitting crossed legged on his table he spent all his time making both work and dress clothes for the locals. The fit of these clothes was often far from perfect but no one seemed to mind this as long as they were hard wearing and covered the parts they were meant to cover. There were also the joiner and wheelwright, very necessary where so much was carried in carts and waggons. The blacksmith, a large, well built man called Tot Miller, was an expert in repairing anything metal and also, again very necessary, he was an excellent farrier.

The local bakery, King and Ward, as well as supplying the village needs also supplied an area from Goathland to Pickering. It was a great treat for us, on the occasions we ran short of home-made bread, to have to eat the odd loaf or two of "boughten" bread. Another treat occurred every Good Friday when we collected hot cross buns straight from the oven and which we ate for breakfast with our home-made fresh farm butter. And in the valley between Lockton and Levisham there was the water mill! When we first went to the farm all corn needing to be ground for feeding animals had to be taken to the mill by horse and cart, left for a day or so, then collected by the same means of transport. Father soon tired of this and got his own grinding machine which was driven by the tractor.

The local postman who used a bicycle where possible to deliver the mail, also kept a small general shop in the village and always carried a pair of scissors on his rounds. A haircut at home cost us twopence in those days. Short back and sides was the vogue, mainly I think because it was the only way he could cut it. Even a special haircut at Pickering only cost us fourpence up to the age of about 18, but after that we had to pay the adult rate of sixpence, or in those days a tanner.

Then there was the "carrier", Edgar Johnson who was ably assisted by his daughter, Mary, and owned a wheezy old open-backed Ford petrol lorry. Daily they made the journey to Pickering where they collected the orders they'd received from the villagers of Lockton and Levisham the previous day. Anything not available at either of the village shops, from a bag or two of coal, a pound of mince or a few fencing posts, to ladies' toiletry or a reel or two of cotton etc. These were then delivered to the customers, payment collected and orders taken for the following day. Once when Edgar was ill I took over his driving duties for a week or two and found it a very welcome and interesting change from the work on the farm.

I remember vividly the day war was declared in 1939. We were out working in the fields that day and our eyes were never out of the sky. We were so sure that there would be hordes of Germans flying over us. Where we thought they would be going I have no idea, but we were all very disappointed when the day passed without a thing happening.

Then there was the LDV – the Local Defence Volunteers – who in the course of time developed into the Home Guard. Shortly after that I joined the RAF and only saw the farm on rare occasions during leave, or when I managed to fly there from some distant aerodrome where I was stationed. On these occasions most of the village knew I was in the vicinity as low flying planes were very rare over Lockton. There are still a few of the villagers who do remember these fly-overs, particularly those who were members of the Observer Corps which had a post on the outskirts of the village and, guessing it was me flying the plane, kept their peace and did not report a low flying plane over Lockton.'

A WORKING VILLAGE

'Well is still called a working village, but in the early years of the century this surely had a different meaning. Apart from the shop-keepers and tradesmen needed by the community almost everyone else worked on the land. There were four farms within the village and each employed a good number of men, who were specialists in their own field. The shepherds, stockmen and horsemen had to work every day to care for their animals, and this was accepted – there was no extra pay for extra hours – it was almost as if the farmer owned his workmen. In the 1920s there were 16 horses at "Mowbray", and these had to be ready for whatever was required by 7 am, so the horseman had to make a very early start to feed, water, groom and harness the teams in time. At the end of the day, 5 pm, his work was not done until the horses were settled for the night. They were his charge and his pleasure and pride was to keep them fit and handsome. Blossom is still remembered with affection and also Beauty and Boxer, and many more.

Winter work could be cold and wet; there were no wellingtons or mackintoshes in the early days. The men usually worked in teams and developed a routine and rhythm to do the job efficiently and with minimum effort so that the pace could be kept up all day. The local blacksmith made a special tool so that turnips could be snagged (trimmed top and tail) at the same speed even when wet and muddy, ready to be put into the "pie" or clamp at the side of the field, near the gate. Potatoes were also stored in a "pie", and careful handling and the building of the pie with both frost protection and ventilation were essential for spring supplies. During the winter hedges were "slashed" with a vicious slasher like a long billhook, and ditches had to be cleared and perhaps dug out to improve drainage in the wet months.

As soon as the land was workable the ploughs (single share) would be out, usually drawn by two horses; the higher fields ie up the "bank" in this area, had fairly light fertile soil with many stones and boulders, and stone-picking was a perpetual job. The stones were used to mend roadways on the farm and some were broken for chippings. The seed was sown as soon as the land was ready, with crops of oats, barley and wheat. The land on the lower farms was heavier and liable to flood so timing there was variable.

The hay harvest was crucial with all the animals to feed, and farmers themselves sometimes worked long hours from dawn to get it in, if the conditions were right. The horses might be rested during the day, but not the men, who might easily go on until dark. The farmer's wife would provide drinks at intervals, and men's wives or daughters took out food and big bottles of tea, and later on thermos flasks. Drying the hay was an anxious time and many hands used to turn it – there was always the risk of damp hay overheating, and setting fire to the rick, or going mouldy and sour.

Harvest was the peak of the farming year, and everyone available was involved. The reaper drawn by four horses, followed by the binder, went round the field in decreasing circles, and six to eight sheaves were collected into stooks. When the middle was reached, the small animals broke cover, and there was pandemonium as boys and men chased the quarry and clubbed rabbits and hares for the pot. (There was no shooting as it was dangerous with so many folk about.) When really dry the sheaves were loaded, stalks outwards, onto a waggon and carted to the rickyard, where the base would be ready. One man supervised the positioning of the sheaves as they were passed up on forks so that the rick was well balanced and would keep its shape until it had to be dismantled for threshing. That could be several weeks away, as the great steam-driven monster worked its way around the area.

This dusty and sweaty job was made easier by the company of neighbours, and the good cooking of the farmer's wife. The corn was taken in sacks to the mill at West Tanfield, two miles away along a winding lane, and the straw was stored on the farm for many purposes including animal bedding.'

'SHEEP AND BARLEY LAND'

'The farm was situated on the top of the Wolds between Scarborough and Driffield. It was what you called "sheep and barley" land, thin soil with a lot of white chalky little stones covering the ground. After you ploughed, the surface was a lovely dark brown, but come the first rain and back were the stones looking as if Christmas had come early and it had snowed.

We grew mostly barley in 1950 but also a few acres of wheat and oats. All crops could easily be flattened by a freak thunderstorm or strong wind, and as this was before the time of pick-up reels on the front of combines, we waited with bated breath for the day the kernels of barley would crack between the teeth showing they were ready to be harvested.

As crops were cut by binder there was much preparation of machinery: the cutter blades to be sharpened on the binder, the canvases upon which the cut corn travelled like a conveyor belt to be examined for splits and holes, and make sure the binder had plenty of Massey-Harris band in it to tie up the sheaves. Band made of hemp fibres was affectionately known as "Farmer's Friend" due to the number of uses it could be put: holding up trousers, tied round the bottom of trousers instead of bicycle clips, thousands of jobs in the garden, even tying down the boot lid on the car.

Corn was cut early, bound into sheaves known as "shavs", and stood up in stooks. Stooks were ten sheaves stood up in a row in "A" formation. They were then left for several days for the corn to finish ripening and drying out. Sometimes the knotter in the binder missed a sheaf and threw the corn out untied. When this happened you took a handful of long straw, bound it round the loose sheaf, twisted the ends and tucked them in.

Barley only had short straw and usually a lot of thistles in the stubby end. All the helpers used to come garbed in thick trousers, tucked into socks, the whole thrust into wellie-boots. Old pyjama tops protected the arms from scratches with rubber bands making a neat finish at the wrists. Of course leather gloves were essential.

When the stooks were ready to be stacked we went out in teams. The oldest or most fragile drove the old Fordson tractor which pulled the large four wheeled "rully" or trailer. At each end of the rully were the "gormers", large wooden frameworks against which you piled the load. This had to be done systematically. First with a person working from each end towards the middle of the rully you "square-coursed". This entailed putting two layers of sheaves around the edge of the trailer with the thick bushy ends out and the heavy heads inwards. This formed a raised edge to keep the load from slipping out. Then facing the gormers you placed the first sheaf at the extreme outside edge, heads upwards, grasped a handful of the heads and turned them in towards the centre, laying the next sheaf on top, thus trapping the first in place.

You repeated this at the other side working towards the centre.

Each person worked their way backwards, row by row until you

Loading up the haycart, a skilled task, on a 'sheep and barley farm' outside Scarborough in the 1950s.

bumped bottoms, then you returned to the front again. Usually the two women worked on top whilst two men forked the "shavs" from the stook up onto the load. A good, well laden rully finished up looking like a gondola basket and could safely negotiate the humps and hollows onto the road without "pigging it" or losing the load.

As a young farmer's wife, harvest was suddenly thrust upon me and I was informed I must make 'lowance for the helpers. The strong hot tea into billy cans was easy enough but what is 'lowance? "Well, 'bait'!" I was told. "What is 'bait'?" I asked. "Summat tae a-et. Chee-ase or summat!" Cheese I understood. "Summat" I did not.

So into the sandwiches went cheese, the thickness of the bread widening from my dainty tea-time sandwiches to doorstep variety as I began to understand the capacity of the workers' appetites.

After several days of cheese sandwiches one of the helpers remarked, "Bluidy chee-ase agean!" "Why, don't you like cheese, Jim?" I asked. "Naw," he replied. "Ower much bungs her up!"

I later became expert at bacon and egg pie and crisp bacon sandwiches.'

THE HORSES

'The shire horses were my favourite animals. There were eight to ten of them on the farm at any one time in colours ranging from black to grey, roan and bay. They had names like Damsel, a black mare, Beauty who was indeed a beautiful roan, Nancy, Charlie, Bonny and Prince who were bays and a lovely grey mare called Dutch. One day she was in the yard when a gypsy woman called, selling her clothes pegs and other wares. When she saw an auburn haired girl who was working in the house she was ecstatic. Apparently to see a grey horse and an auburn haired woman at the same time meant great good fortune to the beholder.

When we moved to Moulton Dad bought a horse from the outgoing tenant, Mr Simpson Dunn, at the farm sale. His name was Boxer, 17 hands high and built like a stone barn, with enormous feet the size of large dinner plates, and as strong as an elephant. When the horses were in the stable which adjoined the church, on Sundays, Boxer stamping his great feet could be heard and made light relief during boring sermons. The horses certainly deserved their Sabbath rest, because they worked very hard pulling carts, ploughs, harrows, grass cutters, hayrakes, sweeps and binders. Three horses were yoked abreast to pull a binder, which cut the corn and tied the sheaves with binder twine known as "Charlie Turner". This was a name widespread and probably originally derived from the name of the merchants who sold it.

Each horse had its own stall and its harness designed to fit was hung on the end. The bridles had eye pieces called blinkers which restricted sideways vision. Maybe so that they could not see how big the load was that they were straining to move. The collars were put on upside down and then turned upright on the narrow part of the neck, and fitted comfortably on the shoulders. The exterior of the collars and saddles was leather, and the inside was stuffed with straw and lined with a checked woollen cloth to prevent sores when the horses were sweating, which was most of the time during a long working day. Metal hames (known as "yams") were clamped round the outside of the collars and from hooks attached to these the traces, saddles, etc were secured, so that all the traction came from the shoulders. The plough cords were slotted through rings on the hames, to bits, for driving. The leather straps round the rear end were known as britchings and these steadied the load going downhill and gave backwards traction.

The mares produced foals that were sired by a stallion which would travel round the farms with his grooms at mating time. When the foals were young they had their tails docked, so that they didn't trail in the mud, and at about a year old they were "swung" to teach them to lead. This was a job for a few of the strongest men in the village, and was virtually a tug of war between horse and man. When the foal found it could not win it would eventually capitulate and, acknowledging who was master, would allow itself to be led by the halter. Why they were not taught to lead from an early age I don't know, perhaps there was not enough time. The horses were broken in to work when they were about three years old, and quite wild they could be too.

Because life on the farm depended on horse power they were well cared for. A man took pride in his team, so many hours were spent in the stable grooming in the evening, as well as playing cards on the corn bin lid! The horses always had liberal quantities of best hay and oats and sometimes boiled linseed which was reputed to give their coats a wonderful gloss. A pan of linseed on the fire bars was nearly a permanent feature on the kitchen range and the liquid was also fed to the calves in their milk.'

A HARD LIFE

'My first recollections of how hard life could be in the Dales were of wakening one winter's morning at about 6.30 am to the sound of the wind howling. On going downstairs I saw my Dad going out of the door into a blizzard. There were drifts as high as the door, and it was still snowing. He was going to do the milking, which meant that he had to walk to each of the cow byres scattered around the farm in different fields, where the cows were housed for the winter. He milked each cow by hand, and then had to carry the milk home in a "back can". The milk was then poured into the milk kits, and taken to a place of collection, or milk stand, where each day a waggon collected it and left empties to be filled.

In spring the lambs appeared. The pregnant ewes were brought in to the fields at about the beginning of April, to await the birth of their lambs. The farmer began his day at first light, when he went to check his flock. If the weather was bad, as it often was in early spring, some of the new-born lambs had to be brought into the farm kitchen to the warm fire. Some of them were so cold they had to be brought back virtually from the dead. The sheep needed constant attention from dawn to dusk. If a mother didn't have enough milk for her lambs then cow's milk was used, and to make it safe for the lambs a red-hot poker was plunged into the milk for a few minutes; this was supposed to kill all the impurities which might have harmed the lamb.

About the first Tuesday in July most of the farmers would go to Hawes on market day, looking for haytime men. These were Irishmen, who would descend upon Hawes in the hope of being hired for two weeks or a month, and they would live as one of the family.

Horses were still working this farm at Bedale in the 1950s.

They were expected to do the hard work, such as scything the hill-sides, which in those days were all mown. Later they had to fork the hay into the hay mews.

If the weather was good during this time the hay would be gathered in and the farmer got his money's worth from his hired hands. But sometimes it could be wet for a whole month, and then the farmer and his family would have all the haymaking to do, after the hired hands had moved on. These were pre-tractor days, and cutting the grass had to be done in the morning as early as 5 am. The farmer would do this with horse and grass cutter, to get the work done before it was too hot for the horse to work. After cutting the grass was strewn about to dry, this usually being done by members of the family. Next day it was turned over, and when it was eventually dry it was rowed up and then swept to the cow byre, with a horse, and forked in through the forking hole.

Haytime was hard for the farmer's wife too, with all the food to prepare; and most of the meals were packed into a basket and carried into the fields. Many times she had to help with the milking so that the menfolk could carry on with the haymaking.

The only time the farmer could take it easier was the "backend", the autumn, after the harvest was all in, and he could have a few days away visiting the local agricultural shows.'

DAIRY FARMING

'We had a farm in the centre of the village at Myton on Swale. We had a dairy herd and also grew potatoes, turnips and mangolds, rye, wheat and barley. All the field work was done with horse-drawn equipment. Two boys lived in the house as well as Mum, Dad and four daughters all of school age. Milking was done by hand into pails, carried into the dairy and the milk was filtered, then poured into the cooler which was a large hopper raised high from where the milk ran over a corrugated plate containing cold water and finally into the churn at the bottom.

It was Mother's job to bottle the milk and put the cardboard discs onto pint and half pint bottles. Half pints were often called gills. We girls then delivered the bottles round the village, going to the further away houses on our bikes carrying the crates. Cold frosty mornings made us get the job done quickly. I well remember breaking the cobwebs between the bushes on either side of any paths. Friday was baking day for many homes so the customers then had a bottle of skimmed milk to use in their recipes. So that we knew which bottles contained skimmed milk the cardboard tops were put on upside down.

Having finished our milk deliveries we went to school, the older ones by bicycle to Easingwold grammar school whilst the younger ones went to the village school. In very bad weather cycles were left at the station and the branch train, "The Coffee Pot", was used for the journey.

Four horses, Clydesdales and Shires, were kept for farm work. Their names were Bonny, Blossom, Darkie and Violet and I remember them as very docile creatures.

Around ten years old my job was to take the empty cart back to the hay field. The horses knew the way and the width of the gates so we always got through all right. At the end of the day, after taking off the harness, I led the horses to the stone trough across the yard for a well earned drink and then took them back to the stable where their feed was ready for them. On other occasions I was sent off with one or other horse to the blacksmith for shoeing. The blacksmith, sleeves rolled up and wearing a large leather apron, tied up the horse while I watched over the top of the door. Amid much cursing when the horse would not co-operate, he stoked up his furnace, heated the iron and manufactured the shoe of just the right size. The sizzling of water in the trough as he cooled the shoe, and the smell of filed hoof are still clear memories with me. All finished, he handed me the halter and we clip-clopped back home with no anxiety about traffic.'

A FAMILY CONCERN

'I was married in 1941. We got a small farm adjoining my husband's parents' farm, and so were able to use their implements until we could afford to buy our own. To start with we bought five cows and my mother in law gave us a chicken house and 20 hens.

Tom, my husband, did some contract work, leaving home at 7.30 am after doing the milking, and I was left with the feeding and cleaning out.

We bought a mare in foal, and after the foal was born I used to feed them both and turn them out into the paddock. Tom said that it was the last time that I could look after a foal as I had spoiled it, and when it came to breaking-in time all it would do was follow me! I worked on the land helping Tom. He ploughed the sugar beet out and I pulled it and led it off with a horse and cart.

In summer I had to pull the weeds out of the corn and put them in a bag tied round my waist. My husband bought an Allis Chalmers tractor so I could do more work at harvest time. I did all that for three years, until I started a family.

On a Saturday I used to go into Malton with 30 shillings in my purse, to do the weekend shopping. When the money ran out we did without! It was hard work, but we were both very happy.'

'My mother and her sister and their only brother worked hard on the farm at Easingwold, but they have all enjoyed life to the full. They pulled and topped sugar beet by hand, and pulled and chopped mangolds for the cattle in wintertime. In the summer they cut the corn with a binder and had to stand the sheaves in stooks to dry in the field before taking them into the Dutch barns ready for threshing. Other jobs that had to be done in season were haymaking in summer and potato picking in autumn. My mother, who is now over 80, often talks about the old days and says she wonders how they ever managed to get through all the jobs they had to do with no "mod cons".'

A WORKING LIFE

'One villager at Hinderwell told me he was recruited for work one day in October outside the school gate. He was not due to leave school until Easter but as his birthday was in January, he was allowed to leave at Christmas. Until then, he said that he helped at the farm every morning, dusted his boots at 8.30 and then went to school. After Christmas he lived in, as was the custom, and was paid one shilling and sixpence for a seven day week, with time off on Sundays between eleven and three o'clock. The farmer used to rouse the lads every Monday morning by calling up the stairs: 'Ha'wae lads, it's half past five on a Monday morning. Day after tomorrow's Wednesday, half the week's gone and there's nae work done!".'

'Bert, who was born in 1918, remembers the hard times following the First World War. A large number of his relations emigrated to Canada to find work, but his father was disabled through the effects of poisonous gas during the war, and was not able to do a full day's work on the farm. His wife and children were dependent on help given by neighbours, which, Bert remembers, was freely and generously given.

Most people at Marton grew their own food and fodder to keep a few animals, so there was always extra milk, eggs and vegetables to pass on to others in need. Farmers would confer with each other before killing a pig, so that the benefits of extra meat and offal could be shared by their neighbours at different times of the year. Bert's mother practised the same generosity too. However simple the meal she had prepared for her family, she always set an extra place at the table for any visitor who might turn up, whether it was an itinerant worker, a carter or even a passing tramp. Journeymen travelled from village to village getting work where they could, often sleeping in barns and joining a village family for a meal. Bert remembers many more strangers working casually or seasonally in this way than nowadays, yet doors were left unlocked and property was respected.

Bert started working on a farm when he was 14, living in and earning five shillings a week. But he had been doing odd jobs long before that, as all children were expected to, without being paid in cash. He would take a neighbour's cows out to pasture on his way to school each morning and back to the byre on his way home again, with maybe a piece of apple pie every so often as a reward.

Every autumn, a hiring fair was held in the local market town, Knaresborough, and farm workers and girls in service wanting a new situation would line up to be inspected by prospective employers. When he was 16 Bert was encouraged to go along to see if he could better his position. A farmer from a neighbouring village needed a worker good with horses; Bert found himself being appraised and then suddenly felt a coin being pressed into his hand – it was a shilling, the sign that a bargain or a contract was being sealed. His new job brought him ten shillings a week with board and lodging provided.'

THINGS COULD GO WRONG

'My mother told me of a brave rescue which happened in 1904. At that time the Hugill family lived at Cote House Farm, Busby. One day Mrs Hugill, the farmer's wife, was attacked by a bull and would have been killed if it hadn't been for the bravery of her daughter. Hannah was only 16, but she rushed to her mother's rescue and managed to fight the bull off with the only available weapon, which was a pitchfork. The bull was very large and fierce but the girl drove it away, saving her mother's life and risking her own. Her brave deed was the talk of the neighbourhood and was mentioned in the newspapers. Hannah's bravery was officially recognised when she was invited to London to receive a medal from King Edward VII.'

'My father, born in 1905, was one of ten children. He left the village school on his twelfth birthday and the same day he began his first day's work on a farm near Pickering.

It was February and root crops were being taken up and carted home to feed indoor stock. His first mistake was to find, after struggling to get the heavy collar on the big horse, it was back to front and much harder to get off. Finally the horse was yoked properly in the cart and he reached the field, but a bit later than expected.

After loading with swedes he drove back to the yard where they were to be tipped and stored under straw. He got the horse to back the cart to the right place, loosened the pin at the front and managed to tip up the swing body with its load. Only then did he discover that he had forgotten the importance of first taking off the back hatch, so much of the load had to be thrown out by hand and again he was later than he should have been.

A bad beginning but the farmer was a kind man and he stayed for four years.'

'The summer I was ten I was allowed to drive the horses in the shafts if Dad was there and thought it safe. He had an idea to ease his workload feeding his root crops.

One fine and calm Saturday he borrowed our near neighbour's high two-wheeled tipping cart, our quiet horse Punch was yoked up and the cart was backed up under the door to the granary over the barn. While Dad handed down the bags I placed them to the front of the cart. Our horse was unused to this and as more weight was added to his back he took a restless step forward and a lot seemed to happen in the next few seconds.

I reached forward for the reins but too late, the stone chocking the wheel had shifted, and with another step on the slope the topside wheel hit the midden wall. I heard an anguished cry of "Oh, mah bairn" as boots clattered down the steps in the barn. I was thrown clear luckily, but horse, cart and sacks finished completely upside down. The heavily built animal was firmly fixed in the shafts with all his dinner-plate sized feet thrashing dangerously.

Dad rushed to hold his head down as he knew by experience Punch would then keep still, and he did, but then of course that only gave us time to think. Our neighbours always milled corn on Saturdays so I was sent on to get help. I gasped out my tale and the farmer and his son hurried to help. Neither horse nor man had moved though both must have been uncomfortable.

Chains were prised loose with a crowbar and once the undamaged shafts were lifted Punch was able to stand up. After a good shake like a wet dog and a rest in the stable while the cart was uprighted, the split bags sorted out and reloaded, he was no worse.

Reaching the top field at last a large empty oil drum stood at the back of the cart with a metal scuttle fitted in the top to hold the powdered top dressing. I sat at the front driving up and down, carefully turning at the ends and enjoying my useful task while my resourceful parent stood at the back and did his arm waving, feeding winter-needed root crops on a warm summer's day.

It all went like clockwork and we rattled back down home to return the cart and enjoy our delayed dinner, Father was singing his favourite hymn and in a good mood. It sobered him though when passing the barn he picked up the wedge-like peg that should have been holding on the cart wheel!

Ironically I had seen it fall when the cart was righted but thought it was but a piece of dried mud.'

THRESHING DAY

'The harvest was safely gathered in at Claxton and stacked in the Dutch barns, then came the first threshing day – a big event! The steam engine and threshing machine were ordered and coal brought from the nearest railway station by horse and cart to fuel the engine.

In the early evening before threshing day, the engine was heard chugging up the lane drawing the machine. The farm gateway proved rather tricky and manoeuvring through could take quite a while. On arrival it took a long time to set the machine very precisely in the stackyard, ready to start work early next morning. The engine driver and machine man would then be provided with a farmhouse tea in the kitchen.

The next morning they arrived to start work at 6 am to stoke up the engine, and would be given breakfast. Extra men would be hired for threshing day for seven shillings for the day (in the 1930s), and would bring with them a packed lunch and their own tea and sugar screwed up in a piece of paper, to be made up at midday; this was all brewed up in the same jug and shared out!

There were two men to fork the sheaves of corn to the band cutter

Threshing day at Claxton in the 1940s, when the steam engine had been superseded by the tractor.

who would cut the twine and pass them on to the feeder who fed them into the machine, which all the while emitted a constant humming noise. The two corn carriers who manned one end of the machine would be the strongest men, as they had to carry 18-stone sacks of corn up the steps into the granary. Men at the other end of the machine used a straw jack to jack the straw into a stack for later use as animal bedding. A straw jack was a large pitchfork needed for handling the "loggings" of straw which came out of the machine. The waste chaff was also carried away in a chaff sweet.

The machine was surrounded by a cloud of dust all day, and by 10 am a welcome break was taken for "drinkings" which consisted of pint mugs of tea with bread and cheese, also apple pie. Dinner later was usually Yorkshire pudding, followed by roast beef and home-grown vegetables, and yet more tea.

Without breakdowns, one corn stack could be finished in a day, and the farmer would take a sample of the corn, which later he would take to the corn merchant. The day's work done, the steam engine and threshing machine would then move on that evening to another farm ready for another similar day.

A sad day for the rats and mice who lived in the stack, but great sport for the terrier and farm cats!'

'As the fine winter day was drawing to a close at Newton on Ouse we noticed "it" crossing the railway line and trundling down the lane to the farm. The threshing machine was on its way. Female members of the family could only think of the four or five hectic days of cooking, washing up, and cleaning up the chaff and barley haulms.

With a lot of puffing and bellowing of smoke, the machine was set up for an early start the next morning, but the men must be fed, and when they had eaten their tea they left with a "Thanks, see you at seven in the morning".

In for breakfast they came. Meanwhile, bread was baked, scones and apple pasties made, to be washed down with mugs of tea. These were enjoyed at 'lowance time, followed at twelve by an invasion of all the extra helpers, for dinner. At three it all happened again, not tea this time, but buckets of beer. Threshing was dry, dusty work! Believe it or not, they were all back at five for tea.

Threshing done, what a welcome sight to see the machine puffing and blowing over that railway crossing again, going to someone else's kitchen for tea! There is a lot to be said for the combine harvester.'

'While the threshing was going on, my mother was busy in the farm-house kitchen. During the morning work stopped for a short time while the men had sandwiches made from home-made bread and home-cured bacon. Later for dinner my mother always cooked a large tin of stewing beef with onions and gravy, on the coal-fired range, and this was accompanied by mashed potatoes and carrot and swede mashed together. Home-made apple pie and custard followed. There were usually about twelve men to be fed. As soon as they went back to work my mother washed up and started to make scones for them to have with their drinkings in the afternoon. The threshing men had a grading of the quality of the food supplied by various farms, and we were fairly near the top of the list.'

MIDWIFERY WITH A DIFFERENCE

'It was in the late summer at Kilburn that we found ourselves in possession of 28 gimmers. A gimmer, for the benefit of the uninitiated, is a maiden sheep, that is, a female sheep with two broad teeth, which has not yet been mated.

All we had to do, or so we thought, was to leave everything to the shepherd and take pretty pictures of little lambs gambolling in the spring. Came the New Year the shepherd left us and we were left with the gimmers, all 28 of them now well and truly in the family way. If we had had any foresight at all we would have sold those dear pregnant creatures while they were each and all of them still in one piece; but after misguidedly listening to a short lecture from a vet on how simple it all was – "nothing to it" – we felt confident that we could cope.

The first birth was calculated to take place on Valentine's Day, and as we thought that a maiden could be anything up to one week late we were still in the throes of anticipation on 10th February when things began to happen – very fast indeed. I was lying in bed in the early morning when a voice called upstairs: "Get up, we've got a lamb and there's another coming." Clad in pyjamas, dressing gown, mackintosh and wellington boots I skidded through the puddles to the sheep house to find a ewe – no longer a gimmer – licking a little black lamb. One look at her opposite end told me where the other lamb was coming from. There was this little black head hanging out of the orifice, actually bleating to be born and mum at the other end trying to make us understand that she wanted rid of it. After a short period of time had elapsed it was obvious that the mite couldn't get out without assistance. Our help was needed.

For weeks we had read and re-read *The Practical Shepherd* so, following the instructions we prepared a bucket of warm soapy water well laced with antiseptic and opened a bottle of Lambing Oils, a very highly antiseptic lubricant. One look at this hunk of mobile mutton told us it needed a man's strength to hold her down while being delivered, so I was instructed to scrub up and feel inside. Here I was, literally up to the elbow feeling amongst the gathers, pleats and tucks of the warm wet tissue to ascertain in just what position the little animal was resting. Our worst fears were confirmed, he had both legs back, firmly wedged horizontally to his tummy, instead of taking the sensible nose dive out, with his chin on his forefeet as his little sister had done a short while before.

The book advised to run the hand gently round the shoulders stretching each leg forward from underneath the elbow, pushing the head back inside if necessary. Now *there* was a problem, how to push back his little head without actually smothering the poor thing. However, ten minutes later he had made his debut, but the stormy passage had left its mark. He was very weak, so, resting myself against the warm kitchen cooker, a limp lamb hanging over one arm and the book of instructions in the other hand I proceeded to read up "Methods of Revival". Whisky and warm milk from a bottle it said, but he was too weak to suck. Whether it was the gasping following the neat brandy I administered we shall never know, but this was quite the quickest resuscitation I have ever witnessed. One hour and three brandies later he was bleating to be back with the mother he had so ardently bleated to be extricated from earlier.

This was only the beginning, there were still 27 more to be attended at birth. From now on it meant a two hourly round night and day. These ladies got on with it once they really got the notion. At ten o'clock each night I would sit on an upturned feeding trough with a pocket full of sugar lumps, which the creatures loved, and as they came nuzzling the back of my neck for the goodies I would focus the beam of the torch on to each posterior as it came into view in order to assess whether we were likely to have a parturition party that night. Some nights were like a busy maternity ward, one would start labour and soon there were more paining in sympathy and so we would get three or four off the list in a very short time.

As each lamb was born it had the umbilical cord cut and treated with iodine, a vaccination against tetanus and pulpy kidney and, within 24 hours of birth, all had their tails "ringed" between the third and fourth coccygeal vertebrae in order that the tail sloughed off; much kinder than the old fashioned "cutting". In the case of the male lambs, castration by the same method of ringing, within three days of birth. Quite busy at times, but it was worth all the sweat and tears – yes, I actually wept when our one and only was born dead. Some things never become commonplace in this materialistic world, the greatest of these things must surely be the miracle of birth.'

CLIPPING DAY

'Our Clipping Day at Pickering was always the first Wednesday in July. It really started the evening before when the sheep and their lambs were brought down from the moor into the farmyard where they were confined for the night. Father was apprehensive if the weather was unsettled as it was difficult to house the sheep in small farm buildings to keep them dry.

The sheep shearers arrived – uncles, cousins and neighbours, with their shears wrapped in their overalls. My brothers in their early teens or younger usually had a day off school to be sheep catchers, and there was a lot of banter and teasing if a sheep got away from anyone. Uncle John was an important helper, usually bringing lettuce and new potatoes for dinner, which Mother and an aunt prepared for between twelve and 20 people. We always had cold home-cured ham, new potatoes, lettuce salad and cold pease pudding – the peas to make the pudding having been boiled in the ham-flavoured water. Afters was probably apple pie and cream.

During the afternoon the men had a break for a glass of beer or home-made ginger beer or lemonade. When all the sheep had been sheared and marked with a red rud mark down the flank the lambs were marked the same, then it was lovely to see them wandering up the fields bleating and finding their own mothers.

After another good feed the men went for a walk round the farm and we children with neighbouring children used to play cricket, with the men joining in as they came back from their walk. I don't remember many wet clipping days, but guess there must have been some.'

IN SERVICE

Many girls found that the only work available to them when they left school was to go into service, either at a farmhouse or in the 'big house'. Experiences were as varied as the families they worked for, and it was hard work for little pay.

THE WORK WAS HARD

'At the age of 14 I moved to the village of Newton le Willows, in lower Wensleydale. I went to be employed at a large boarding school for boys; in those days it was known as going into service. The school employed a large staff, both indoors and outdoors. The work was hard, rising at six o'clock each morning and there were many chores to be done before breakfast, such as blackleading stoves and scrubbing floors. Yet we enjoyed our working hours and our leisure. If we went out we had to be in by 9.45, or else!'

FROM FARM TO HOUSE

'Alice went into service in 1927 at the age of 14. Her first position was in a "hind's house" or farm foreman's house where the farm lads lived. At that time there were nine lads living in the house. She was up at 5 am to lay and light the open fire and prepare the lads' breakfast consisting of cold meat, bread and butter and tea. The stoves had to be blackleaded, flues cleaned and the steel fender and fire irons burnished. She had to help with cleaning the bedrooms, scrubbing the floorboards as they had no covering. She remembers harvest time being particularly busy with "allowances" (lunches) to be taken to the men twice a day. Another memory is of scrubbing the kitchen table which was so wide that she couldn't reach across and had to kneel on it. The Mistress would come with a sewing needle and run it along the grooves to see if all the dirt had gone.

Alice next went to work for the "boss" of the British Oil and Cake Mills at Stoneferry, Hull. She was a maid but was asked to take over the cook's duties when Cook developed asthma. Unfortunately for Alice she didn't take over Cook's wages.

After two years Alice moved on to work for Doctor Gillespie, who in fact had brought Alice and her eleven brothers and sisters into the world. Here she was employed as cook with two other girls helping in the house, but her duties included much more than cooking. A typical day started with the cleaning of the consulting room, front doorstep, bells and door plate, followed by the cleaning of the dispensary, not forgetting to wash the bottles, then cook the breakfast, all for 8.30 am. She had her own breakfast, then upstairs to make her bed, clean the room and bathrooms. Downstairs again to clean the two kitchens, the front one housing the big oven and the back one containing the sinks where the washing up was done and vegetables prepared. Next clean the pan cupboards, pantry, other cupboards and ovens as necessary. Lunch was then prepared, washing up done and supper prepared.

No extra help was available for entertaining, Alice did it all. She remembers once a tennis party and a bridge party on the same day. Another memory is of a new china dinner service with four tureens with knobs on the lids and Alice knocked off one knob at four consecutive dinner parties. When Alice first started at the doctor's, Madam worked out the menus but later this was left to Alice too and she also did the ordering. Meat, vegetables and groceries were all delivered to the door. If steamed chickens were on the menu for lunch she had to draw and prepare two chickens before breakfast. The staff didn't eat the same things as Dr and Mrs Gillespie, tomatoes for instance were only for "the room", in fact Alice remembers once Madam removing tomatoes from their plates. They were not allowed fresh eggs but had to eat ones preserved in waterglass and when "the room" had pork sausages the staff ate beef ones.

The two girls always had their time off together, then Alice had to do their work as well. She herself had two nights off one week, the next two nights plus a half day either on the Saturday or Sunday. The half day started when the lunchtime washing up was finished. She also had one week's holiday a year. For this she was paid £2 17s 6d a calendar month. She had to provide her own uniform comprising three morning dresses, six big white aprons, three caps and three sets of cuffs, an afternoon dress, six afternoon aprons and three afternoon caps. One Christmas Madam gave her an afternoon dress, cap and apron as a present. When she had been with the Doctor for five years, her mother was invited to tea in the dining room with the silver service and Madam gave Alice a bankbook with £5 in it.

At the outbreak of the war the family was evacuated to Scotland and Alice was out of a job. She married in 1940 and continued her work on a daily basis at a farm at Summerbridge near Harrogate. Although the hours were long and the work hard Alice says she would do the same again.'

LIFE IN THE BIG HOUSE

'From the late 1920s I spent nine years in service. Life in the big house was well organised with a total of six servants to look after the master and mistress and two children in the house, and nine outside servants including stable staff, gamekeepers and gardeners. The gardens supplied virtually all the food for the house, including exotic fruits such as figs, grapes and peaches, all grown in glasshouses in the walled garden. Altogether the estate, which included two farms, provided a living for 20 families. As nursery maid, and later a nanny, I helped to look after the two girls, much better than having to get up at 5 am to clean out the kitchen fireplace and light the fires, as the kitchenmaid had to do.

The Swiss governess taught me to sew, and one of my jobs was to make all the clothes for the children. I also went on holiday with the family, looking after the girls and staying in hotels. This was a change from being on the top floor of the house where the stair carpets stopped on the floor below – bare boards for us.

Life had its lighter moments, such as trying on the fancy clothes of the mistress when she was out.

I was treated very well, and when I got married and left service, I was told to go through the estate house into which I was moving and say what joinery work and decorating I needed doing. They also took me to a shop selling sewing machines and let me have my choice for a wedding present. I chose one of the cheapest models, but it has been superb and is still doing good service today, 60 years later.'

IT CAME IN USEFUL

'Annie worked in a munitions factory during the war but before that she had been in service as a parlourmaid in a large, old-fashioned house. Her employers were two elderly sisters and their invalid brother who also enjoyed the services of a cook, a kitchenmaid and a nurse.

Annie's day would begin at 6.30 am and rarely finished before 10 pm, when her last task of the day was to collect up all the silver –

tureens, candelabra and all – wrap it carefully in special cloths and take it up to the mistress's room for safe keeping overnight. Every morning it all had to be brought down again.

The two maids shared a bedroom and had the use of a hip bath, though later two bathrooms were installed in the house, one for the exclusive use of the staff. Otherwise the regime was an old-fashioned one with plenty of scrubbing and polishing to be done. Annie's most hated job was cleaning the numerous pieces of silver, which left her fingers blackened and rough.

Annie had one half-day off a week, which began at 2 pm, and one full day off every month, but this did not begin until after 10.30 am, when all the early morning chores had been completed. In recompense for these long hours of duty, Annie received the sum of £3 a month. She was given board and lodging, of course, but had to buy her maid's uniform out of her wages. After marriage, Annie's domestic experience in service came in very useful in running her own home.'

VILLAGE TRADES AND CRAFTS

Many jobs were to be found locally, from craftsmen such as the village blacksmith or wheelwright, to the road lengthsman or the local shopkeeper. Villages were often closely connected with the surrounding farming community and were busy places.

DIFFERENT OCCUPATIONS

'Farming played an important part in village life at Brompton on Swale in the early 1900s. The mill owned by Mr R.H. Layfield continued to operate until 1947. A threshing machine business owned by Mr J. Hugill ceased in the 1950s when farmers purchased their own harvesters and other machines. The brewery owned by the Fryers closed in 1956. Other trades continued, such as joiners, blacksmiths and builders. Employment was also available at the nearby quarries, the railway and Catterick Camp.'

The blacksmith at Spennithorne, high in the hierarchy of village craftsmen.

A BUSY PLACE

'Newsham was a small village but it had a working water mill in the 1930s, where my mother bought large white linen sacks of freshly ground flour. When the sacks were emptied they were often made into aprons, pillowcases or cushion covers. There was a village pub, and below this was Coles' haulage garage. This garage became the dance hall for the villagers, when the waggons were removed and a wooden floor placed over the concrete. It was also the headquarters of the ARP during the war, as it was one of the few places with a telephone.

There were three shops, a blacksmith and a bus company. This bus company carried passengers to and from Darlington, picking up the fares in the villages between Barmingham and Darlington, a distance of about 20 miles.

The blacksmith's shop was over the road from our cottage and I loved to watch the two farriers using the huge bellows to blaze up the fire, then thrusting the horseshoes into it and getting them red hot. With sparks flying from them the shoes were hammered into shape, then with a lot of hissing and rising steam they were plunged into a trough of cold water and cooled down.'

'We had quite a few shops in Middleton St George which served all our needs, including a small draper's shop run by Miss Millar. She sold some jewellery, cosmetics, sewing aids, traced articles ready for embroidering and the silks to do it, crochet cotton, wool, various patterns, as well as some clothing and haberdashery. There was the post office, newsagent's, greengrocer's, two general grocery shops in the square, as well as a Co-op stores. Mr and Miss Robinson (brother and sister) had a shoe shop and shoe repair business. Then there was Pennocks fish and chip shop – oh! those scollops, slices of potato dipped in batter and deep fried; they were delicious and you got a big bag full for a penny. Next door, Pennocks had a baker's shop. Old Mrs Pennock used to get up at about four each morning and bake the most wonderful bread and teacakes, scones, and a variety of cakes. Her rice cakes were the best I'd ever tasted! Sadly, owing to the depression, they moved to Redcar in the mid 1930s and set up in business there. In the mid 1950s my mother and I called into their shop in Redcar. Their children and grandchildren were running the business and they were doing a very good trade with the tourists.

There used to be a round trough in the middle of the Square with a signpost on it. Mother would despair of us and got very irate; when the weather was fine and the trough dry, we used to sit at the base of the signpost with our feet in the trough and talk, while the traffic just went round us. If Dad came up to the pub, I was quickly despatched off home.

The industries were mostly farming, plus some light engineering. Just beyond the Old Row there was some stone quarrying from the slag left from the ironworks; the stone was crushed for roadworks. It was trundled round to the crushing plant, across the main road, to the crusher on a miniature light railway. The little steam engine was rather like Thomas the Tank Engine! The stone crushing plant ceased some time after the Second World War.

Up to the mid 1930s Dinsdale Ironworks gave a great deal of employment for the villagers, but in 1936 the company was wound up and it stood derelict until after the Second World War. Dinsdale Ironworks were known locally as "the works" or "the Blast".

At Fighting Cocks was a small firm of Arnott & Young who dealt in scrap metals, pipes, etc. This was taken over by another company in about the late 1960s.'

THE LENGTHSMAN

'Some of the occupations prevalent in rural areas during the 1920s and 1930s died out after the Second World War. One of these was the job of lengthsman, responsible for the care and maintenance of a fixed stretch of road. He could be seen at Marton with his spade, broom and barrow, sweeping, cleaning and filling potholes. As he lived near his length of road, he took a personal pride in doing his job well and his neighbours knew whom to approach for immediate action if the road needed attention.

Grass verges would be grazed by farm animals, horses, goats or sheep, and these would be looked after, or "tented", by village children. The schoolmaster would often have to complain to parents when children missed school because they were tenting the animals.'

CONNECTED WITH AGRICULTURE

'Most of the village workforce at Moulton was employed in agriculture or connected employment and supporting services. There were two blacksmiths in the village, one mainly engaged in shoeing horses and the other, who also owned a threshing machine, repaired farm implements. The clang of hammer on metal was heard around the village on most working days. There was also another threshing machine owner living in the village, but he worked in another area and travelled to work every day on his bicycle.

The joiner's shop was housed in a medieval chapel. Herbert Pinkney was also a wheelwright and the local undertaker. There was always a wheel of some sort on the verge outside his shop, waiting for new spokes, felleys or rims. He made coffins and organised funerals so that everyone had a dignified end. The chapel of ease at Moulton was not dedicated for funerals so that the bodies were transported by horse and cart for the service and interment at Middleton Tyas. When anyone in the village died everyone drew their curtains as a mark of respect at the time of the funeral, and the curtains of the house where the person had died were kept closed from death until the funeral, usually three days.

Quite a few men were employed by the local council to mend and clean the roads, and others as labourers on local farms. Farm "hinds" lived in tied cottages and had to move their place of abode when they changed employers.

Mrs Ireson kept the village shop, which stocked all the groceries one might need and was also the post office. The postman, Tom King, came from Middleton Tyas and walked with his heavy bag from the post office to Scotch Corner, south to Morris Grange, down to Moulton, along past the Hall towards Uckerby, across to Lingy

Moor and back to Middleton Tyas via Kirkbank, every day including Christmas Day and in all weathers.'

LIFE IN A VILLAGE SHOP

'Looking back on 30 years of shopkeeping in a village store in the Yorkshire Dales, I have so many memories of a life far removed from present day standards.

It all began in the 1930s when, after eight years of marriage and with a five month old baby, we heard of a store for sale in Hampsthwaite. Excitedly, one evening we went to view the property with its many outbuildings, orchard and garden. The stock was very limited, but there were drawers filled with hundreds of linen buttons, hooks and eyes and packets of pins; there was a large box containing assorted oils – linseed, lubricating and the rest; there were buckets and brushes dangling from the wooden ceiling; there was an off-licence with beer at sixpence a pint, Guinness, Hall's wine, Invalid Port.

Undeterred, we decided to buy and were promptly told by well-meaning relatives that we should have to "put our backs into it". Being young and enthusiastic, we did just that.

Only one day was set aside to clean up – a dreary, wet day in May. I arrived, armed with brushes and other cleaning equipment, to find my husband on his knees, chipping away layer upon layer of linoleum from the stone floor in the living room. The walls were painted a drab buff colour with a very wide dado of oranges; the doors were a dingy brown – like chocolate exposed too long to the sunshine; the large black fireplace had a high mantel, with a deep plush overhang. Collapsing on to a tea chest, my mother gasped, "Whatever will you do with this place?" Dismayed I may have been, but I rolled up my sleeves and set to work with a will, tackling first the food stores and then one of the five bedrooms.

The removal day dawned, fine, thank heaven. I took a lingering farewell of our first home then, clutching the baby and a large glass shade, was driven away in state in the furniture van! What chaos followed. There must have been ten people milling about "helping", but eventually peace reigned, except for the odd creaks – and I grew accustomed to those in time, for after all every old house is haunted.

Each morning was a mad rush. I had to bath and feed the baby before my husband left to seek and deliver orders, leaving me to watch the shop. I well remember my first venture into shopkeeping. A man came for a pint of vinegar. Simple, you would have thought, but I could not find the funnel and his bottle had a very narrow neck. Result? – a flood of vinegar. It was only later I discovered the man was totally blind, but could find his way to the shop alone.

152

One day in particular I shall never forget. Glancing out of the window, I saw the orchard full of sheep from a neighbouring field. As they pulled at the blossom-laden boughs of the trees, I dashed to chase them out, leaving the gate open so that about 50 hens invaded the garden and began to scratch in the flower beds. My shouts wakened the baby, who howled lustily – and the shop bell rang!

On the top shelf in the shop stood a row of chamberpots. One special one, decorated with garlands of roses, caught the eye of a dear old lady, who said, "Missus, do you think yon up theer would fit me?" I can't remember my reply.

Some of our customers were maiden ladies, who used to arrive dressed in their rather tall black hats and gloves, bearing flat baskets covered with newspapers under which reposed empty Guinness bottles! They insisted upon waiting until the shop emptied before slipping their replacement "tonics, so good for the health" into their baskets.

A hole in the boxroom floor above the shop gave a bird's-eye view of children – and others – stuffing their pockets with goodies when the shop was unattended. We decided to have that room and the next one converted into a large bedroom. The workmen arrived one Saturday afternoon to take down the dividing wall, oblivious of the "peephole" until down came a cloud of dust on the irate customer below.

In those days we sold loose syrup. It came in large tins and had to be run off into jam jars by means of a tap. In cold weather this was a lengthy process, so occasionally we left it to trickle into a container. One night we completely forgot that we had done this. My husband went into the dark warehouse and lost his slippers and socks in a pool of syrup.

There was a very large key to the beer cellar and it was a favourite trick of my young son to drop this down a grating, forcing my husband to lower himself through the aperture to retrieve it. Once his heavy overcoat caught and nearly strangled him. The next time the key disappeared he said, "I'll teach that boy a lesson." He tied a thick rope around him and lowered him to the key. I can still see the frightened look on his face – but the key stayed in its assigned place after that.

Next to the shop we had a tiny cottage. This was let to a rather strange woman, who had a permanently fierce expression. She would march up to the counter and throw down her rent book and money without a word. She had a weakness for dandelion and burdock and would plonk down her empty bottle, saying, "Another"! Truly a woman of few words. In summer she wore a very short, tight dress stretched around her ample form and a sou-wester hat.

Growing up the front of her tiny home was a plum tree, from which a loose branch once dangled over her door. To be helpful my husband went for a ladder and sawed it off. She was furious and accused him of taking the branch with her one and only plum. Stick in hand, she was positively dancing with rage, whilst poor hubby was caught by his trousers on another branch in mid-air!'

THE CORNER SHOP

'Going into business at 20 years old was a real eye-opener especially as the war had just ended and rationing was still in operation.

The truth was we needed a house of our own, having been married only six months, so we applied for the tenancy of an off-licence and grocery store which opened from 9 am to 10.30 pm every day except Sundays, when we had five hours off.

Ration books were a puzzle at first, as my mother had dealt with mine. However, I soon got used to them.

Friends and relatives we hadn't seen for years came to visit in the hope of a little extra butter or sugar or anything else that was on ration or in short supply. But this was not on as we were allocated just enough for the customers who were registered with us. They soon faded from the scene.

The customers were lovely and we made many friends; there's nothing like a shortage to draw people together. One lady had six boys. Every Friday she would buy a bottle of bleach and a sixpenny packet of Oxydol washing powder to use to bath the boys in the dolly tub. She literally scrubbed them, and strangely enough they all had lovely complexions.

Within nine months the takings had doubled. We introduced a Christmas Club for toys and fancy goods and this proved most successful. The business continued to improve so that my husband had to give up his job and work full time in the shop.

Apart from serving the customers, many other things were requested of us: midnight runs to the maternity hospital, urgent telephone calls to make and receive, letters written and advice on spots and sore throats are just a few. But in return we had loyalty, help when needed and a kind of protection.

Of course there was gossip, but we had to be neutral at all times – that was sometimes difficult. The nodding and shaking of one's head had to suffice.

Sunday opening was the norm, and we often had a queue waiting for us to unlock the shop door on a Sunday morning. Customers didn't buy in bulk then; they didn't think that way, neither did they have the money. On Sunday morning they would come in for one egg and a pound of flour. You knew it was Yorkshire pudding day. They'd buy a two ounce packet of Bisto for the gravy.

The ordering of bread at Christmas nearly drove us mad. Somehow we could never get it quite right, and we often ended up letting irate customers have our own just to keep them happy.

Sweets were still rationed and to see children's faces when we got something different in was a delight. One gentleman spent his sweet coupons on creamy toffees and allocated himself three a day.'

WATERCRESS AND BESOMS

'The majority of the men at Pickering worked on the land, mixed farming mostly, so there was a busy weekly cattle market. One of our local industries was, and is, the growing of watercress. Situated at the west end of the town is Keld Head springs and from there flows the Costa beck; outlets of this are used to grow the watercress, which is despatched worldwide. We had a local blacksmith in the town, the smithy a meeting place for old and young alike, where all the cart horses and ponies were shod. A local family had a small business making besoms.'

OTHER WAYS WE MADE A LIVING

There were, of course, a multitude of other kinds of work and the following are just a few memories of times past – from working in a bank to a chocolate factory, from the Merchant Navy to collecting bait.

FARMING AND QUARRYING

'Jobs at Harmby were mainly in farming and quarrying. There was a quarry at Harmby which supplied stone to the steelworks of Tees-side, taken by rail, and in later years the stone was mainly used for road making. The quarry closed in the 1950s and is now two caravan sites.

Robingarth, built 1920–21, was the last house in the village to be built from stone taken from a small quarry in the Ghyll – there was also a lime kiln here and during the war years the area was used as the village tip.

There were six farms of a decent size, mainly dairy farms but chee-semaking was stopped in the early 1940s when the Milk Marketing Board started and all milk was sent to the dairy.'

IN THE LIBRARY

'Today we take the wide choice and availability of services provided by the County Library for granted but, in days gone, the library pro-vided only books and the choice was limited.

In 1930 when I joined the staff of the North Riding of Yorkshire County Library at the age of 14, the headquarters was located in the old Deeds Registry building in Zetland Street, Northallerton. There was the county librarian, a chief clerk, three clerical staff and me. It was a two storey building with a central staircase. On the ground floor on the left side was the general office with the county librarian's office and the new book room above and on the right was the packing room and fiction stock room with the old book room and non-fiction stock room above. There was a cloakroom with hand basin under the staircase and an outside toilet. Only the non-fiction room was available to the public.

The local branch library was housed on the ground floor of the town hall and was open two evenings a week. It was manned by unpaid volunteers whose reward was the use of the fiction section at headquarters. The book stock was changed twice a year.

Books were provided to schools throughout the county and branch libraries were set up in village halls and institutes. The number of books available was dependent on the number of readers and the variety (romance, mystery, western, etc) was provided as evenly as possible subject to guidance by the volunteer librarians as to their readers' preferences. The county library had no transport of its own. Books were packed in wooden boxes with hinged lids that could be padlocked and each box held about 75 books. The transport was hired from the local garage and was a coach with the seats removed. The emergency exit door was at the rear and was useful for loading and unloading the boxes. The chief clerk went on the runs about twice a week and each branch library and school had their books changed every six months. On those occasions when the load excee-ded 20 boxes, I was sent to assist with the lifting. No mechanical aids were provided. It was an opportunity to visit many unspoilt villages in the Riding.

We did simple repairs to books with loose or torn pages whilst books with damaged covers were sent for rebinding. Books beyond repair had their hard backs removed and went for salvage. There were never any book sales. Except for the odd borrower of non-fiction we had very little contact with the public and the job was very monotonous. Selecting books, packing boxes and typing lists for each centre. Unpacking boxes, checking the books for condition, and replacing them back on the shelves in alphabetical order of authors. However, we did have the opportunity to read new books when they were purchased. In addition we dealt with requests for non-fictional books by post and I learned to pack a neat parcel.

We worked a five and a half day week and my salary, at £26 per year, was paid monthly.'

GARAGE MATTERS

'One of the difficulties which faced us in the motor repair trade in Ripon during the war was the shortage of spare parts. I must have spent hours searching through the local scrap yards in the hope of finding useful spares.

Tractor spares were somewhat easier to obtain. Fordson tractors were the most popular, and these were reliable machines which gave little trouble apart from the occasional difficulty with starting, and almost invariably this was due to a fault with the magneto. It was a source of delight to be called out to a Fordson which, despite all efforts, refused to start. It took only a few minutes to check that it was in fact the magneto that was at fault and remove it, fit a replacement, then one quick pull on the starting handle – an instant start, and a very smug young mechanic gracefully accepting the admiring remarks of all present. Life in those days certainly had its lighter moments.

I remember carrying out some minor repairs to an ancient Austin Seven and noticing that one of the spokes of the steering wheel was heavily bound with raffia. Thinking that the spoke was either cracked or broken, I cut the binding off in order to check, but could find nothing wrong. When the owner called to collect the car she was most annoyed at what I had done and insisted that the binding be replaced immediately, saying that she couldn't possibly drive without it. She went on to explain that when that particular spoke was at twelve o'clock she knew that the road wheels were facing straight ahead. The fact that she was the wife of a local vicar, and perhaps had divine protection could explain why she never had an accident in the whole of her driving career.

The incident which I will never forget involved a motorised cultivator owned by a local market garden. The owners had asked us to give the machine a complete overhaul and had promised to deliver it on a low horse-drawn cart which they used in the garden.

Our boss was out when it arrived, but this was no problem; no lifting was involved and it was only necessary to slide the machine off the end of the cart. I asked the youngster in charge of the pony to back it so that the cart was just inside the building. This he did, then the trouble started; we had unfastened the cultivator and started to pull it off the cart when the horse reared and began to prance about. This unloaded the cultivator more quickly than we had intended, but we managed to swing it out of the way as the horse continued to back until all too soon he was over the inspection pit and his thrashing hooves had dislodged a couple of pit planks. It didn't take long for his hind legs to disappear down the pit. He was still thrashing around, obviously in a panic (he wasn't the only one believe me!) and the only thing that I could think to do was to get the cart off him. This I managed to do but it proved to be a mistake as once free of the cart he slid backwards down the pit.

The boss arrived about this time and fortunately saw the funny side of all this; in fact he was still laughing when he rang the local knacker yard and explained the situation to them. They were customers of ours and not only came straight away, but much to my relief carried out a rescue operation with speed and efficiency – a couple of ropes around him and they quickly pulled him back onto his feet, then placing a wide plank down from the end of the pit, they walked him out with no trouble.

Fortunately he had not injured himself in any way, although for months he could not be persuaded to go anywhere near the garage. We took the cultivator back in the shop van; obviously I was much better with things mechanical than livestock!'

PING AND SHOTTER

'In the autumn of 1945 I joined a large branch of a York city bank. Although the war was over, it was evident that things were not normal by the fact that the male staff was mostly middle-aged, the younger members were still in the forces. Each morning everyone signed the attendance book, which was whisked away to the accountant's desk at 9 am precisely – latecomers were not encouraged. All the ladies wore overalls, with a choice of navy or dark green. Much later the brighter colours came along, greatly appreciated by the customers! As a special concession, the men were allowed to wear sports jackets and flannels on Saturday mornings. Our messengers too were resplendent in uniform, complete with bowler hat. They were real characters, Mr Fix-its to a high degree.

Work in the general office took place sitting on high stools at equally high sloping desks, using scratchy pens. Once in my junior days I used a fountain pen containing green ink, only to be told:

"Green ink is for inspectors' use only." "Inspector" was also a dread word. They had a nasty habit of arriving, unexpectedly, on a Friday afternoon, just before closing time. That meant an immediate cash count and another late night! The staff knew that for a number of weeks chaos would reign supreme, with everyone running around trying to satisfy the whims of the inspector and his assistant.

Behind the general office was the machine room. Here all ledgers and statements were posted on NCR machines, and it tended to be very noisy. Each day all entries, debits and credits from various sources were listed and had to balance. Everyone breathed a sigh of relief when it did, otherwise it meant staying until the error was found – yes, even a penny. Standards were very high and statements were not issued with even one typing error (yes, it was possible to ask for, and get, an up to date statement over the counter!). We machinists were very proud that we could recognise the signatures of all our customers, and forgeries did not get past us.

The holiday chart's arrival caused mild excitement and much disappointment. Choice was made in strict order of seniority, and for some years my two weeks' holiday was taken in early May or late September. The end of the year balance was always a nailbiter, what time would we get off to the New Year's Eve party? Usually about 10.30 pm. Fortunately our friends understood.

During the winter of 1947 and the power cuts, I remember working by candlelight and dashing to use the machines as soon as the electricity came back on.

We used to dread the frequent Bank Rate changes, which always came at noon on a Thursday. Every account had to be ruled off by hand.

Ah, the "Ping" was the noise of the chief cashier tapping his pen on the scales to signal that all customers had left the premises, and smoking was now permitted. "Shotter" was the cry of a cashier balancing his till at the first attempt.'

THE HARD LEVEL

'When I was at school, soon after the Second World War, I often walked with family and friends in Swaledale. I was fascinated by the remains of the lead-mining industry that were clearly visible on the valley sides and moors. My favourite ruins were of the Old Gang Mine where the lead ore had been crushed and processed; also Surrender Bridge, where the ore was smelted into metallic lead.

However, my greatest fascination was in the mine tunnels themselves – dark, cold and eerie entrances, with well-built arched stone roofs, and a chilly stream of clear water pouring from them. They were called "levels", even though the water drained gently outwards into the daylight. One of the best known and easiest to enter in those days was the Hard Level of the Old Gang Mine.

Preparations for our mining expeditions were minimal. Lighting was traditional with a candle on a stick, sometimes protected in half a baked bean tin with a front window of perspex. The water level was lowest in the mine after a long summer drought, and it was always preferable to emerge from the cold, dank tunnel into a hot summer's afternoon – our back-up team preferred to wait for us in similar conditions.

In those early post-war years, before Swaledale was a mecca for tourists, and the Yorkshire Dales had become a National Park, these mines were not so well publicised as now. A narrow-gauge railway with some ore tubs was still in place in the level. We splodged forwards through the ice-cold water for hundreds of yards, and often saw tools of various kinds on ledges along the side of the level, just as though they had been left there shortly before. In many places water poured down from above – down old ventilation shafts full of rotting timber that looked every bit as dangerous as they must have been. Often there were side branches of the tunnel that were full of still water, usually deeper than our "wellies", so never fully explored.

The final thrill of our long trudge was reaching the main junction of the mine, where three tunnels branched out. The left-hand one was most accessible, and often the walls glistened in the candlelight – rich in galena, the lead ore the miners had to search so hard for. In places the tunnel had been cut upwards to follow the rich vein of ore – so high it was beyond our lights. To us, seeing this working face of the mine was better than finding gold, and it made our cold, wet feet easier to bear.

We had to admire the fortitude of the miners, who had worked there year after year, in all conditions and much danger. We were equally amazed at the courage of the mine owners, who pressed on with this level, hoping to cut across the rich veins of lead ore hundreds of feet under the moors. No wonder its name was changed from Force Level to Hard Level!

I don't think the level is easily entered now, for the entrance has collapsed, and caused deep water to back up inside. There is no sign of our little railway and the tubs. Walkers on the Coast to Coast Path – that passes only feet away – may not even realise the significance of the small landslide, and will never see the wonders that lie behind, deep in the hills.'

NURSE AT THE COLONY

'Edna left school at 14 and went to work at a farm not far from home in Penshaw, Co Durham. She helped with morning milking and had to do all the cleaning of the farmhouse. She worked really hard and was given fat bacon sandwiches to eat. At a family funeral, her mother was told nurses were needed at Claypenny Colony, Easingwold, so she came down on the bus to Easingwold with her sister. Young men of Easingwold would meet the bus and used to help the girls carry their suitcases up the hill to the Colony. This was how Edna met her future husband.

The nurses' accommodation was on the very top floor of the ward blocks in those days. The patients were all female, some of whom were only in there because they had had illegitimate babies. They did all the ward cleaning and only needed supervision. In later years a lot of these young women were released to domestic service.

I was told the site which was latterly the kitchen block was known as Cotton Chair, with spastic residents. The floors were scrubbed and washed and highly polished. One day after trying to remove the effects of urine without success, Edna gave up and went off duty, to her bed in the nurses' quarters. She was sent for by the ward sister and had to get up and go back to clean the floor again.

The matron was very strict and the girls had to be in by 10.30 pm unless they had a late pass. The matron would often walk down the road in her dressing gown from her quarters in the main block. Couples would do their courting in the gateways of the houses. She would pass each saying, "You, in. You, in. You, in" along the row.

Once there was a dance in the town hall and one of the girls went to ask for late passes, but was refused. They were all stamping their feet and rattling the fire irons in their quarters. Matron came and said, "If you are going to carry on like that, you had all better go!" She often said no but then gave permission.'

THE LOCAL CHEMIST

'After I left school in the early 1950s I worked for about two years in the laboratory of a York manufacturing chemist. The company produced, among other things, cough linctus, ointments, vinegars, gripe water and the tinctures and extracts used for medicines. Everything had to be analysed, accuracy being essential, and I helped the pharmacist in that. In the manufacturing laboratory huge steam-heated vats with paddles to stir the contents held syrups, emulsion which looked like white custard, or herb decoctions – a great variety.

On a small scale, I watched orders for special pills being made by hand (possibly opium pills – opium came in large blocks, looking like linseed cow-cake stamped with a hammer and sickle). The constituents were mixed with a pestle and mortar, transferred to a tray with brass grooves at one end, pressed with a similar tray to separate small balls of even size which were then rolled in a shallow round box to perfect the shape. I think talc was used to prevent the pills sticking together. I also saw suppositories made with a gelatine or a cocoa-butter base, shaped in two-piece moulds. Looking back, I feel very lucky to have seen these old methods before the age of mass-production and computerisation killed them off.'

THE CHOCOLATE FACTORY

'I started working at Terry's chocolate factory, York, in 1936 when I was 16 years old. My wage was eleven shillings a week and out of this one shilling was taken for my stamp. I worked from 7.30 am until 5 pm during the week and from 7.30 am until noon on Saturdays.

I had to wear an overall and a cap at all times and I was given one of each. Extras had to be bought at two shillings and sixpence for an overall and sixpence for a cap.

As a beginner at the factory, my first job was to assemble cartons from flat pieces of cardboard, already cut into shape. After several weeks I was moved on to wrapping cellophane round the boxes, by hand.

Eventually I was put to work on the conveyor belt. Chocolates were fed onto the belt at one end, automatically wrapped in foil, and then I took them off and put them into tin trays. The next job was to gather the chocolates into an assortment for boxing, and then weigh them, adding a makeweight chocolate button or two when necessary. Chocolates which were not wrapped in foil had to be polished by gentle brushing with a camel hair brush.

Before starting work each morning, we all had to be inspected. Hands were held out and nails had to be short and clean, and not a stray hair must be peeping out from our caps.

Most of the workers were women. The few men employed pulled trolleys, maintained the machines or were foremen in charge.'

LADIES' OUTFITTER

'My first job after school was in Woolworths, where I earned £1 12s a week. Later I answered an advertisement in the local paper for an assistant in a ladies' and babies' outfitters. I got the job and was there until I got married.

We sold navy, dark green and brown knickers for school girls, with a pocket in, and liberty bodices both button front and slip-on.

Boys' and girls' tweed coats had velvet collars and were fitted at the waist.

We sold lots of hats, as every lady who bought a coat would also have a new hat. Corsets sold well too, evil looking monstrosities with bones and laces and all a peculiar shade of pink. Ladies' stockings we had in pure silk, rayon, lisle and wool. There were no such things as tights. When customers were purchasing stockings we had to put our hands inside them so they could see how fine they were; and we were not allowed to wear rings in case they tore the stockings. Stockings were either seamless or fully fashioned, some had black seams and others had what we called "clocks", a fancy piece on the ankle.

There were two fitting rooms, one with rails of coats in and the other with dresses, suits and skirts. If both fitting rooms were full other customers sat on chairs on the landing, and sometimes when we were busy the queue used to line the stairs. Alterations were done above the shop by one experienced lady and a young girl who had started the same time as me.'

HIGH CLASS MILLINERY

'I left school when I was 14 years old in 1920 and although I wanted to be a tailoress, millinery was considered to be more suitable. My sister, who had brought me up since the death of my mother when I was seven, took me for an interview at a high class millinery shop. The owner, Mrs Annie Holt, answered the door dressed in an emerald green dress with a long train.

I started work the following Monday as an apprentice in the downstairs workroom. My brother paid a premium for me and I received no wages for 18 months, and then got two shillings and sixpence a week.

My first task each morning was to light the fires before the other apprentice and two milliners arrived. I was then given a reel of white millinery wire and told to copy hat shapes. I was expected to buy my own wire scissors. At first the hats were made from wire shapers covered with velvet or silk. Only later, bundles of straw were delivered to the shop to be used in hat making.

I learnt to use the crimping machine with its many wires, and had to make sure that the material was perfectly straight. I then pressed it with a damp cloth and an iron. I made white lace mob caps for old ladies (no lady would answer the door in those days without a cap on!), also christening veils. Sometimes I was "put on funerals" and had to go to the homes of widows to discuss the style of mourning bonnet required, and the length of the black crepe strings.

When I was 16, a new shop opened and a friend and I were taken on as apprentices where we earned three shillings and sixpence per week. Here we made everything for hats and their trimmings. Later a shop called "cheap Wilsons" opened in the next town and we went for an interview because we "fancied travelling". We got the jobs and were amazed to be offered eight shillings and sixpence per week. We worked with ten other girls in an upstairs workroom. Our hours were 8 am to 8 pm and we wore skirts and blouses and simple white aprons. There was a small lift in the workroom and the customer chose and bought a hat in the shop and then it was sent up in the lift to the workroom to be trimmed.

Long boxes full of foreign straw hats were delivered to the shop and they cost a shilling each. The apprentices trimmed each hat with a yard of ribbon and a bunch of flowers, and they were put on show in the shop window priced at two shillings and elevenpence. This was done just before Easter and they sold "like hot cakes".

I left my employment when I got married in 1929 and the head milliner made my wedding hat for me – of black panne velvet with a large white osprey feather curled round the brim.'

AT SEA

'In 1931 my husband, Stanley, joined the Merchant Navy as an apprentice. It was during the depression when jobs were hard to get and it offered an adventurous life for a young man just leaving grammar school, who had lived up till then in a small village on the North Yorkshire Moors.

He joined a Whitby shipping company which had 19 ships, all named after local villages. With a total crew of 34 men, each ship included six apprentices. His total wage for the four year training period was £40, cheap labour disguised as training. Even though the work was hard and the food poor – never mind braving the elements – he managed to see all kinds of exotic places. These same destinations are now commonplace to air travellers.

When I first saw the foc'sle head where they lived – all six of them – even though they kept it spotlessly clean, I wouldn't have put animals in there. The beds were iron cots and to heat the area there was a big coal burning bogey (stove). When the weather was bad they shipped big seas and that meant sleeping with water swilling round.

There were no fridges on ships in those days and the meat was kept in ice boxes. As the voyage to Argentina lasted about 31 days, by the time they got to the hot weather, the meat was not in the best condition. The steward overcame this by scraping, and washing it in a weak solution of Condey's Fluid!

The apprentices were always hungry and one day when the cook had made a jelly for the "Old Man's" tea (the captain is still referred to as this) one of the apprentices reached through the port hole in the galley and took it along for'ard to share with the others. Next day the steward went along to see them and said, "Now lads we don't expect to get the jelly but we'd like the dish back." Unfortunately it had gone "over the wall"!

The owners were always anxious to see the ship away by Christmas Eve to save the expense of having it idle over the holidays. One particular cook had celebrated too freely before leaving port and on Christmas Day he put the turkeys in the oven complete with feathers and innards so the dinner that day was a failure. The Captain, however, made him replace them out of his wages when they got to Buenos Aires so the crew didn't miss their seasonal fare.

The war changed so much in the Merchant Navy, pay and conditions rapidly improved. One of which was that bedding (the mattress, made of straw, was colloquially known as "the donkey's breakfast") was provided (made of flock by this time), instead of buying it from the local ship chandler. Fridges were installed so the food was better, which recompensed a little for all the wartime dangers they endured.

He assures me that he enjoyed those times, and after much training and study he went on to become a ship's captain.'

SKAINING, BAITING AND FLITHER PICKING

'In the early 1900s it was the womenfolk at Staithes who had to collect the bait for their fishermen husbands. They would go down to the beach as the tide was going out, wearing heavy boots, with their long skirts tied up to keep them dry. Each lady wore a cotton bonnet on her head and on top of this she placed a wooden ring. As the bait (and worms etc) was picked up, she would put it in the ring. It fascinated me to watch them bending at the knee and with such a straight back that nothing spilled out of the ring. They walked home with the ring of wriggling bait still on their heads.

Fishermen's wives spent their days collecting bait, baiting lines and mending nets. All the women of Staithes wore special white bonnets with a frill at the back of the neck (many ladies still own such a bonnet today).'

'In the 1930s, boxes of mussel bait were brought by train to Staithes and taken from the station, by carrier's cart, down to the harbour where they were piled up on the staith ready for collection by the fishermen's wives – each one taking enough to bait her husband's lines for the whole week.

The mussels were then "skained" – the flesh removed from the shell with a sharp knife, shells and flesh being dropped into separate

Staithes harbour and the muddy track which led down to it in 1930, before the road was made.

buckets. The shells were used for covering muddy footpaths and for decorating gardens and flower boxes.

Baiting was done by attaching the flesh to hooks on the long fishing lines and after each mussel the women fixed a "flither" (limpet). This was to prevent the mussel from falling off the hook when in the water, as the limpet flesh is much tougher.

Flither picking was done when the tide went out. The sharp pointed knives used for skaining were now used to prise the limpets from the rocks. The flesh was put into buckets but the shells were thrown away as they were too heavy to carry home.

When all the lines were baited the women carried the remaining boxes on their heads, supported by a circle of plaited rope, to "The Scar". Here the boxes were packed into deep square holes which had been cut into the rock and heavy rocks were piled on top of them. When the tide came in, sea water filled the holes and kept the bait fresh.'

WAR & PEACE

THE GREAT WAR 1914–1918

Almost every household was affected in some way by the war, from those who lost members of the family to those who suffered the bombing from the air brought by the Zeppelins. When at last it was over, we celebrated with relief and with some sadness.

FATHER WAS A WARDEN

'Our father was an air raid warden at Scarborough. When the "buzzers" went he would get the three of us up and help Mother get us ready for "off", then we walked two miles to Grandma's. One brother was in a push chair and we two holding on. Father then went on duty.

One day we heard the Zeppelin and saw the bomb drop. We were all dragged to safety, into a wallpaper shop and hid amongst the rolls of paper. The blast shook the rolls off the shelves and we were buried. We scrambled out and continued our pilgrimage to safety, quite fearless. The three of us were soon lying under the huge dining table between eiderdowns and Mother and Grandma and Auntie were in the cupboard under the stairs. The all clear went after midnight which meant no school till afternoon. We walked home after breakfast. Our house was damaged, all the windows were out onto the pavement and the doors open. The men came and boarded up the windows and Father came home to tell his stories. He didn't go to work that day. We got used to these raids before the war was ended.'

HE RAISED HIS HAT

'On going to the shop in Carlton my Aunt Dorothy (who is now 101 years old) saw an approaching figure who raised his hat and said, "Good afternoon." Dismounting her bike and crossing over to speak, Aunt Dorothy realised it was Winston Churchill, who was staying at the manor house with Anthony Eden. This was during the war and the Chief of Staff from Berwick on Tweed to the Wash was staying at Busby Hall.'

THE MYSTERY SHIP) AT MANCHESTE

A Scarborough man served on the Mystery Ship during the First World War. It became a tourist attraction as well as an ingenious war weapon and attracted crowds wherever it put in along the coast.

THE MYSTERY SHIP

'My father, from Scarborough, joined the Navy as an engineering artificer when he was 17. After his initial training he served on the *Hydrabad*. This was a "Q" or Mystery Ship, looking like an ordinary cargo steamer but specially built so that it only drew a draft of four feet of water. The sailors wore cloth caps and had mufflers around their necks to be in keeping with the role of cargo steamer. When an enemy submarine surfaced to fire its torpedo, the crew would watch with bated breath as the torpedo rode the waves towards them, and heave a sigh of relief as it passed underneath the boat and out to the other side. Within seven seconds the "cargo steamer" was converted into a fighting appliance. The deck lifted up and out rose the bomb-throwing machine and the guns which were trained on and destroyed the enemy submarine.

Naturally, being in the Navy my father learned the Morse code. When she was a young girl, my grandmother was the first lady telegraphist in the local post office, thus she also knew the Morse code. My grandfather was a very strict local preacher and when the young Navy lad came home late for lunch one day, Mother thought to warn him he was in trouble with Father by tapping a message to him in Morse. He replied in Morse saying he had a valid excuse. Meanwhile Father was furious at not understanding the Morse code messages.'

171

ALMOST EVERY HOUSEHOLD

'My mother was born in 1900 and told the story of how the women in her street would stand on the doorstep each morning looking for the telegraph boy, who brought them news of their sons and husbands from the war. There were, she said, three words on the form: Wounded, Missing, Dead. The appropriate one was ticked and this was the way the news was broken. If it said Wounded, you were too relieved to wonder where or how bad because you knew it meant they were out of the line of fire and safe for a little while. My mother told us that almost every household either lost men in the war, or members of the family in the dreadful flu epidemic. No wonder, therefore, that when it became the turn of her sons to defend their country in 1939 she found it so upsetting.'

WHITE FEATHER

'There were twelve children in my aunt's family and one of her brothers worked on the railway at Pilmoor at the time of the First World War. One day a lady got off the train and gave him a white feather, because she thought he ought to be serving in the war. He decided to join up by giving a wrong age, went off to war and was killed when he was 19.

Over the years, no one in the family had ever seen his grave as they couldn't afford to go to France. Then one year the local Lions were having a "Jim'll Fix It" type of event and I thought of a way I could repay my aunt for all she had done for me while I was young. The Lions arranged for her go to out to France to see her brother's grave. It was a very emotional moment when we got to his grave, but I think it was one of the best days of Auntie's life.'

BEGINNING TO END

'I was ten when the war broke out and it was brought home to me when I saw the head boy of the boys' high school visiting the head girl of our school. They lived near us and he was there to tell her that he had joined up and to show off his new uniform – khaki, with puttees on his legs. He was just 18 and was killed almost as soon as he landed in France. I can still see him as he said goodbye at the gate. He looked such a hero.

My chief memories of that time are connected with *Keep the home fires burning* and *It's a long way to Tipperary* and other songs. Kitchener's face with a pointing hand was on every poster saying "England needs YOU"; it was a great shock to everyone when he was drowned. Food was scarce as there was no rationing, and the horrible taste of the new Blue Band margarine is still very vivid!

We were on the netball courts at break when suddenly a window was flung open and our headmistress appeared shouting, "Girls! The war's over! Listen..." It was eleven minutes past eleven on 11th November 1918 and all the bells were ringing. In the evening all the lights went back on. It really was magic.'

THE SECOND WORLD WAR 1939–1945

Only two decades later we were at war again, and the bombs soon started to fall over Yorkshire. Even the tiniest village was liable to see great changes and we all became used to the sight of soldiers and prisoners of war, and to the wail of the air raid siren.

THE WAY WE HEARD

'On Sunday 3rd September 1939 I was sitting in chapel with the rest of my family at Kirkby Malzeard. Suddenly the village policeman came into chapel, strode up to the pulpit, stopped the service and informed us we were at war with Germany. Immediately, the sirens sounded and we were all terrified.'

'I was at home at Wass, helping my mother with vegetables for lunch and we were listening to the radio when the announcement came. I didn't fully realise the awful thing that was happening. I looked at Mother and silent tears were rolling down her cheeks. I said, "Oh, Mum." I knew her thoughts – her favourite brother killed in the First World War and two sons now growing up.'

GOOD LUCK, LADS

'The planes, loaded with bombs, used to fly over our house at Snainton every night at about dusk on their way to Germany. We would all go out into the field and watch them go and my mother said every night: "Good luck lads, and come home safe tomorrow." Some days we would count them, but we were never awake to count them coming back in the very early hours. One morning one of the planes landed in the field next to our house and we had visitors for breakfast. My mother provided them with a cooked meal and those lads never forgot it. Another night, incendiary bombs were dropped all around us and very near to our house, which lit everything up. Later that night a bomb was dropped on the village, over a mile away, and my parents got straight onto their bikes and rode on to see where help was needed. There was a big hole and the house was gone along with the occupants.

Another night as we were watching the planes go over, my grandfather was coming along the farm road on his bike. He had put his lights off as the planes were enemy ones, but he was smoking a cigarette and you should have heard my father shout: "Get that cig out, the enemy will see you." We thought it was funny but my father was very, very annoyed about it. How on earth a pilot or anyone else up there could see the light of a cigarette we shall never know, but my father was adamant that it would be seen.'

PIGEONS AND BOMBS

'I had just had my tenth birthday when the Second World War was declared and I suppose I was lucky in that my father was too old to be called up. Instead he became the "pigeon officer" for York which entailed collecting together all homing pigeons for use by the services. The birds were collected regularly by the Army and the house was connected to our own pigeon loft by a bell. When a bird returned my mother had to remove the small red canister from the bird's leg and take it down to a special room attached to the old Melbourne Street church. This was also quite near the "War Office", ie the Northern Command Headquarters.

Naturally, in those days we didn't go far from home except to school. The street lights were non-existent and all front cycle lamps were hooded. My father made removable shutters for all our windows with bitumen paper and Mother made thick blackout curtains. After the war, when materials were scarce, coloured bands were added to brighten the curtains.

In April 1942 during the blitz on York we had our first bombs locally. A house in Crossland's Road, across an open space from our house, was destroyed, killing a small boy. The "open space" was our allotment – part of the digging for victory campaign – and I was out there with my father during the raid. He was on air raid duty. I can still hear that awful whistling sound from the falling bomb. We spent the rest of the night in the John Fenby playing field watching the lights being dropped over the city and shortly after that we applied for an Anderson shelter. This was partly underground but our neighbours had a Morrison shelter indoors. You can imagine that they were put to good use.

We all knitted gloves and balaclavas for the forces and my mother knitted all our jumpers, socks, gloves, hats and scarves. Old garments were "pulled out" and the wool reused again and again. Nothing was wasted and my father also bought two lasts to repair all our shoes. The squares of leather and rubber were bought from the City Leather Shop in Church Street.

During 1942 we acquired our first wireless – a neighbour's broken one which my father repaired. We had many happy hours together listening and joining in with the hymn singing; all content to listen to the same programme.'

BOMBS IN YORK

'I left school at Easter in 1939, and five days later became an apprentice milliner and shop assistant at "Miss Anfield's" in Blake Street, York.

My apprenticeship entailed serving in the shop, and learning to make hats, which meant decorating basic "hoods" which were the felt crown and brims. These hoods were stored at the shop ready for decoration when required. During the war I helped to safeguard the stock by storing 24 hoods at my parents' home, in the country ten miles north of York, in case there should be bombing.

People over 18 had to fire-watch in York during the war. Although I was only 17 at the time I volunteered with the shopowner's 19 year old daughter. This duty was shared with Munby and Scott, solicitors, who were housed on the first floor above Anfield's shop. When on duty we slept on camp beds in one of the offices.

My friend and I were on duty the night York was bombed in 1941. The first we knew about it was when the caretaker (who lived in an attic room above) shook us awake saying, "Come on lasses, bombs are dropping." We all went down into the cellar and only minutes later a bomb dropped in Blake Street, outside the City Garage, 50 yards from us.

When the all clear sounded and we emerged from the cellar, the shop door and windows had been blown in, and the shop bell was continually ringing, until one of the ARP wardens stopped it. We had then to make our way to my friend's house in St Olave's Road, in Bootham; but as incendiary bombs had been dropped in the Lendal area, the only way was a detour down Stonegate, and up Low and High Petergate, and past the Minister. Glass was strewn everywhere.

My family had spent the night, away up the Vale of York, worrying and wondering, as they could see the flames over York and could hear the aeroplanes and bombs. When morning came I went out to catch my bus home, and when the Reliance bus drew into Exhibition Square I was mobbed by villagers who had travelled in to work on it, asking how I was and what had it been like.

When the bus turned round I boarded it and went home, where my relatives and friends were anxiously waiting and hoping that I would be on the bus, and not injured or worse.

When I was 18½ years old I was "called up" and had either to go into the ATS or do ammunition work at Handley Page on Rawcliffe aerodrome. I chose the latter. My day now started at 6 am when I cycled the mile to Sutton on Forest, where I got a lift to work by car. I helped to repair Halifax bombers, riveting centre sections onto planes. I left work at 4.30 and worked Monday to Friday, and thoroughly enjoyed the work, feeling that I was actively contributing to the war effort.'

'One day, August Bank Holiday, my parents and I took the bus to Poppleton for a picnic by the river. As we sat, I saw a plane dropping something and remarked on it. My father realised it was dropping bombs so we packed up and set off home. The city had been hit and as our bus drove along Coppergate the tyres crunched on broken glass from shop windows.'

'I was born and brought up in York. In April 1942 I saw the bombing of York station. We lived in a flat above a corn merchant's in Holgate Road, just up the street from the station. When the siren went, my family and I all stood at the door and watched the flares come down and heard the drone of the aeroplanes. A neighbouring family of six joined us and my father ordered us all to go under the stairs, which was prepared with corn bags for protection. He and a friend stayed on the doorstep and when a bomb dropped on the station the impact blew the pair of them backwards into the cornstore.

I wasn't at all frightened, with my family and friends there, a child on my lap, listening to the whistling bombs.

The convent in Nunnery Lane was bombed and nuns were killed, and there was devastation all around us, but in the two hours before the all clear our house wasn't touched. My father told us to go and look at the station, as we would never see a sight like it again. We saw all the guns and soldiers coming up Blossom Street, the whole of the station afire, the roof ablaze. It was a tragic but wonderful sight.

I went to bed in the blackout that night, thinking we had escaped lightly, not even a window broken. Next morning when I went down for breakfast, my parents couldn't stop laughing at me. All the bombing had shaken the flat and I'd gone to sleep on a bed of soot. And we never saw our cat Felix again.'

'The morning after the York blitz an unexploded bomb was discovered nearby and we were hurriedly evacuated from that part of Poppleton Road where we lived. Our family of five moved up the road to my grandfather's house where we three kids slept on a single mattress on the living room floor. It was hard!

Apparently my father sneaked back home when the policeman wasn't looking, to rescue the budgie. "Our bomb" was used outside the Mansion House as a collecting box for a while.'

WAR AND PEACE

'The time and place – a small street south of the Thames on the night of 10th May 1941. I was staying with my mother in law in a terraced house just off the Lambeth Walk in Southwark, across the Thames from the Houses of Parliament. When the sirens went, notifying us that once again the German Luftwaffe were threatening to bomb London, we all went to the reinforced shelter under the stairs. The bombardment was heavy, and soon after midnight the ARP wardens, who looked after us so well, called for volunteers to help put out small fires caused by "Molotov Cocktail" bombs. I left my small child with her grandmother and went into the street during a lull.

Imagine my surprise to see what seemed like the whole of London alight, with a very large school opposite on fire from top to bottom, and only a couple of sandbags stacked nearby. There was no water to be had anywhere. We were instructed to drop sandbags on the small fires in the roadway, caused by incendiary bombs jumping – due to a very small charge inside them. Close to me was a First World War serviceman, who eagerly took up his sandbag, carefully judging where to drop it, only to find the bomb had "jumped" another yard or two away. This happened several times and I learned more swear words in a short period that night than I ever knew in my life up to that time. The air wasn't blue, it was multi-coloured purple!

After what seemed like hours, but could only have been about 20 minutes, the barrage started again and we were warned to get under cover. I was forcibly pulled into a house and thrust under a shelter table. In the clear light of morning, I was reunited with my family none the worse for wear.

The biggest irony was that within days I left the capital to return to my husband, billeted before going overseas in the reasonable peace of South Craven, Yorkshire. And what was the first thing these kind, generous folk wanted to do when I got there? They used their

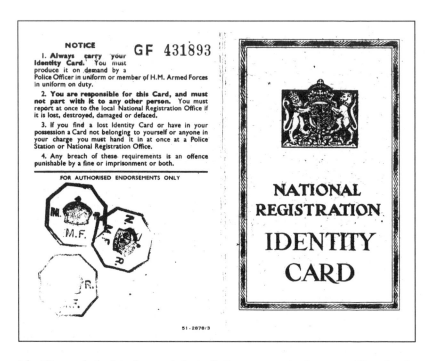

Identity cards had to be carried at all times, some traders providing handy holders in which to keep them.

small amount of rationed petrol to take me to where "their" bomb (singular) had fallen in the centre of the local moor!'

THE RADAR STATION

'Danby was dominated by the eight towers on the skyline at Danby Beacon connected with the radar station up there, where a small "town" of RAF huts and offices had grown up among the heather and bracken. Entertainment for the personnel stationed there was very limited but in one hut was a cinema screen where films were shown, and occasionally we civilians were invited up to see a special film. We were delighted, and went up on our bikes. Probably few people remember that time now, and looking at today's bare expanse of heather, home of sheep and grouse, it is hard to realise it happened.'

WAR IN THE VILLAGES

'Our village hall at Newton le Willows was commandeered by the military forces and soldiers were billeted there, some of whom made life-long friendships with local people. We had big trucks parked all over the village, their duty being to transport ammunition from the station to places of storage, notably in lay-bys on the country roads.

The soldiers had ENSA concerts and all the local people were invited, and they held dances too. In our homes we sat and knitted balaclavas and gloves for the soldiers, and towards the end of the war we held whist drives in our own homes for the "Welcome Home Fund" for when our men came home from the war.

We had double summertime in these days, and beautiful summers they always seemed to be. There was rationing to contend with, but in our close-knit community everyone helped everyone else. To boost our fuel we had sticking days, when we roamed about the countryside in search of wood for our fires.'

'When the aerodrome came to the edge of Dishforth lots of alterations were made, especially to roads. The cemetery was also enlarged later, as we have a lot of RAF graves. The bombers from further north came over before dark and the planes from our airfield took off and joined them and went over Germany to carry out their raids. When we saw them go we wondered how many would come back safely. One morning one crashed on the edge of the airfield and burst into flames. We were very fortunate that we had no damage in the village. On one morning eleven Wellington bombers were forced down nearby having run out of fuel crossing the moors.

The arrival of the Canadian Air Force brought changes to village social life! There were parties in the school with games and dancing, and the Canadians also organised a baseball team.'

'At the beginning of the war two houses on the Scorton road at Brompton on Swale had to be demolished to clear a flight path for the planes on Scorton Airfield (the Americans were based there). A German bomb was dropped at the top of Parkgate Lane which fortunately did no damage. An unexplained explosion in 1944 partly demolished Catterick railway station and the Railway Hotel, and there were several casualties, some of them fatal.'

SIGNS OF CHANGE

'I was nine years old when war broke out, and remember being very apprehensive. The first visible sign of change at Austwick was the disappearance of the iron railings and gates, to contribute to muni-

179

tions. Young men and some women were drafted into the armed forces, and others into the munitions factories. Some stayed at home in reserved occupations to keep farms going; those not eligible were formed into the Home Guard, ARP wardens and special constables in the police. The Home Guard began to drill and go on manoeuvres, a constant source of amusement to the children.

Everyone listened avidly to the progress of the war on the radio, and the stirring speeches of Winston Churchill, the Prime Minister. We were urged to collect waste paper and jam jars, the latter being used by the Women's Institutes to produce endless jars of jam.

We were also urged to "dig for victory", and grow more vegetables on all available land. Flowers were dug out and thrown away; oats were grown on local farms on land hardly suitable in a highland area.

The Land Army girls helped on farms; many of these girls had never seen a field before, but buckled to and soon adapted to country life. Economical recipes were broadcast by the Ministry of Food, and dried egg became a familiar sight. Ration books were issued and food had to be obtained on coupons.

Petrol was available for essential journeys only, so local buses were full to capacity, especially with workers and schoolchildren, night and morning. There was no driving test, so a driver automatically received a licence by payment.

Pupils from Hove and Bradford came to us to share our schools. The Ministry of Information sent out films to help our education; a strange choice of film was one on "Hedging and Ditching". Air raid practice was part of the new routine, including the use of gas masks, and finding the safest place in an air raid. Anti-splinter cover was fitted to the windows; everyone learned to knit, including the boys, and mitts and balaclavas found their way to the forces. There was great excitement when a letter of thanks was received. Teams of children led by local naturalist Chris Cheetham collected sphagnum moss, which was dried, packed and sent to hospitals for use in place of cotton wool.

We didn't suffer much from bombing, but we did quake in our beds when the "jerry" planes went over to bomb the Barrow shipyards. There was great excitement when a Whitley bomber had to land near our village, having run out of fuel. The local farmer held the crew at gunpoint, until someone in authority came, in case they were the enemy. The "Reccies" (reconnaissance troops) were billeted in the parish hall, their hobnailed boots wreaking havoc on the wooden floor; some returned after the war to marry local girls.

The chapel schoolroom was requisitioned for the use of the Home Guard and Ambulance Brigade, and there was no shortage of volunteers for first aid practice.

Eventually prisoner of war camps were set up and German and Italian prisoners helped on the farms, some of whom preferred not to return to their own countries after the war.

When peace was finally declared on VE and VJ days, which represented victory in Europe and in Japan, everyone celebrated. There was dancing in the streets, bonfires on the hill tops, and street parties. The men eventually came back home to their loved ones. Some, of course, never came back.'

EVEN OUR TINY VILLAGE

'Who would have thought that residents of a tiny village 60 miles from either coast, east or west, away from industrial towns, and 15 miles from Catterick army camp would have anything to fear from air raids? Fear struck at Carperby when Lord Haw Haw announced over the radio that the Germans were going to destroy the flour mill at Aysgarth; this being only half a mile away from us was a cause for concern.

During the early part of the war two incendiary bombs were dropped. One was a direct hit on Mr Wiseman's joiner's shop, and the other landed in a field causing an enormous crater within 30 yards of buildings. This terrified a lot of the older generation, and it is said that many of them never went upstairs again to sleep until the war was over.

Many families took in evacuees from Gateshead and the neighbouring village of Aysgarth had evacuees from Sunderland, both very vulnerable towns in the North East. The children settled well and there was only one case of a child running away, to Sunderland. This put great strain on the village school which managed somehow to cater for the increased numbers. The children must have enjoyed their stay for quite a few returned later to visit those who had taken them in.

An army truck from Bellerby delivered prisoners of war to local farms, and came back to collect them each evening. Most people remember the German prisoners as very hard workers, who did not appear to cause any trouble while on the farms. In fact many people remember how they collected bits of wood, metal and string, and took them back to camp, returning them made into toys for the farmer's children, or string bags or slippers for the farmer's wife. A local farmer had a tractor that was always slipping out of gear. It didn't take his two prisoners long to fix the problem which the farmer had been unable to do anything to improve.'

I WAS VERY GREEN

'In 1941 I left the civilised world of nursing to move, with my new farmer husband, to a 112 acre farm in the Yorkshire Dales. I was very, very green; I had to learn the hard way – and I did!

My husband was excused military service because he was engaged in food production. "Food" was the operative word. If food wasn't growing in the soil it walked about all around us. Ducks paddled in puddles waiting for Christmas, hens cooed and cackled after depositing the latest egg in a remote hiding place, cows mooed at the gate waiting to be milked and pigs grunted impatiently in their sties as they waited for the next meal.

Now all these creatures left residuary jobs. The surplus milk was set up in large shallow bowls until the cream set on top. The cream was skimmed off daily for a week and collected in a white enamel bucket, stirred regularly several times a day, after which my worst weekly chore was to churn it into butter. Oh! the memory of that cold wet dairy floor, the monotonous swish-swish of the cream going round in the churn as I turned the handle for what seemed an eternity, followed in due course by the thud-thud of the lump of butter as it fell around in the buttermilk. The buttermilk was drained off and kept for use in cooking. The butter was then washed in cold water, salted, kneaded and made into pats.

The eggs which the hens produced had to be gathered, washed, stamped and packed ready for collection each Friday morning. When the hens had completed their laying cycle they were killed and prepared for the pot.

Pigs were killed on the farm. A licence was required from the Ministry of Food and issued according to the size of the household. I used every part of that pig. Head, ears and feet made brawn; the fillet I used for sausages, having first cleaned the intestines for skins. All the offal was made into parcels for "pig fry" and given to friends and neighbours. This was always served with hot bread cakes straight from the oven. The hams, shoulders and sides were dry salted for three weeks on the large stone slabs in the dairy. The trimmings were made into luscious pork pies.

All this produce was very precious during a time of severe food rationing with very little access to refrigeration. For haytime, harvest and threshing days the Ministry of Food gave coupons for a small extra ration of cheese, margarine, sugar and tea for each worker. This had to be applied for before the event.

Threshing days were a real party. It was the custom for neighbouring farmers to lend their men to anyone who was threshing. Workers descended upon us from all points of the compass; the better one's reputation for the food provided, the more willingly they came. No money changed hands but the hire was reciprocated until all the corn in the Dale was threshed. Providing two "drinkings" and a hot meal for at least 14 men was a marathon. Rabbits were plentiful and I had lard from the pig, so rabbit pie with home-grown vegetables and a good milk pudding took care of the midday meal. At 9.30 am and 3 pm I sent out sandwiches and scones, apple and curd pies, all made from our own produce, with a large can of hot steaming sweet tea.

A succession of land girls and students lived in the house with us and we had all nationalities of prisoners of war for casual work. The POWs loved being sent out to the farms because the food was such a treat. I was horrified when I first saw the doorsteps of bread they brought with them from the hostel. We had Italians, Poles, Lithuanians and Germans all in their turn. It was when we had one group of Germans that we thought we had added to our German vocabulary. Whenever I sent out ham or bacon sandwiches they would grab one greedily and exclaim "pigaarse". It took us some time to realise that this was their English for the back-end of a pig.'

SHARING AND CARING

'When the war began many of the men in Poppleton worked on the land, while others were employed by the railway and the chocolate factories or the retail trade.

Most of the houses and cottages were old and all had gardens or crofts, so all were self sufficient in vegetables, fruit, eggs (from their own hens) and usually a pig was fattened each year. All bacon coupons had to be surrendered if one had a pig. Rations were rigidly kept, but it was possible to supplement the meat ration with rabbit, hare or pigeon.

When one household had a pig killed the sides and hams were salted down, but as no one owned a fridge the liver and offal were shared out amongst neighbours and this was reciprocated when they killed their own pig, so nothing was wasted or went bad. Wives made pork pies and brawn, and lard was kept in a bladder!

A platoon of Local Defence Volunteers was formed immediately after the appeal by Sir Anthony Eden, and although they were ill-equipped they were very enthusiastic. They met and drilled at the White Horse Inn and their headquarters was at Long Marston – Colonel York was their Chief. Gradually they got their uniforms and arms.

The air raid wardens were very particular about blackout regulations and patrolled the streets on bicycles.

There was a look-out post on Kettlewell Moor just outside the village. This was a permanent dug-out manned 24 hours a day, only the chimney from the fire being visible from the road. The men were there to switch on dummy lights which resembled York railway shunting yards in the event of air raids. This was to divert the bombers away from York station. Unfortunately on the April night in 1942 when the Baedeker raid took place it was bright moonlight and the bombers followed the moonlight, gleaming on the river Ouse, to bomb York, without much opposition. After this one barrage balloon and a few soldiers were placed in a field in Knapton!

The Women's Institute did many things in addition to meetings. Making and mending, including making rugs from old blankets (thrift rugs) and we exchanged recipes for cakes using grated carrots, dried eggs and liquid paraffin. The WI hired canning machines and women spent many hours in the church hall canning their raspberries, plums, pears and other fruits – very successfully too. Other fruits were jammed or bottled using sugar which was obtained by surrendering the jam coupons. Beans were sliced and salted, and eggs, which were plentiful in summer, were preserved in crocks containing a solution of waterglass. We made wine too, but our special whiskey wine made from wheat and raisins was eventually made illegal!

Church and chapel groups continued as normal, as did the Scouts and Guides. No one feared going out in the blackout as we knew everyone in the village and we had never had any street lights anyway. We cycled, using a very small lamp, half blacked out, and there were no cars, except for some officials.

During the first week of the war evacuees came from Leeds. As all was quiet they returned home very quickly, but in 1940 we had mothers and children from London. Many had been evacuated twice before and had hoped to arrive in Blackpool. They were very dissatisfied with rural life and their habits and lifestyle were very different from ours. The Poppleton mothers were most helpful and equipped the children with clothes and shoes – but when the blitz abated they all went back home.

There were many special events during the war, such as "Navy Week", "Salute the Soldier", "Wings for Victory"; and everyone was exhorted to buy National Savings Certificates and have sales to help the war effort or "buy a destroyer". During the last effort the money was saved and the returning servicemen and women were each given £5 (quite a sum in those days) and £100 went towards the village hall fund.

Newspapers were collected and stored in a Georgian barn in the village. We collected aluminium pans and hot water bottles, and the beautiful Georgian railings round many houses. These were given willingly, but sadly. They were stored by the blacksmith and eventually taken away, but we believe that they were unsuitable for recycling and were dumped at sea.

The village suffered no enemy damage, but every summer evening we saw the bombers from Linton passing over the church every three minutes. One of our soldiers was killed, and many of our young men and girls served overseas. George Richardson, Yorkshire Hussars, was the first to go abroad in January, 1940. He was only 19.

There was much sharing and caring and with the coming of VE Day in 1945 the tempo of life had slowed down – we had grown weary, but were glad that we had suffered no great hardship.'

TRAVEL WAS DIFFICULT

'During the war travel was difficult, especially by train in the blackout. Towards the end of the war I worked in the Midlands, and whenever possible travelled to my home at Flaxton for weekends. My usual practice was to catch a train at New Street, Birmingham at 10.45 pm and so I arrived in York after 4 am. This train was from Bristol to Newcastle.

One night it arrived at the platform at New Street, and seemed packed. Every door was blocked solid by troops, kit bags etc. I could not find a door where it was possible to enter and as I rushed along, my fear could be imagined. The station was blacked out, no waiting rooms open and I must have looked very distressed. A large female porter in her navy uniform came along and offered assistance. She asked if I could get in through a window, if she helped me. I was so desperate, I said "Yes". With her help I managed to scramble up to a window which was opened by sliding two sections apart, above a table in a carriage. I passed in my handbag, case and a bunch of flowers I was taking home to my mother. I was hauled in by the people inside and there was space to stand when I did get in. A never to be forgotten journey, but a safe home coming.'

OUR POLISH FRIENDS

'During the war years we had various soldiers billeted in our home, but my strongest recollection is of the 800 Polish officers who arrived in our village in 1940. These older men were the top politicians, many of whom I came to know quite well.

In spite of rationing, my hospitable mother had open house every Friday evening, when several Poles dropped in for supper. They liked to walk about the room whilst they were drinking their tea.

My father was a dentist, and had many of these officers as patients. How they loved to have their mouths filled with gold! In common with most dentists at that time, the workroom was in the house and all the work was done there. Very often there were language difficulties and it was not unusual for me to be called in to the

185

surgery when I arrived home after school to translate German or French, and sometimes there was a great deal of miming between dentist and patient!

I was helped with German by Captain Joseph Wasserberger, a Jewish judge from Warsaw, and in return I helped him with his English, which was not an easy job as he asked many questions, especially about our peculiar grammar! Colonel Blozirski assisted me with my French. He was a sad and lonely man who had been head of the army before General Sikorski. He returned to Poland after the war, but died of a broken heart. One of the few who had his wife and child with him was a Jewish colonel, who had been head of the Intelligence. He was the only one to keep in touch with us after he went back to Poland.

Chopin was often played beautifully on our lovely Challen piano by expert exponents of the composer's work, which gave me a real appreciation of his music.

We had quite a bit of fun with the language. My mother quite upset one officer when she accused him of "pulling her leg"! She used to be very embarrassed when she met a Pole that she knew, as the hand of a married lady was kissed in greeting. I think that I was a little bit envious!

Looking at my autograph book I am reminded of so many of these aristocrats of 50 years ago.'

HARRY'S MEMORIES

'All farm workers were entitled to one week's holiday with pay at Martinmas and in November 1939 I got married to Lily at Ample-forth. Lily was working at the White Swan as a cook and after the ceremony we had our reception there. We went to stay with my sister at Nidd for a few days before returning to live at Providence House, Kilburn where Lily looked after my father and me, and ran the village shop with us. I was still working on the farm at Wildon Grange too and keeping a few animals on my own land.

Rationing was a nightmare, we had all the coupons to count and the supplies never measured out correct, we were always short measure for weighing the last pound. In the end we gave up the shop, it wasn't worth all the trouble.

There were prisoners of war, German, Italian and Hungarian at Thirkelby camp and the guards used to come with them in a lorry each day to the farm fields to work. The guards didn't work the fields, they guarded the prisoners with guns while the prisoners worked. We were allowed only margarine in our rations but the prisoners were allowed butter in theirs and come dinner time in the fields they would make a fire and cook potatoes. If there was a cow nearby they would quickly milk her to use with their butter ration to mash their potatoes. They sometimes managed to get the scraps from the abattoir and made a stew to eat. They were very clever with their hands and if they could get hold of a piece of wood they would carve the most lovely toys with moving parts. I remember seeing some carved chickens on a board and if you pulled the string these chickens just looked as if they were pecking the ground.

Just a few months after I was married the army came and covered the White Horse at Kilburn with camouflage nets; they pinned the nets down with great big metal stakes driven into the ground all over the horse. The Horse was a real good landmark for the Germans as well as our Air Force lads who always knew they were home when they could see the White Horse. There were airfields at Dishforth, Topcliffe, Leaming, Dalton and Linton on Ouse. Bombers used to go out at night loaded with bombs and we could hear them droning as they left and I'd say, "They're off". When we heard them coming back I used to clap my hands and say, "Good lads, you're back".

There was a couple of nasty incidents at Kilburn, one when a mine got dropped. A chap lived at a house down by West Parks and a lot of people blamed him for it happening. They said he was out that night with a stable lamp while there was a convoy moving on the road and the Germans were out that night looking for it. They dropped a mine about 80 yards from his cottage, luckily the wind was blowing away from the cottage or it would have been blown down. By it was a big hole, it was about 40 feet across and as deep.

Another time there was a plane came real low up Kilburn and I mean real low, everybody was out to see it. At the top of Hoodhill Plantation there was a big stone about ten feet high by about 14 feet across and this here plane hit that stone fair on and smashed it to smithereens. The people in the plane were all killed. There's parts of that plane up there yet, kids keep finding bits. The stone was called Hoodhill stone and when I was young we used to climb up on top of the stone and play marbles, there was a flat bit on top.

During wartime I rented the field in front of the vicarage from the vicar. He was real High church, and this particular time I was piking hay on a Sunday, there would be about twelve or 15 of us and we were just finishing the field when Parson came down the field in his robes. He said, "I can't do with this, you piking hay on a Sunday, you can work in here but you can't come to church in the morning." So I says, "Oh, I haven't time to come to church, I'm busy working." He were ower late when he come, we'd finished t'field which was just as well 'cause he would have stopped us if he'd come earlier. So I said, "Howay men, we're out of here", and we went across the road and did somebody else's haytime and then the next day it

187

poured down. My hay was all right, it was all piked up and tied down, it was beautiful.

So I got my hay led into the stackyard and all made safe for winter and it was a very heavy snow that year, it was knee deep all over. One day I was foddering the cattle in the fields during wintertime and the Parson came across. He had two goats. He said, "I wonder if you could sell me a hundredweight of your hay?" I says, "Your goats won't eat my hay." He says, "What for?" I says, "My hay was got on a Sunday! What's wrong with your hay?" He says, "My hay's all mouldy, they won't eat it." I said, "My hay would have been all mouldy an'all if I hadn't got it in on a Sunday." That's Parson for you.

Most people used to kill a pig and cure their own ham and bacon. During the war I was only allowed to kill one pig, farmers were allowed to kill two but we all killed more than we were allowed and when the inspectors came round to check, all the extra was hidden in the corn.

After the war finished the army took the camouflage off the White Horse and it was all completely overgrown with weeds, so a squad of men from the area went up and redug the outline of its shape and took all the weeds off. We all had to weed in a line because if some got below the others and a rock came down it would hit you, and up there you had no chance. The rocks and stones would bounce and you couldn't tell which direction they were coming. All the older men were on the Horse's back where it was a bit easier and all the young ones were on the breast where it was real steep. We didn't have no safety ropes or anything, we had a hoe or a rake in one hand and hung on as best we could with the other, till we got the job done.

At the end of the war we had a big tea party in the village institute, Lily boiled the ham in the copper and everybody contributed something for the tea.'

RATIONS AND MAKING DO

We still had families to feed and to clothe, whatever happened, and ingenuity was called for as food and other goods became scarcer.

RATIONING CAME IN

'When food rationing was brought into effect each household was issued with ration books for a certain amount of, for instance, meat, sugar, butter and lard each week. Clothing coupons were also issued. The amounts were very small to cover a week and ways had to be found to make food go further. Dried eggs and milk became common, and it didn't sound very exciting but the dried eggs could be made into fritters with onions added and tomatoes to make them tasty, and cakes could be made with them and dried milk added.

Recipes were broadcast over the radio, giving people ideas on how to stretch the rations, such as adding grated carrots to puddings and cakes to keep them moist and save on fat.

When the German submarines started sinking the cargo ships, tinned foods from abroad started disappearing from the shop shelves and the rations became very boring – we seemed to get a lot of tinned prunes and tinned sardines. Our back garden had to be sacrificed to grow vegetables and fruit, as the Ministry of Food asked everyone to "Dig for Victory".'

EGGS IN WATERGLASS

'Eggs were in short supply so people who kept hens were very popular. Whenever we had some spare eggs my mother would preserve them for future use by making waterglass, which was bought in a tin and mixed with water in a bucket. The eggs were then added and the bucket left in a cool dark place. The waterglass set to a clear jelly and the eggs kept in it for several months.'

CRIME DOESN'T PAY!

'Each household was allowed to kill two pigs yearly, by permit. One Yorkshire farmer who was accustomed to selling several hams would kill an extra one and sell the hams for cash on the black market.

When the pig was out of the salt and dried, the hams were taken and hidden under a large corn heap in the granary ready to be collected when convenient.

Eventually the customer came, he and the farmer went off to the granary but to their dismay, the hams had gone. Someone else had fancied the taste of Yorkshire ham. It does not always pay to try to beat the law.'

THE PARCEL

'I had an American pen-pal and she and her family obviously had distorted ideas of how we in Britain were surviving. Apart from two food parcels she sent me a pack containing three pairs of nylon stockings. Imagine my despair when the parcel had been pilfered in the post and the precious nylons stolen. However, she sent another parcel and this time they arrived safely. I was terrified of laddering them each time I wore them, but they really did make me feel like a queen. Until then it had been a case of applying a brown stain to my legs and drawing a line down the centre at the back to look like a seam.'

'My sister, a trained nanny, volunteered for the WAAF in the first month of the war. As a dental orderly at RAF Cosford she cared for the teeth of the hundreds of air crew passing through for training. As the war went on, goods disappeared from the shops and rationing became more severe, then food parcels were sent from the USA and Canada. Imagine my sister's delight when a large parcel arrived for her from the mother of a grateful patient. With admirable restraint, she determined that the parcel must be opened at home so that we could all enjoy the anticipation and its delights.

A 48-hour pass was no problem, but she'd used up all her travel warrants. Transport depot to the rescue, a lorry was going as far as Derby – she would borrow a station bike and cycle the remaining 50 miles. Long after midnight, saddle sore and speechless with exhaustion, she laboured into the yard and fell into the house. Mother put her to bed; the parcel could wait.

Next morning we gathered round the kitchen table. The parcel string was cut by Father and the brown paper carefully removed and folded for future use. The stout box was heavy; did it contain chocolates, dried fruits, jellies? Reverently we lifted the lid and took out layers of cotton wool and tissue paper to reveal a dozen bottles of bright red nail varnish and 20 compacts of pan-cake make-up.

"The cotton wool will be useful for the first-aid box," said my mother.'

Local Women's Institutes had a stall at York market on Saturday mornings, selling surplus fruit and vegetables and the occasional rabbit.

CIGARETTES AND SWEETS

'My uncle kept an off-licence grocer's shop at Gildersome. Because of rationing you had to be registered at a shop for your groceries, and when cigarettes came in they usually went to the registered customers. I got into real trouble one day. A total stranger came into the shop and asked for some cigarettes, to be told that there weren't any. I was in the shop at the time and called out that he was wrong, for there were plenty of cigarettes "under the counter".

My grandfather had a very sweet tooth, and felt the sugar rationing badly. He always had one "good" cup of tea when he got his ration, with two spoonfuls in it, and then became a miser with the sugar until the next week's ration was due. Then he discovered that if he bought jelly sweets with his weekly sweet ration, he could rub them round each other in the bag, and if he was lucky this resulted in some of the sugar in which they were coated dropping to the bottom of the bag. One more "good" cup of tea resulted.

Clothing coupons were a worry, and new clothes hard to come by, so we made do and mended. Shoes seemed to swallow up coupons, especially with children's growing feet, and mine grew at a prodigious rate. One day at school those of us whose feet, because of their size, were a great concern to our parents, were taken on one side. One by one we stood with our heels pressed back against the skirting board, doing our best to make our toes cross a chalk mark drawn on the floor. The prize was extra clothing coupons, and I was a lucky one.'

IT'S NOT WORTH SHARING

'When rationing came in, we had eight ration books in our family and I was at the butcher's shop with my mother one day waiting our turn. She handed over the eight ration books and asked tentatively if the butcher had any beef. He looked at her, bent down to the shelf and slapped a piece of beef on the counter which was just about enough for a family of our size. He looked her straight in the eye and said, "Well my dear, this is my ration and it's not worth sharing. So you might as well have the lot and at least one family will be fed this week."'

LIGHTS AND DOCKETS

'Every Friday, my mother went to the Co-op at North Duffield to queue up for our rations. She started talking to another woman in the queue who had a bigger family than ours. As the ration for butter was less than that for margarine, my mother agreed to swap our margarine for the other family's butter. It was my job to walk five miles each Saturday to do this swap!

I remember "lights", that is the lungs, of pigs being boiled up and then used in a mincemeat recipe with apples, prunes and sugar.

Dockets were needed for curtains and furniture of all sorts both during and after the war. If you had particularly big windows you had to go round all your friends and relatives cadging dockets so that you had enough to get sufficient material to make the curtains.

My sister was very good at dressmaking and was very proud of a "costume" she made from a grey blanket. We had evacuees from Hull and they came from the very poor dock areas. I saw them in jerseys which had a collar and tie attached. When they got a new one, they didn't take the old one off and discard it, the new one was put over the top of the old one and sewn in place. I remember one evacuee boy who was so thrilled to be given an overcoat that he never took it off, even on the hottest summer day.'

LIQUID STOCKINGS

'Stockings were scarce during the war, and on coupons, so we painted our legs with a tan coloured "liquid stockings" mixture, and got a friend to draw a seam line up the centre back. The effect depended on how steady her hand was. When it rained there were "ladders" in abundance. If you were lucky enough to own a pair of real silk stockings it was possible to get ladders repaired in a little shop at Thirsk where a girl sat at a machine doing this tedious job at so much an inch.'

BEETROOT CHERRIES

'It was amazing how ingenious one became – for example, little balls of cooked beetroot became a cherry cake for a birthday!'

DON'T EAT IT!

'Some of the strangest wartime memories are of the ploys that we used to eke out our meagre rations. Perhaps the most revolting thing was using liquid paraffin, instead of margarine, when baking cakes. Our margarine ration had to be spread on bread to supplement the small amount of butter we were allowed. We had a "little butter week" (LBW) and a "big butter week" (BBW). The ration for LBW amounted to what would spread on two slices of toast today, and the BBW was not much better. Bananas were unobtainable during the war years, but we improvised. We made "banana" sandwiches by boiling up parsnips and stirring banana flavouring into the mash!

Thinking of bananas reminds me of a wartime story. A family with two little boys was travelling on a train in the same compartment as a sailor going home on leave. He produced two bananas and gave one each to the goggle-eyed children. Never having seen such strange objects before they hadn't the faintest idea what to do with them and they watched in amazement as he showed them how to peel back the yellow strips. Before their eyes was something looking like an exotic flower and it was inconceivable that it could be something to eat. Just as the sailor had assured them that it was, and the first boy had taken a bite, the train entered a tunnel and the compartment was suddenly plunged into darkness. With a yell of horror the boy screamed to his brother, "Don't eat it – it'll make you go blind!"'

DOING OUR BIT

From the Home Guard to the Women's Land Army, from voluntary service to firefighting, no matter how small our contribution, we all did our bit for the war effort.

GIVEN THE CHOICE

'When the war started we had to go either into a reserved occupation or into the forces, so I went to the flax factory. I worked in the canteen so didn't know much about the factory, apart from the fact that the flax was pulled, brought into the factory, went through the machines and was eventually made into parachutes. Sometimes I would go to the farms around Easingwold to make the tea, when the girls went to pull the flax. I used to take all the food with me as well. Some of the farmers would lend me a copper which had previously been used for boiling water on wash day, so then I would have to wash out the boiler, light a fire underneath and boil water for tea. The flax factory closed down in 1947.

I also joined the Red Cross during the war, and at night when the siren went we had to put on our tin hats, take our gas masks and go to a place in the market and wait to see if we were called out. I used to be very frightened going up the street in the blackout. We were once there all night and I had to ask if I could go home to get my breakfast so that I could catch the 6.25 am bus to work!'

'We were given the choice of the forces, Land Army or munitions. On munitions we worked twelve hour shifts seven days a week, travelling long distances in the blackout. No lights anywhere and no signposts or names on stations.'

WARTIME ENTERTAINMENT

'By 1942 the war was three years old and the blackout was a way of life and something to joke about. Public entertainment in rural areas was non-existent and petrol rationing meant entertainment in towns and cities was inaccessible to country folk. So they had to make their own. A remarkable lady schoolteacher in Brompton called Miss Elford ran an amateur pierrot show for several years.

Brompton Breezes Concert Party usually had about five or six youngsters between 14 and 17 years. Their rehearsals took place in private houses in the evenings. They wore costumes of tall conical hats supporting pom-poms, ruffles round the neck, and satin tunics and trousers, and the act consisted of monologues, duets, song and dance routines and usually a one-act play.

Using any available transport, but usually all piling into the local taxi, they gave concerts at the village halls of Yedingham, Wykeham, Ebberston, Wetwang, Langdale End and many others. All the village halls were constructed out of corrugated iron and the stages were low platforms, the dressing rooms also the kitchens or even outside.

The performances were amateurish to say the least, and in some cases horrendous. Lines were forgotten and ad libbing took place with frequent prompting. But in spite of all this the halls were always packed out, people standing in the doorways and steam running down the windows. No wonder when such gems as the following were in the show:

"Noo yar day i' Reichstag jus' a bit sen,
Twa fellahs sat baith laiking glum.
Yan was gree-at Adolf 'Itler
And t'other were Goring, his chum.

They talked of invading England,
We'll just adopt same procedure
Drop parachute troops in't backyard,
But then Goring said to 'Itler,
It's awright but thoo's fergotten yar thing ... t'Home Guard!"

The programme always ended with *There'll always be an England*. Such was the cheerful spirit that helped England survive the war.'

INTO THE NAAFI

'In August 1943 I was called up to do my bit, and I was offered work in a munitions factory at Aycliffe, or a conductress on the trolley buses in Darlington, or as a counter assistant in the NAAFI. I chose the latter and spent from September 1943 to September 1945 in service with the NAAFI as a counter assistant with the Canadian Air Force at Goosepool aerodrome (now Teesside Airport).

We said we joined the NAAFI to scrub it out! One could find oneself up at 6 am lighting fires – two of us got up to clean out and light four fires. The counters were open from 10 am to 10.30 am for refreshments, after which one could be on bedroom duty up to dinner time cleaning out the bedrooms, ablutions, bathroom etc. The counters were all open again from 12.30 pm to 1.30 pm, then one could find oneself on "tea duty" – two stones of potatoes to peel, tea towels to wash, all four fires to keep going, make the manageress her afternoon tea and take it into her office on a tray, then make the tea for all the staff ready for 5 pm. The tea duty girl was then off duty until 7.30 pm when she came back on to the counters. These were all open from 5.30 pm until 9.30 pm – the Corporal's Bar stayed open until 9.45 pm. After closing the pots were to be collected and washed up, all food was to be put away off the shelves and stands, the kitchen to be left tidy – only then could you retire to bed!

Each morning two counter hands went out with the NAAFI mobile at 10.30 am round to Flight where the aircraft were being repaired, and then to the bomb dump, to serve tea, coffee, cakes etc. At the bomb dump the lads stood in a row and threw the smaller bombs from one to the other to load them up on to the planes – I used to hope that none of the lads had "butter fingers"!'

THE CANTEEN

'A canteen was opened by the YMCA in the reading room at Top-cliffe to cater for the servicemen stationed in the area and a rota of volunteers ran it each evening. The equipment was very limited, comprising a toaster which did two slices of bread at a time and a rather battered saucepan used for poaching eggs. I was still at school but fitted in my turn on rota by doing homework as soon as I came home from school. I well remember the night I poached 60 eggs, one at a time, broken straight into the pan of water and I only broke one. We also served beans on toast and various sandwiches and it was at the canteen that we first saw peanut butter, which was popular with the Canadians. Horlicks was a favourite drink and several Canadians asked for a mug of their special brew which was tea with a flavouring of coffee and drinking chocolate!

There were some special events held during the war. I remember "Wings for Victory" and "Salute the Soldier" weeks when people parted with prized possessions to raise money for the war effort. On the night of VJ Day, a huge bonfire was lighted on the sheepwash near the river and crowds of airmen came to it. One Canadian said as he watched the blaze, "Five years, eleven months and twelve days have I been fighting for this day and it sure has been a great day." We all agreed with him.'

ARP WARDEN

'When the war broke out, two days after my second birthday, my father volunteered for the army, and was eventually given a medical. He was dismayed to be classified as C3, his services under no circumstances to be required in His Majesty's Forces, for he looked and felt well at that time. He had been found to have a heart complaint of which he was totally unaware. So he threw himself into the Air Raid Precautions duties when he returned from work each day.

We had the ARP first aid box in the hall of our terrace house at Horbury; it was as long as a coffin, though deeper, a red cross on the lid and two rope handles at each side. I was fascinated by this but never got to look inside. From time to time there were first aid exercises in the local park, which were at once useful and a spectacle for the village to watch. The first aid box would be loaded on a lorry and we would follow it. I remember being absolutely horrified to see our friendly local butcher lying on the grass, covered in what looked like blood. It took a lot of comforting from my mother to persuade me that he was only a pretend casualty.

If it were not my father's turn to be on ARP night duty then he got to sleep at home; but should there be an air raid warning he had to turn out immediately, to supplement those already on duty. We suffered mainly from incendiary bombs, aimed at the busy main line railway a mile away, but we never had any personal damage.

The warning siren would blow – a fluctuating, up and down the scale noise that no one could possibly sleep through – and my father would jump out of bed, don his navy-blue battledress and tin hat, and leave hurriedly. My mother would snatch me from my bed, wrap me in an eiderdown, and take me to my grandfather's house, next door but one in our terrace. There we sat at the top of his cellar steps, under the well of the staircase. This was thought to be the safest and strongest place, if of course you didn't have an Anderson shelter. My aunt did have a shelter dug in her back garden, but it always seemed to be knee-deep in water, and consequently didn't smell very nice; so we were rather glad we didn't have one.

During the period of the air raid, or until the danger from passing enemy planes had gone, we played snap, ludo or I spy, or sang songs; sometimes if it went on a long time my mother would make a hot drink. Then it would be all over, and we would hear the continual high-pitched tone of the all clear blowing. By the time it died away, we were ready to leave for home. Within a few minutes, should there have been no damage that night, my father would be dropped off by a lorry, and we would resume our broken sleep.

I was never fully aware of the danger of it all; there was no television to bring what would have been the harrowing pictures of death, injury and damage into our homes several times a day. Parents had the newspapers and wireless to keep them informed, but children were not as aware. To me the air raids were an exciting adventure, an excuse to be up in the middle of the night, and if a night went by without one I was almost disappointed.

*Air raid wardens became familiar figures to us all, immortalised by their cry
'Put that light out!'*

When we had once gone almost a fortnight without a warning I
was found pacing up and down in my bedroom, with my tiny
attache case packed with toys and games, demanding: "Are they
never going to blow the siren again?". But of course my parents,
especially my father, were glad to have their sleep uninterrupted.'

FOR THE WAR EFFORT

'Our little village WI at West Witton was the keystone for all the
local war effort events – knitting for the troops, firefighting, caring
for evacuees and egg collecting for the local hospital. We were also
responsible for the obtaining and distribution of the "jam-making
sugar". This system worked on the lines of no fruit trees, no extra
sugar.
    One month we had a party for the soldiers stationed nearby. Plain
but wholesome refreshments such as rations would allow were produced, and we all sat waiting for our guests. Sad to say, only one
poor chap turned up. However, he could play the piano, so he
volunteered to oblige, while the ladies showed their heels doing the
ribbon dance! The entry in the minute book says: "A good time was
had by all".'

'My mother found herself setting up the jam-making operations at
Sowerby. Jars were urgently required, and a handful of boys and
girls, calling ourselves grandly the Youth Service Squad, set out with
a handcart to invite the housewives of Sowerby to bring out their
spare jam jars. We paid a penny for a two pound jar and a halfpenny
for a one pound jar. The jam was sold in local shops.'

COLLECTING HERBS

'During the war my mother organised the collecting and drying of herbs from which valuable medicines could be prepared, since such materials could no longer be obtained from abroad. My sister and I, together with our friends, were the main collectors. We dried colts-foot leaves, raspberry leaves and wormwood in an attic over the bar of the local pub at Gargrave. The leaves were spread on frames covered with coarse netting. The wormwood was tied in bunches and hung from the beams.

Our most valuable item was foxglove seed. It was sold at £1 for a pound, a lot of money in those days, which was sufficient to cover any expenses. The seed, which looks like finely ground coffee, contains digitalin; this is still used in the treatment of heart disease. We used to shake the dead flower stems over sheets of newspaper, the seed dropped out of the capsules and was tipped into a box. It was slow and not very efficient, but one summer we managed to collect five pounds. The fine seed is very lightweight and this quantity filled a seven-pound biscuit tin to the top.

Another major effort was the yearly collection of a hundredweight of rose hips. The whole family was roped in to pick them over and remove all the stalks. They were used to make rosehip syrup, a valuable source of vitamin C, given to young children as a dietary supplement.'

VOLUNTARY WORK

'My husband joined the Royal Air Force in 1936, and we were married in 1938. By then my husband was a fully trained heavy bomber pilot, stationed at Leconfield near Beverley. We had rented a fully furnished house for £1 per week, including rates, so we were very lucky.

The week before war was declared in 1939, my husband was posted to an operational squadron at Linton on Ouse. We packed up our furnished house and I went home to Poulton le Fylde, wondering when we would ever be together again. However, the policy at that time was for air crews to live out, so within a week I joined my husband, having obtained board and lodgings in York with some very homely people, with whom we are still good friends.

I then continued doing voluntary work, as I had always done since being 17. The time came for me to register for war work, but in the circumstances I was not called up to go into a factory, providing I continued to do voluntary work, e.g. WVS, Red Cross, canteen meals etc. When York had the flooding we went out in amphibious boats taking soup and food to the people marooned in their bedrooms.

This was followed up by helping to issue clothing and footwear to the people who had lost so many of their clothes, and particularly to the menfolk, so they could have trousers and wellingtons to clean up their homes.

After a short posting down south, when my husband was doing anti submarine patrol work in the Channel and outskirts of the Bay of Biscay, he was posted back to York, and was on bombing raids over Europe. We stayed with the same friends in York, and I continued to do voluntary work. These were anxious times, not knowing when the men would return, but realising that many bombers had gone out each night. By this time my husband was commissioned, and on occasions when crews were reported missing, I had the sad task of breaking the news to the wives that their husband's aircraft had not returned. I broke it as gently as possible, assuring the wife not to give up hope, as it was only "missing". Then of course the official Air Ministry letter came confirming the crew was missing. Then the wife or wives returned home to their parents. One wife had a baby when her husband and crew went missing over the North Sea, and unfortunately they were never heard of again.

When this tour of "ops" was finished my husband was posted to Abingdon, instructing new pilots, and whilst there he flew on the three 1,000 Bomber raids.

The station did have a few fatal crashes, whilst training, and again I had that difficult task of breaking the news, and comforting the wife of the pilot instructor, but this time with no hope of him coming back. These wives were wonderfully brave.

After a while my husband received notice of a posting to convert to Halifax bombers, at Marston Moor, and later to RAF Burn near Selby on to operational flying again. All this time he was in 4 Group which operated from Heslington Hall, York. At Burn he was in 578 Squadron, which had been formed in 1944 and was disbanded in 1945, a short lived squadron but a most successful one, which had the first VC of 4 group and many more war decorations.'

IN THE WAAF

'On 15th May 1943 I had my eighteenth birthday, and as all girls of that age had to register to do war work of some kind, I decided that I would join the WAAF.

I was a very innocent country girl who had hardly ever been out of my home village, except to go to Richmond, six miles away, to work as an apprentice hairdresser. We were brought up very strictly in those days, and with no television to watch, we knew very little of the outside world. As I was the eldest of six children, I had to help Mum wash and bake and look after the younger children.

200

The prospect of joining the WAAF was terrifying, as I had to make my own way to join up. However the day arrived and in February 1944 I received the appropriate papers. I had to get myself to Wilmslow, Manchester, to start my six weeks' training. A few days later I received a travel warrant to catch the train from Richmond to Manchester; I had never been on a train. It was a cold winter's day when I set off, Mum crying at the station as she saw me off, and me wondering what was going to happen. When I arrived at Manchester along with several more recruits, there was RAF transport waiting to take us out to Wilmslow.

On arrival we were herded into a Nissen hut, there were about 20 in ours; here each of us had an iron bedstead with a horsehair mattress. Dropping our luggage we were marched to the Stores and each given two army blankets, two cotton sheets and a pillowslip; at least we got sheets, the RAF only got blankets. We then marched back to our hut and made up our beds. The place was freezing even though there was a stove in the middle of the hut; it was so cold very few of us got any sleep that night.

Next morning we were up at six and out across the road to the washhouse for a wash and brush up, before being marched down to the large cookhouse for breakfast. We were then taken to be kitted out with our uniforms, none of which fitted very well, but we made do. I well remember the grey Air Force bloomers, with elastic in the legs, and the long grey lisle stockings.

Then on for our medicals. We had our hair searched for lice, and quite a few girls had them and had to have their hair disinfected, and a few had to wash their bodies a bit cleaner. Back at home not all girls had even the most basic washing facilities, and you could not call it their fault.

We were marched everywhere in threes, doing our best at the beginning as we tried to get it right. I enjoyed the drill, but woe betide you if you got it wrong. About the third day we were given our injections, to combat various diseases. Oh, did we suffer; our arms were so sore, and we were expected to drill just the same. Soon we were given an intelligence test, to sort out where they were going to place us after training. We had a preference in what we wanted to do, but it depended on your intelligence test. I decided I still wanted to do hairdressing, for which I was trained, and the WAAF needed hairdressers. So I did a test at the hairdressing shop and passed.

How I longed for home in that first week and was terribly homesick. There was no going out to ring Mum up, for we had no telephone. But as each day wore on, with the companionship of the other girls, and lots of laughter, we all began to settle down and to enjoy ourselves, and to make lifelong friends. I would not have missed it for anything.'

FIREFIGHTERS

'After the first half of the war at school, I spent the second half in different uniforms as a firewoman. Fortunately I was treated like a daughter by some of my colleagues who had been at school with my father. Being on duty (48 hours on and 24 hours off) was somehow more acceptable than leaving home for a full service life!

Now, everybody knows from television what a tough and dangerous job firefighting is. One of my 30 year old colleagues had been unfit for the forces, where he might have spent the war years pen pushing. Instead, this unfit man was drafted into the Fire Service where he risked his life two days out of three every week. The training was very strenuous, and even in peacetime the work was often exhausting. Many, especially the self-employed, also worked on their rest days.

During the blitz, in addition to our own, mainly rural, areas, our firemen fought fires in distant cities under heavy bombardment. They had to drive out to where they were needed, put out the fires, drive back again, then clean and polish the appliances and equipment before going off duty. They worked amazingly hard, and sometimes the public, not realising, said that they were lucky to be in a rural area!

Throughout the war, local farm, heath and hill fires, which could be enclosed and left to burn out in peacetime, had to be extinguished by dusk so that they did not provide a guide for enemy bombers.

We often saw masses of German bombers overhead en route to industrial sites, unaware of the secret radar development under their path. Not many rural fire stations had a red telephone like ours from Radar Research, knowing only that it was crucial to the war effort. We were greatly relieved that all the calls were only practices.

Women mainly manned the control, although some became dispatch riders or canteen staff. They worked with extreme speed and accuracy in receiving and passing on messages, and plotting and directing manned appliances. Timing became vital, especially in a rural area where we often dealt with several fires simultaneously, and dispatch riders could spend several minutes finding a telephone. Delays or misdirection of firepumps, mobile water tanks or turntable ladders could be fatal, and keeping an accurate log of each incident often proved difficult, but was essential in case of legal enquiries.

For the men, one of the worst fires was a crashed aircraft. They couldn't rescue the crews, and couldn't get rid of the smell for days. There were many local training airfields where accidents happened.

Firefighters had one of the most dangerous jobs on the home front.

On "test turnouts" each station had an "allowed time", in our case mainly for indoor and outdoor stairs. We were proud that our men often achieved "minus time" and our mainly middle-aged regulars and auxiliaries won cups at Area Speed and Efficiency competitions. This especially delighted our favourite Area Officer who always brought his golden labrador, which had a huge scar on its side. He had left the dog in Shaftesbury Avenue fire station when fighting fires in the blitz and returned to find the station bombed and the dog injured. He never left it again.

When in 1944 my family suffered several tragic losses, my second "family" gave us enormous support, and I am forever grateful that my higher education was in the NFS – the National Fire Service.'

DREAMING OF CORNWALL

'My friend joined the Land Army dreaming of Cornwall. She got a fourpence ha'penny railway warrant from Thirsk to Topcliffe, so went on her bike! They started the gardens on the aerodrome, and reared pigs, chickens and ducks, much to the amusement of the Canadian airmen. As I marched to the office in the Army, I thought of her picking frozen brussels sprouts without gloves. The land girls had a hard life and most suffered arthritis in later life. They got no gratuity for their service, just a letter of thanks from the Queen.'

I JOINED IN 1939

'I joined the Women's Land Army in October 1939 and was very fortunate to go to Askham Bryan agricultural college to train. In early January 1940 there was a very severe spell of weather, with snow and ice and on several occasions no buses were running in to York from the Tadcaster area owing to the slippery road surfaces. The river Ouse was frozen over and the ice had to be cut every day for the swans and ducks to drink and feed. We tried one day to snag the turnip swedes but they and the land were too frozen.

I spent four of my five years in the WLA on two farms in Danby Wiske doing general farm work, which was tiring, but never boring as there were so many varied jobs, milking and feeding daily, with other jobs in their season. In haytime there was the hay to cut, turn it to dry it, make into haycocks, then load the loose hay onto carts and pitch it onto the stacks. Threshing days were busy for everyone, especially in the days of the steam engines when water had to be carried to keep the engine working; cowling (raking) the chaff from underneath the thresher was a dirty and dusty job, pitching the sheaves from the stack was cleaner, but my main job was to cut the sheaf bands before the straw was fed into the machine.

I remember one threshing day seeing a bomber nearby in trouble, and coming down in flames at Birkby. The Canadian crew were all killed. Another day with a colleague we saw a German bomber and shortly afterwards heard the explosions as he dropped his bombs. As the bomber returned we crouched down hoping that he would not see us or have any bombs left. We learned later that Leeming airfield had been bombed and a number of our aircraft had been destroyed.'

TO MY SURPRISE

'As a young girl at the beginning of the war, I spent much of my spare time helping out firewatching at Wakefield cathedral, at a first-aid post two or three nights a week and auxiliary nursing. Then, in 1940, almost to my surprise, I found myself in the Land Army!

My journey began by rail from Wakefield to York, then to Alne, which I managed to mispronounce, and finally by a train called the "Coffee pot" to Easingwold. I was placed in a hostel which now is the site of the fire station, along with about 40 other girls.

We were a mixed bunch, some of us very "green", some very worldly. We worked on different farms every week; regular hours eight until five except haytime and harvest when, of course, it was much longer. Every morning we would be taken to the farm by lorry, but as petrol was scarce short journeys would be made on men's bicycles. Each of us was responsible for a horse and cart. The horse had to be harnessed and the cart filled with muck before the spreading could begin. Eventually I was sent to work regularly at a local farm, living in with another girl; two other girls came each day from Farlington.

We had to endure initiation rituals – like being sent for a "long wait" and when the men thought we'd waited long enough they told us so! Also, we were given the dirtiest and most uncomfortable job of clearing out the chaff-hole on the threshing machine, where all the dust and rubbish is thrown. On the whole we were accepted for doing a good job, one exception being the vicar, who thought our hedge-cutting wasn't worth the money!

We went to Husthwaite to dances and were brought back home by the boys on the cross bar of their bicycles. The shortage of stockings meant that we had to colour our legs with a gravy salt solution, on one occasion mixed with ochre sheep dip! At weekends we went home, returning on Sunday night, that is until I met Phyllis, who talked me into getting back on Monday mornings on a workmen's bus. Quite a bad influence. Amongst the brighter happenings was meeting my future husband on the farm; we celebrated our Golden Wedding last year.'

A WARTIME ADVENTURE

'I well remember my first day in the Women's Land Army. It was dark when a small group of us arrived at the end of our journey. Here we were at last in a tiny North Riding village, on the edge of a moor in midwinter with a covering of snow. Everything was strange and new to us, all city girls from Bradford and Leeds and as green as grass on country matters. It was very cold when the wind swept off the moor but we were warm in our thick uniform; the strong shoes and boots took a lot of breaking in, but they were made to withstand a lot of hard wear.

Our first job was reclaiming land ready for growing corn, this meant chopping down gorse bushes and burning them. This proved difficult if a gale was blowing at the time and it often was; I don't know how many matches we must have wasted before the fire got going well.

Threshing days became our lot very often during the winter months, and being the most inexperienced members of the team, it was usually the girls who had to keep the chaff-hole cleared out. It was certainly an endurance test because besides the black smoke from the steam engine getting in our eyes we had to contend with the swirling chaff and the agony of barley awns getting down your neck and everywhere else.

Making the acquaintance of heavy horses for the first time was rather frightening, they were so big and their huge feet were likely to squash our toes at any time as we led the carts loaded with corn to the stackyard. One of my jobs was to ride the cart horse from Greta Bridge to the blacksmith's at Cross Lanes for shoeing. This was very pleasant if the weather was fine, but sometimes I would meet an army tank on a training exercise, the noise would strike the horse with terror and I would take a detour into the fields if I could.

I will always remember the Italian prisoners of war who came to work on the farms, they always appeared happy to be out of the camp and sang operatic songs most of the time. The German prisoners were not so cheerful but were good workers. The war seemed very remote and didn't concern us very much except when we saw the convoys of lorries filled with waving soldiers going south. This continued for many days in the preparation for D-Day, but we didn't know about it until afterwards.

When we were issued with cycles a few of us had to go down a quiet lane to learn to ride them, it took a few tumbles before we became proficient. Then it was the joy of free-wheeling down the hills to work in the morning air and the slow walk back to our billet at night, with aching muscles, blistered hands and very tired but content to know that we had done a little bit to help the war effort. No matter how weary we were after a day's work it was surprising how we found the energy to go to the village dance held in the reading room once a week. We danced the night away to Mrs Preston's accordion band and thoroughly enjoyed it all.

We learned to plough, sow, reap and mow when farm work was not so mechanised as it is now. It was a wartime adventure none of us would ever forget, and most of all it is good to remember the warmth of the friendship which we received from the village people as we were absorbed into their little community.'

A CHILD'S WAR

Children soon came to accept the war as normal, and many who were too young to understand found great enjoyment in everyday life. The war deprived us of many things, but how strange that the banana became the symbol of all that we had missed!

A TIME OF AUSTERITY

'The war was a time of austerity, when we made our own fun. Mother made wonderful rag dolls with composition heads, and dolls' clothes strong enough to stand up to much pulling on and off, with dolly washdays being a favourite game – I had my own little line and pegs! I enjoyed pretend dolls' tea parties on the floor with prized china tea sets. Dad made delightful wooden toys. I was fortunate in having quite a few dolls but our teddy bears had to go to the War Effort – we were asked at school to give them up to help. I was told my own (a hard but pretty bear with yellow head and legs and a pink and blue body) would go to some poor child in Holland. My brother told me his would be shot out of a gun!

We had few attractive clothes. Mother made most of mine, often from her own or other family cast-offs, also making aprons from cotton curtains, etc. There were no pretty undies for us, only liberty bodices (plus Thermogene vests after illness!) and plain school navy or bottle-green knickers. For grammar school, gymslips with white or pale blue blouses for winter, gingham dresses and blazers for summer. Very little was wasted in those days. We never thought of complaining about our plain clothes since we were all in the same position.

Being wartime, all windows had to be blacked out against air raids, so we had large wooden frames covered in thick brown paper to put up at night. It was obviously an anxious time to grow up, but York only had one major blitz, when Dad as an ARP warden was out on duty. The railway station was badly damaged, and Dad who was a carpenter on the London & North Eastern Railway (thereby exempt from active service) had much work for weeks in the repairs to the large arched roof.

Mother looked after the children at home bravely, and part-dressed us (nighties tucked into knickers!) ready to get out quickly in case of air raids. My brother wore a toy tin helmet. At the dreaded sound of the siren, we came downstairs to makeshift beds in the recesses either side of the fireplace, and one night I remember watching the tall bookcase swaying ominously with vibration. However, we were fortunate. We all escaped fairly lightly, although did have a near miss when an enemy fighter plane crashed only half a mile away from home, destroying several houses and dropping the pilot's logbook and gloves and lots of silver foil in our garden – all being collected by "officials" in due course.

Our family had two different evacuee London families to stay with us for a time, and we made friends with children coming to stay in the area whom we would never have known otherwise – we were very conscious of their southern accents being different from ours, and they were much quicker-witted than us!'

BLACKOUT AND BANANAS

'One of my strongest memories of the war years was the blackout. The procedure of ensuring that no chinks of light emanated from within the house was a ritual carried out every day before dusk, come what may. My father had a reserved occupation and he always checked the curtains from outside before going on duty as an ARP (Air Raid Precaution) warden.

Whenever the dreaded air raid siren sounded it meant a hasty retreat to the air raid shelter with its own peculiar aroma. At the beginning of the war when I was only two years old I was carried to the shelter wrapped in an eiderdown and set down on a bunk bed head to toe with my sister. Later on in the war I could walk into the shelter and felt very adult on the first occasion I was allowed to. In a childlike oblivion I fell asleep to the constant clattering of my mother's knitting needles. It nearly always seemed that as soon as I dropped off to sleep I was disturbed again, this time by the all-clear siren. One of my father's friends made me a small bell which I would ring as loudly as possible, calling out "all clear – all clear" at the same time.

When I first went to school I had to carry with me a gas mask. All small children were issued with a "Mickey Mouse" gas mask but whilst I do not recall much about it, I do remember that it was housed in a square cardboard box which had a cord which I had over one shoulder and across my body. In the first few weeks at school we had a rest after lunch and we had to lie down on a raffia mat. Each child had a mat with different colour variations and it was considered to be a big step in learning for us to collect our own mat and know where to position it, as well as putting our shoes on without help.

Although sweets were rationed throughout the war and for a long time afterwards we tended to find alternatives, the most popular of which were Ovaltine tablets and liquorice root. Ice cream was not very nice, being made with dried egg, but we still ate it. One of our local shops sold pink wafers and white wafers at threepence or sixpence but we soon realised that the threepenny wafer was better value. If you were caught eating ice cream whilst wearing school uniform you were in trouble but the risk was well worth taking as I remember walking out of the shop licking two threepenny wafers on top of one another, both being different colours.

I remember how much dried potato was part of the diet and how horrible it was and who would have thought that this food would still be available today though of much better quality and taste. On the subject of taste, one of my favourite foods at the time was bread and dripping and I looked forward to a plate of this on arriving home from school.

On the birthday of a friend of mine her father treated the two of us to an afternoon at the pantomime and I saw on the stage a large canvas banana with a long zip. This was my first recollection of a fruit that I had never seen for real.'

FREE SCHOOL MILK

'During the war years a number of evacuees arrived at Low Mills Farndale school from Hull and Middlesbrough, plus two of their teachers. It was a very trying time for them, coping along with Mrs Appleby our headmistress with three classes of children between five years and 14 years, all in one small room.

Food rationing was introduced and Lord Woolton was concerned that we country children were not supplied with enough vitamins and proteins. He said that all children must have free school milk in one third pint bottles. Pasteurised milk was brought by train into Pickering and Kirkby stations at about six each morning. We in Low Mills were seven miles out and so we had to have Horlicks to drink instead. Mrs Tinsley, our school caretaker, had lit the big iron round-barrelled stove early to heat the room and at 9 am Mrs Appleby placed an urn full of water on top. By the time it was mid-morning break (playtime) the water would be about boiling. She would add measures of Horlicks, use a plunger to mix and ladle out into beakers for us all to enjoy. This was, of course, if the wind was in the right direction for the stove, but if not, the Horlicks would be cold and we were all shivering anyway.'

IN THE CELLAR

'School dinners started during the war, ours at Follifoot came in containers. They must have had problems the first day, because the dinners did not arrive until 2 pm so those who had elected to go home for dinner felt very superior. Eating up your meal was important. I was once kept in until afternoon playtime to eat up my jam roly-poly pudding. I hated it for years afterwards.

Then there were the gas masks, what a funny smell they had when you practised putting them on. You had to carry them all the time, hooking them on your chair back at school. We had to prepare for the possibility of air raids. The school house next door had the roof of the cellar specially reinforced to make a shelter. We also had to practise getting under our desks in case there was no time to reach the shelter.

One day at playtime we heard the sirens sound very briefly. We rushed into school to tell our teacher. The rest of the afternoon was spent in the cellar singing *One man went to mow* and *Ten green bottles*. Home time came and no all clear, but no sound of aircraft.

What could have happened? There was no school telephone in those days so no way to find out and we were instructed to go home as quickly as possible. It turned out that the siren had been turned on by accident!'

A STRING OF SAUSAGES

'When I was a little girl, in the 1940s, my mother would say: "I'll pack a picnic tea, meet me on the beach after school." There was no fear of rain as most of the summers had good weather, or so it seemed!

I was at school throughout the war, and I had to take my gas mask every day. We lived over a mile from the school at Fylingthorpe but we walked the distance four times each day, as my brother, sister and I returned home for lunch. In winter we took a packed lunch.

One day when my brother, Edwin and my sister, Audrey were at school, I was at home with chickenpox, and Mother and I went to the garden for some vegetables for dinner. Our allotment was halfway down a field in front of our house and the army were using the field. Mum was passing the time of day with one of the soldiers when a plane flew over. I looked up and saw something coming from the plane and said, "Look Mum, a string of sausages!" The soldier said it was a rope ladder, but my mother gave me a big push and said, "Run, it's bombs!" She was right, it was! They exploded before we reached the house and Mum said that they were on or very near to the school, so we waited for Audrey and Edwin to come home.

Looking back my mother must have been out of her mind with worry. Our neighbour went dashing off to find her son, missed him, and was in a shocking state when she arrived home. After a long while the schoolchildren arrived home covered in dust and with some very grizzly tales to tell. That was not the only time that I saw bombs being dropped, but afterwards I knew what they were.

During the war my mother worked as a cook at Sneaton Castle. All the nuns would go into the kitchen to see her, and when I was about seven Audrey, Edwin and I would go there after school. I can remember the smell of new bread today, and Mum was such a good cook that Father Armasted used to arrive at our house on most Sundays for his tea.

My father was in the RAF, and when the first enemy plane was brought down on British soil he was at home ill in bed, but he gave the British plane plenty of encouragement by hanging out of the bedroom window shouting, "Get 'em, lads!" whilst Mum hung onto his legs to stop him from falling out!

When I see my six year old granddaughter, who has masses of toys and clothes, I think of the contrast with our family of 50 years ago. We relied on the RAF for our only Christmas present, and my sister and I went to bed in Mum's old dresses as we had no night clothes. Our school gymslips were washed (by hand) until they were threadbare, and in summer we only had one dress each which had to be washed, dried and ironed after we had gone to bed so we could wear them the next day. We had no television, and our wireless required an accumulator which had to be taken to the local garage to be recharged. We were quite able to amuse ourselves, and couldn't have been happier.'

TOO YOUNG TO UNDERSTAND

'My first memory was Christmas, 1939. The war had started and the War Office had commandeered eight acres of my father's farm land at Ingleby Arncliffe for searchlights. There were 52 men billeted there and on Christmas Eve they had their Christmas party, after which they took down all their decorations and brought them to our farmhouse and decorated the rooms for me on Christmas morning. As Mother carried me downstairs and into the room I will never forget the sight – it was like being in fairyland. Those decorations were used for about 40 years until they dropped to pieces, but the memory of them will live for ever.

Another memory of the war days was when I was about three or four years old and the bombers came over the house and dropped three bombs at the Cleveland Tontine about one mile away. My father was out on duty as an air raid warden and my mother and I were in the house with my elderly grandparents. After the first bang my mother pushed me into the dining room and sheltered me under the sideboard – we often laughed about it years after, but it was very frightening at the time, especially as the tiles on the fireplace cracked with the impact.

I can remember standing at my bedroom window watching the criss-cross of the searchlights and thinking what a lovely sight – I was too young to appreciate the seriousness of it all. To me the war meant fun and lots of company and comings and goings. We had evacuees from Sunderland, who didn't stay long, and two teachers (who were twin brothers). They played with me and took photographs of me which I still have. A major, his wife and family stayed in the house with us and each evening Mother had some of the soldiers up for supper. They used to take it in turns. One winter the weather was so bad that they used my sledge to walk to Stokesley, eight miles away, to get their food rations.

One highlight was being taken down the field to the camp and allowed to sit in the "spotting chair".

Toys were hard to get and money was short, so my father made my dolls' bed and cradle, and my sister, who was nursing in London, had dolls made for me, Red Riding Hood and a WAAF doll. I still have the dolls today. As food rationing was very much part of my childhood, sweets were very special and I never see a Mars Bar today but I think of the war. Mother used to cut a Mars Bar into thin slices and I had one a day for a fortnight until the next ration came.

I would love to meet some of those soldiers today to thank them for the kindness they showed me in my childhood, but unfortunately many of them were killed in France.'

AT SCHOOL

'I was born in 1937, and so had a wartime childhood. My two brothers and I attended the old Romanby Church of England school, which is now the church hall. There were over 70 children aged from five to eleven with only two teachers.

When I started school the infants still used slates occasionally. The infants teacher had a bad temper and if you got your sums wrong she threw your book across the room and rapped your knuckles with a ruler. I was terrified of her. The girls' toilet was round the back of the school, and I remember queuing for ages in all weathers.

The classrooms were heated by large black coke stoves. In winter, when it snowed, not many children got to school because they had to walk a long way. One day the snow was so deep that only a few children arrived and we all sat round the stove whilst the teacher read us stories. The teachers must have worked very hard because a lot of children passed the scholarship.

The older children had a small piece of garden, and we all enjoyed sowing seeds and watching them grow. In autumn we collected rose hips and took them to school to be made into rosehip syrup – we were paid for them. Once we all had to take a container to school and we were given drinking chocolate powder which had been sent from Canada. In summer we were taken for nature walks when we collected and pressed wild flowers. We always took our gas masks to school. They were kept in coloured metal cylinders, and my brothers and I had different colours.

The war did not affect us very much. I remember a bomb dropping on South Parade, Northallerton which blew all the glass out of the windows in my great-uncle's grocery shop, but my aunt and uncle were not injured. When a German plane was shot down in Romanby my brothers pestered my mother to take them to see it, but I was frightened that there would be dead men in it!

My father was the manager of a mill which sold flour and animal feeds, which were all on coupons. They had to be sorted and counted each evening.

My grandmother lived next door to us. She had evacuees – a school teacher, his wife and baby. A whole school was evacuated from the coast to Northallerton grammar school. One school had to use the buildings in the morning and the other in the afternoon.

When we were small my brothers and I all had a bath together, and we had to hurry up and not use too much water because a soldier came to have a bath later in the evening.

My Dad made our garage into an air raid shelter, surrounded with sandbags. We children slept in it during the war so that we wouldn't have to be woken if there was an air raid warning.

Everyone had to dig up half their garden to grow vegetables. We often played hide and seek with our friends and a favourite hiding place was behind a row of peas, which we could eat while waiting to be found! We kept hens and ducks at the bottom of the garden, and a friend of Dad's shared a pig with us. My mother baked all our bread and buns and the smell was lovely when we came home from school on baking day.

We were never short of food but only saw oranges occasionally, and there were no bananas during the war. My Dad loved bananas and often said how good they were. I was disappointed with the first one I tasted after the war – I expected it to be juicy!'

ALL RATHER FUN

'When war was declared in 1939 I was playing with a school friend of mine about 20 houses up the road and it was announced on the wireless that our country was at war. I ran back down the road to find my aunt running up to meet me wearing her gas mask. We had been expecting war and she had obviously been expecting the gas to follow too!

On arriving back home with my aunt we rushed down into the Anderson shelter in the garden. These crude corrugated iron constructions were to become our nightly bedroom for six years. My father had tried to camouflage it as best he could with his usual flair for a rock garden, with old chimney pots on the roof and what I as a child thought was a door with a knocker, but was really a protective door against blast. Inside we heated it nightly with a candle under a flower pot and it was amazing how hot it became. The air raid warning would go on a regular basis every night at eight o'clock and you could set your watch by it! It was all rather fun at my age and I never realised the seriousness of the war, especially one night when I had forgotten my teddy bear and expected my father to return to the house to fetch it for me. In my naïve state I never thought that my father would allow the Germans to capture me and anyway I had my wonderful collection of German stamps which I would show them, and then they would think I was a nice little girl!

After the nightly bombing became really intense, the following morning the gardens would be covered with large chunks of shrapnel from the exploding shells and my sisters and I would collect it and take it to the local police station where they had a large empty shell case into which the pieces were thrown and they would then be sent to be melted down again to be made into more live shells. We were expected to help the war effort in many small ways, for instance we had to collect tins, paper, bones etc in separate sacks as they all had different uses.

Our houses had to be protected against glass damage from blast, so every window was taped with two inch wide brown paper strips. Blackout blinds had to be put up each night and woe betide anyone if the air raid warden spotted a chink of light, which could be reported to the police. There were no street lights in those days, hand torches had to be covered with red paper to dull the light, and the few cars that were allowed petrol coupons for important work had to have mere slits for headlights. It was a very gloomy time yet crime did not increase, and somehow it brought the best out of people, not the worst.

During the war my mother concocted wonderful meals from mere vegetables and made delicious soups. Likewise we got used to powdered egg, with which to make cakes, and sandwiches of mashed banana-flavoured parsnips! Coupons were needed for clothes, furniture, food, sweets etc and yet we did not starve. I grew up with a weekly allowance of a quarter of a pound of sweets. Today I buy a pound of cheese at a time, and yet that would have been the ration for our entire family for a week and a half during the war.'

WRITING TO THE SAILORS

'During the war Whixley school adopted a minesweeper and we used to write to the sailors. A blanket was knitted and made into a parcel with a cake and sweets and sent off. Unfortunately the ship itself was lost, but the parcel was received safely and distributed amongst the crew. A Petty Officer received the cake my mother had made and he wrote to my brother. Later I became his penpal. One day on his way home from leave he called to see us, staying overnight. He did this several times and later his younger brother joined the navy and did the same. After his demob the brother returned to York and married my sister!'

POWs AND SOLDIERS

'One of the many people who worked on my parents' farm in wartime was an Italian prisoner. He had been a motorcycle courier and was quite relieved to have been captured, but he didn't like the uniform that showed him to be a POW, so he took off the patches and boiled it in the copper. Then he wore it proudly, saying, "Now me like British soldier!" He would entertain us by standing on top of the granary steps, waving his arms about and giving an impression of Mussolini making a speech. When letters arrived from his Mama Marguerita he shed a few tears of homesickness. In the evenings he liked to go to Pickering on a bike to meet girls, but one day he fell off going down the bank and broke his arm. He was taken back to the camp and we never saw him again.

Beside our farm was a tree-lined lane, where some camouflaged British army vehicles were parked at one time. Our hen houses were on the other side of the hedge, so every time a hen cackled we had to rush to collect the eggs before the soldiers got there. Our barn was used as the cookhouse and had a large "Keep Out" notice on the door. One day my mother saw a soldier in the garden looking puzzled, he had been sent for some potatoes, but as she was showing him that they grew under the soil and he had to dig them out, an officer came and shouted at her that the man was supposed to use his initiative.'

BOMBS IN SCARBOROUGH

'We were playing in my Grandma's garden at Scalby Nabs on the morning of 3rd September 1939. It was a lovely sunny day and

Mother called us in just in time to hear the announcement by Mr Chamberlain that war had been declared. We didn't really know what it meant. When we went to school we were issued with gas masks, each in a cardboard box and Mother had to buy a case to put them in. We were supposed to carry them wherever we went. We had to try them on and they smelt awful!

When I was at Falsgrave school a lot of children were evacuated to Scarborough from Hull. Until things got organised we went to school in the mornings and in the afternoons we went to All Saints church hall where we played games and did country dancing. The next week games were in the morning and lessons in the afternoon, alternating with the evacuees. Sometimes the siren would sound during lessons and we all had to go into the brick built air raid shelters in the schoolyard until the all clear went. We sang songs while in the shelter.

We had shelters built in the streets and before that we used to go to St James church hall. The night of the Scarborough "blitz" Mum, my brother and I sat under the dining room table, wondering what to expect when we went out the next morning. The mother and sister of a boy in my class were killed in Commercial Street. We didn't see Dad for two days as he had to stay on duty as a fireman. He had been putting fires out that had been caused by incendiary bombs. Some nights the firemen had to go onto the moors to put out fires caused by the bombs and his uniform would smell of the smoke for days.

We were in our backyard in Spring Bank one Sunday night in summer and we saw bombs being dropped from a plane. They landed on the railway bridge at Woodlands Ravine not far from my other grandparents' house. I was at my aunt's house at Scalby Nabs one afternoon, standing at the top of the hill from where I could see the castle, Olivers Mount and the promenade. Suddenly a plane swooped down over the woods at Olivers Mount and started firing. I found out later that a boy from Hinderwell school had been killed by the bullets. We used to see our bombers flying out to sea, going to bomb Germany in droves, and then hear them coming back damaged. Usually more seemed to go than came back.

My boyfriend and I went to Boots Corner on VE night and everyone was singing and dancing. We joined in as we were all happy that the war was over.

Rationing didn't end with the war and when I married in 1951 I had an awful job to get a pair of navy court shoes to go on my honeymoon. If you went into the "K" shop or any shoe shop and asked for a pair of shoes you would have thought that you had asked for a pound of butter or something. "Shoes?" they'd say. "We haven't got any!"'

A SENSE OF EXPECTANCY

'The Christmas party was the great event of the year for the children of Swainby. Held on the Saturday before Christmas, every child got a present. When you reached the age of eleven you could choose your own, not to exceed five shillings, and the two most popular for boys were an Ingersol pocket watch (exactly five shillings) and a single-bladed bone-handled pruning knife (about four shillings and sixpence). When the war started the watches were no longer available, but Meccano sets were in!

The school population grew when evacuees came to the village, but everyone still got a present of some kind. The evacuees had to learn "broad Yorkshire" which was almost a foreign language to them. The older boys had to clear a patch of ground where the mineral railway used to run, raking off briars and rubbish, and then the four-foot embankment on one side and a stout hedge formed a trench where the children could lie in rows face down in the event of an air attack.

My most vivid memory is of the eve of the Normandy landings. Standing on the railway bridge on my way back to the farm, I counted 38 Lancaster bombers, and three Spitfires above them, coming in from the west and circling over a radius of less than a mile. The noise was deafening and the air heavy with a sense of expectancy.'

PEACE AND QUIET

'My first memories of Yorkshire were of peace and quiet, no more air raid sirens, no more long dark nights lying in the Morrison shelter, huddled in fear with my brothers and sisters, listening to the doodle-bugs overhead, the ghastly silence when the engine stopped, the terror of those silent moments before the horrific crash which shook the whole house and the sighs of relief that it hadn't hit us. As daylight broke on that last day spent in South East London, the chaos was all around and we knew we had been very lucky. It was then that my brave mother who had coped with all the deprivations of war said enough was enough – she would take all eight of us north to Ripon in faraway Yorkshire, where my father was stationed. He couldn't be contacted, we were on our own!

Bags were hastily packed, each child to carry as much as possible, the pram was packed to capacity with little room left for my baby brother. Food was rustled together for the journey, my sister and I made an orange drink with that horrible wartime rationed orange, with added liver salts to give it fizz (I don't remember the outcome). We arrived at Kings Cross station where over the loudspeakers came repeated demands to keep clear of the windows.

I recall very little of the journey except that when we reached York there were no trains running to Ripon that night and so, stranded, we spent the night on the benches in the waiting room. Apparently there was an air raid warning that night and the sight of my immediately elder sister and myself – still fast asleep – diving under the table for shelter was the finish for my mother who in her distress wondered if her children would ever recover from the trauma of war. When we eventually reached Ripon station my father (who had somehow been contacted) took us to the Methodist schoolroom in Allhallowgate where we were accommodated on mattresses on the floor. This was great fun as I remember, although we found the local dialect very strange, as no doubt the locals found ours. I thought we had only stayed there a few days, but my older sister informs me it was six weeks before a house could be found to accommodate all our very large family.

Having reached Ripon, the friendliness of the people was often remarked on by my "very much a product of the South of England" mother, so much so she refused to move again and spent all the remaining years of her life among her many Yorkshire friends.'

THE EVACUEES

Evacuees arrived in villages all over North Yorkshire from the heavily bombed areas such as Hull and London. This journey into the unknown often led to a lasting love of the countryside and new friendships, despite the difficulties of the language barrier!

A BORROWED FAMILY

'Ingleton was judged to be an area safe from air raids, and plans to receive people evacuated from Bradford were soon put into practice. Our home, Moorgarth Hall, was run as a guest house, so we had accommodation to offer. We were allocated seven children and two adults. The evacuees soon arrived by train and we met them at the station, which used to be where our large community centre now stands. We all trooped in a long crocodile to the school, where tea was provided, whilst we waited for our "instant" family. We were given Mary aged twelve, Margaret ten, Malcolm eight and little Alice who was only four and had never left home before. Also Lilian aged nine, an only child, and two mothers each with one girl, who only stayed a fortnight, saying they "could not stick village life", it was too quiet, so they took their children back home.

We soon realised the enormity of the task we had undertaken. Clothing was a major problem, as they brought very little with them. Alice carried only, on a string over her shoulder, a box containing her gas mask, with a nightdress stuffed inside. Not even a doll, or a teddy bear! Their only footwear was the sandals they were wearing. We could not have coped without help from a committee composed of members of the Women's Institute, Mothers' Union, Women's Voluntary Service and their friends, who collected a stock of spare clothing.

Providing meals for this large family was a challenge. Having so many ration books was a help and we were given a small allowance for each child towards their cost.

We had some hens in a hut in the far corner of the garden, so new-laid eggs for breakfast were greatly enjoyed, especially when the children found them laid in cosy nests, not in boxes in shops. They loved collecting eggs, so each day the task was given to the one who had been most helpful. We remember with gratitude relatives, friends and neighbours who were astonishingly generous, bringing jam, packets of margarine, tins of beans, even cakes and home-made biscuits, from their own meagre rations. The small sweet ration was a hardship for children who had apparently been regular customers at their local corner shop. There again we were lucky because Lily Batty at Kingsdale Head kindly offered to exchange tea coupons for their sweet coupons (strictly illegal of course) as her farm men preferred "tea to toffees" she said.

After a few days allowed for settling in they had to go to school. The staff there managed to cope with the influx of dozens of pupils of all ages, without any fuss or complaint. Our children did a bit of complaining though, about having to take gas masks with them every day.

Looking back I remember how quickly we became one big happy family. They were splendid children to care for. Mary was like a mother in the way she watched over Alice. There were seldom any quarrels and scarcely ever any tears. Lilian was a loner at first, but quickly learnt to fit in. They were typical city children, who were soon enjoying room to play freely on grass, amongst pretty wild flowers, and with trees to climb.

219

It was lovely autumn weather and the hedgerows were bright with berries. A collection of rose hips was being made at school, to be processed to extract their rich vitamin C content. Armed with bags and a walking stick to help with high branches, we tramped along lanes and across fields for miles, and gathered dozens of pounds. More rewarding was our search for blackberries as these were for our own use. Stained fingers and mouths, and sorely pricked knees were cheerfully ignored. Also they delighted in finding wild mushrooms, plentiful that year, and learnt how to make them into delicious soup for supper.

We had a specially happy day when, as the rationing of petrol was forecast, Reg suggested taking them to visit my sister on their farm near Slaidburn, while we had the opportunity. As we rode towards Bowland Knotts we saw a horse close by the road. They started laughing and giggling, and Malcolm said, "It is not daft, it is bare!" On enquiry we learnt that at home in Bradford their uncle was a greengrocer who sold goods from his flat cart as he travelled from door to door along the streets. They had never seen a horse without a cart. At Raingill they climbed trees and played hide and seek in the wood, and filled their pockets with hazel nuts. They carried buckets of food and fed calves, and laughed at the tiny pigs with curly tails. They watched cows being milked and caused much amusement by remarking, when offered a cup of new milk, "Not out of a silly old cow; we like ours out of bottles." A small stream runs close by the yard, and as it was a warm late September day shoes and socks came off and they were soon splashing happily, and trying to catch tiddlers. After tucking into a delicious tea of home-made goodies, they piled into the car and sang all the way home. As she was tucked up in bed Alice smiled sleepily and said, "Thank you for my bestest day.'

Mary wrote letters home regularly and occasionally got a reply, but that was the only contact with their parents till the following May. Soon we started planning for Christmas as there was no likelihood of their return home. They wished to make a present for Alice. We collected a bucketful of clay from a seam by the river, near the swimming pool. Night after night, as soon as she was in bed, they set to work to fashion tiny items for a doll's tea set. When complete these were baked in a very hot oven, then painted with any bright colours left in tins after springcleaning. They kept it secret till Christmas morning!

Although all windows were blacked out with heavy curtains to prevent even a chink of light showing, the scene inside was bright, with evergreens, ivy, holly with lots of berries, paper chains and lanterns made by the children; and a tree shining with tinsel and baubles. And a pile of parcels with gifts for everyone to make Christmas Day a very happy one (except for two old birds from the hut in the corner of the garden, whose laying days were over!). That evening as we sat singing carols round a blazing log fire, I remember suddenly thinking of two sad, quiet homes in Bradford.

New Year brought bitterly cold weather and severe fuel rationing. News of the fighting was depressing; and one by one the children fell ill with chickenpox. This was the most difficult time during the 14 months the children spent with us. One of Reg's duties as a special constable was to go with a colleague to guard Ribblehead Viaduct, a vital bridge on the Settle–Carlisle railway, a main line to Scotland. They were to repel any enemy attack armed only with truncheons! Sometimes the wind across the open moorland was so piercing that icicles formed on their eyebrows.

We were glad to welcome the warm sunny days of spring. On the walk to school they saw new-born lambs and baby ducklings and found the first celandines and daisies. They searched for birds' nests in hedges, and found primroses and violets. They visited a pond to see frogs and newts, and to bring home frogspawn. Such was Alice's delight to show her find that in her eagerness she spilt her jarful all over the carpet.

At Whitsuntide the children's parents paid visit and brought new dresses for the girls and shirts for Malcolm. They were greeted rather shyly; eight months was a long time to be parted. The day passed quickly, and as we waved goodbye at night no one minded not returning to Bradford.

We marked out a square of garden for each to use. They dug and planted with enthusiasm. We gave them seeds to make letters of their names in cress. Egg and cress cannot have been enjoyed more than those results of their first garden crop. A few potatoes were planted in each plot and grew quite successfully, except for Malcolm's. He kept digging them up to see how they were getting on.

By the time the summer holiday came they had become strong walkers, so we went further afield. They enjoyed the walk around the waterfalls, and one fine, clear day, the four older ones had a picnic on the summit of Ingleborough, then an exciting adventure in the White Scar cave.

The girls were becoming useful; washing up, making beds and cleaning their rooms. Mary was eager to help with the cooking. She used powdered egg from America and made tasty scrambled eggs. Malcolm spent hours in the garage helping Reg, and was overjoyed if there was a ride to a farm to repair a tractor. Being so busy the weeks of autumn passed quickly. It was in November when news came that they were to go home; and as unexpectedly as they arrived, they were gone. Malcolm returned for a holiday each summer until he started work, but we never saw the girls again.'

FROM HULL TO LASTINGHAM

'On 1st September 1939 I was eight years old and amongst a lot of children who were gathered together at our school, Mersey High in East Hull. We all went on buses to Paragon station where we were put onto trains. We eventually arrived at Kirkbymoorside and were given a paper carrier bag which contained tins of food and a Kit-Kat. Alas, *my* bag did not have a Kit-Kat, which I have never forgotten! We left Kirkbymoorside on buses and I can remember coming up Appleton Common and seeing sheep roaming on the roads. I had only ever seen them in fields at my granny's before.

In Lastingham we were lined up and 39 children went on to Hutton le Hole, the remainder trooped into the village hall which had been turned back into a school again. A lot of ladies were there to choose one or two children and I was taken with three other girls up to Mr and Mrs Alfred Holden, who lived at Moor Royde. We went into the maids' quarters where Amy and Marjorie Fox welcomed us. Later Freda the cook bathed us and I cried because my mother had bathed me the night before and I didn't like other people undressing me. On Friday we used to go into Mrs Holden's bathroom where she washed our hair and then gave us a bag of sweets.

I was later moved down the village to the Stricklands, who lived at Prospect House, a smallholding with pigs, cows and poultry, and stayed with them for six years. Mrs Strickland used to take in visitors, whilst Mr Strickland was a traveller for his brother in law's shop in Rosedale. He covered a lot of the area taking in orders and delivering.

We made a playhouse out of an old incubator shed and people gave us things when they springcleaned. In those days this was an upheaval, taking up carpets, pictures down, drawers scrubbed out, floors scrubbed, curtains washed and all furniture polished. One lady in the village had coconut matting on her kitchen floor and she used to put it in the beck held down with large stones so that the water ran through all morning, then hang it on the bridge to drip dry in the sun.

I used to earn a few pennies by taking milk to two ladies. I also helped Mrs Strickland washing up, cleaning vegetables, collecting sticks and feeding hens. Potatoes were boiled to help with hen and pig food. I used to save money and bought myself a new coat and square-toed shoes with green laces.

There were six farmers, an innkeeper, a few retired folk and a vicar, a church, chapel, shop and post office, and a hostel for sick evacuee children at Lastingham. I returned to Hull in 1945 but never settled there and I came back to Lastingham and married.'

Moving the valuables from Gastnor Castle before the evacuees moved in!

UP FROM BRIGHTON

'I started grammar school in Brighton in 1939, and the following year had many of my classes in the "trenches", during the Battle of Britain.

I was given the opportunity of evacuation in 1941, and left Brighton wondering where I would be sent. After a night spent at a centre near Ilkley I was taken to Gargrave. We sat in the Institute, around the walls, while the foster parents arrived, obviously looking for likely lads. I was taken away to be billeted at High Mill with an elderly couple who looked after me well.

We had a very crusty postmaster, and on one occasion he refused to change my birthday ten shilling note; I asked him for a halfpenny stamp, and he had to give me the change – 9s 11½d.

I used to spend six evenings a week doing my homework by oil lamp, seated in a shippon window-bottom, waiting for the next pail of milk to cool, and smelling the warm smells of the shippon in winter. I helped at lambing time, and at sowing turnip seed, hand pumping the tank, stooking and snagging turnips. I enjoyed the

223

unity of purpose at hay-time, five or six people circling the meadow, hand turning the swathes. I was introduced to nettle beer, and found that our Saturday teas were quite unaffected by the austerity of rationing. It was a real pleasure to work with horses and feel the serene contentment when returning across fields at dusk (double summertime) having taken the horses out to pasture at the end of a hard day's work. On threshing days the War-Ag tractor and thresher came and we had land girls, and then the reciprocal visits to neighbouring farms when they were threshing.

It was a real shock to return to Brighton in 1943 for the sixth form – and the flying bombs.'

OH, MR MURPHY!

'I remember with great affection my old boss at the Co-op at Ingleton. He was very bald with just a dark fringe of hair above his neck. One day he had his head down doing some paperwork on the counter and this little evacuee girl was obviously fascinated. When he looked up she said, with eyes like organ stops, "Oo, Mr Murphy, haven't you got a wide parting!" We simply howled with laughter.'

A COCKNEY LASS

'At the beginning of the war, Scarborough was considered a relatively safe place upon which to billet evacuees from Hull.

As an eleven year old myself, I can remember long crocodiles of boys straggling up our country lane, each one adorned with his cardboard gas mask, and wearing a luggage label tied to the lapel of his jacket. To me they all looked rather big and rough with short cropped hair at one end and big clumpy boots at the other. But big as they were, on each rather grubby face there was a woebegone look and even traces of tears.

The line of boys slowly diminished as in ones and twos they were introduced to their new foster parents by their harassed teachers. By contrast the few girls we saw seemed very grown up and self possessed. They all appeared to have frizzy permed hair and to my envy, sported little gold crosses in their pierced ears. They were very worldly-wise for their years.

We also had to share our girls' high school with the Kingston Girls High School from Hull. Their uniform was a beautiful dusky pink and far superior to our own navy blue. We had to pass each other in orderly lines in the corridors as they had morning assembly in the gym whilst we were in the assembly hall. This state of affairs did not last long as with little bombing in Hull at the time, everyone slowly drifted back home.

The war continued, we grew up, and then the V-bombs began to descend on London and we had our second invasion of evacuees, this time Cockneys.

Once again the girls' high school was used as a sorting centre, but this time as sixth formers we were enlisted to help. Amongst these tiny children was a four year old, Maureen, who had spent practically her entire life down in the Underground sheltering from buzz bombs. With her large brown eyes and fair curly hair I was immediately captivated. I begged my parents to be allowed to take her home, and on condition that I looked after her, she became a member of our family. I suppose as an only child myself I looked upon her as a little sister and lavished my love upon her.

Whilst washing her hands and face one day an aeroplane passed over. She dashed to the window exclaiming, "Is that a doodle-bugger? My Georgie calls them doodle-buggers!" In the course of time we learned that she had absorbed quite a lot of bad language in her short life.

In an attempt to keep her own family in her mind, each night we said prayers. "God bless Mummy and Daddy, Georgie and Pickle Lilli (her older sister) and keep them safe, for Christ's sake, A-men." A day or two later she was playing with a kitten and trying unsuccessfully to make it sit down in a chair. Eventually we heard an exasperated little voice say, "Will you sit down? For Christ's sake. A-men!"

Having attended the local school for a while her Cockney accent became mixed with Yorkshire. One morning she put her hands in the wash basin and exclaimed, "Coo, this woater's cawed!"

She stayed with us for two years when the war being over, she returned to London a thorough Yorkshire Lass.'

HIGHDAYS & HOLIDAYS

WE MADE OUR OWN ENTERTAINMENT

Every village seemed to have a surprising amount of talent, so that in the days before television, and even radio, we found our entertainment in our own locality. Whist drives and dances were very popular and the break from the working week was a welcome treat. Sports were important too, from quoits to cricket, and many of us went to the cinema at least once a week and huddled round the wireless for our favourite programmes!

HOME-MADE FUN

'Dishforth, like many other villages, did not have electricity before the Second World War, nor much transport other than a bicycle or one's own legs, so most of our entertainment had to be of the home-made variety. Parties were foremost, especially in the summer when somebody in the village would offer their garden. Large tents were erected and before an excellent supper there would be games such as "find the parcel", "walking on flower pots" and "dressing up quickly".

There was a party every year for the children. One of the local farmers cut a track down the field for the races and prizes were provided for the winners. Needless to say, everyone enjoyed the refreshments later, which included ice cream, a luxury in those days.

Practically everyone in the village went on the annual outing to the seaside, taking packed lunches with them. Although the village would be practically deserted, no one bothered to lock their doors.'

'Dances, social evenings and whist drives were held in the school at Spennithorne, the entrance fee for the social evenings being sixpence. In the 1940s the van Straubenzee family converted an old loft into a meeting place for the village and many happy times were enjoyed there until it closed when Harmby erected a village hall. There was a drama group in the village and plays were performed to packed audiences. The village also had Scout, Guide and Cub packs up to the 1950s, and a youth club.

The village show, held in a marquee on the football field, was an annual event when villagers got together and exhibited their garden produce and the women their baking and preserves. Ice cream was made by Mrs Mary Elder in a metal container stood in a wooden bucket filled with ice, a treat indeed for the children in the 1940s.

The village seems to have had football and cricket clubs for many years, and a tennis club existed between the wars, the first courts being in a field over the beck at the foot of Mill Lane and later near the rectory gardens.'

'A Boroughbridge doctor's daughter taught the local women folk dancing and the team was good enough to enter a national competition. Their first gathering was at Hovingham Hall and they won a second class certificate. For practising on grass they used a portable gramophone and each paid threepence a week towards new records. The men, not to be outdone, later joined in and a mixed team was formed.'

'In the 1920s the Women's Institute was often the only form of entertainment and instruction open to local women. At Alne most of the entertainment was self-generated and the pleasures of life simple. The National Anthem was sung at all the meetings and often the entertainment was a sing-song, a whist drive or games such as wearing a blindfold and drawing a tail on a donkey. There was a folk dancing team, a group of pipe players, and the women seemed to be able to put on a sketch at the drop of a dramatic hat.'

DANCES AND WHIST

'People travelled for miles to attend the dances in Caperby village hall in the 1920s and 1930s, they were so popular. Out would come the best dresses and many of the men wore patent leather shoes. The MC would be smartly dressed, and his hair sleeked down for these regular dances during the winter months. For a shilling or one and sixpence there would be a dance band (the Nightbirds from Ripon were a favourite), a supper of home-baked savouries and cakes, and dancing until 2 am – and perhaps the chance to meet someone special!

Often whist drives were followed by supper and then dancing until the early hours. But the favourite annual event was the concert party and dance. The concert party came from Swaledale.'

'When I was a child in the 1930s, there was no village hall in Rudston, on the Yorkshire wolds. This meant that the weekly Friday evening whist drive was held in the schoolroom. Late every Friday afternoon a man would go round the village collecting one or two chairs from people's houses, which he took to the schoolroom on his horse and cart. After being used by the card players, they were returned to their owners in the morning.

The drinks of tea provided at the whist drives were also in borrowed cups. Coloured threads were tied round the cup handles and round the teaspoons, by their owners, to identify them.'

'My uncle said that when he was young they walked across the moors to dances, so they were known as "ling hoppers", and they changed in nearby houses.'

FETES AND FUN

'I lived at Middleton St George in the 1930s. Before electricity was connected we had a radio with an accumulator, which had to be charged up at Mr Dowson's garage each week. This radio was a boxlike thing with dials which you twiddled round till you managed to hit a programme. It was known as a "cat's whisker radio".

As in many villages, our church was the focal point for most of our social life. Post war we had fund raising events such as the Harvest Supper and in the summer a garden fete was organised. Mrs Mellanby kindly loaned her garden in Middleton-One-Row for the day. A variety of stalls were set up, with cakes, tombola, ice cream, raffles etc. My friend Joyce and I looked after the sweets stall. We spent the night before making peppermint creams and fudge and collecting sweets from various people who had promised to give – and hoping we would be put under the trees out of the sun. Some of the younger children put on a dancing display and there was a Punch and Judy show for the little ones.

During the 1950s the Caryl Jenner Mobile Theatre Company came to the chapel hall, Middleton-One-Row. I remember three J.B. Priestley plays being put on: *Ever since Eve*, *An inspector calls* and *Summer day's dream*. The players were very popular and their performances excellent. The local people put them up overnight after the shows.

The Lyric cinema opened in the village in the 1930s, when the films were changed three times a week. It was very popular with us. As a schoolgirl I used to go on a Friday night. I never had any money and I had to earn my fourpence for my seat by cleaning every pair of shoes and boots in the house. I carried out this task with pleasure, or I did not get my fourpence.'

CINEMA AND RADIO

'The 1930s was the great cinema and radio age. There were several large cinemas in the nearby town and each suburb also had its own Ritz or Regal or Lyceum. Here the film changed midweek, so if one were especially "flush" one could see two different films in one week. We usually went to our local cinema at Knaresborough on Thursday evenings when I had no homework. I rarely went at all until I was eleven and at secondary school. Before that it was only to see Walt Disney films or Shirley Temple and once a school visit to see *David Copperfield*.

On these Thursday evenings I saw all the Ginger Rogers and Fred Astaire films, *Beau Geste* and *Robin Hood* as well as all the Hollywood interpretations of our history. How glamorous and exciting they were though most were black and white, and what a magically rich world America was on the silver screen. The larger cinemas in the town were rich palaces indeed. Very warm and comfortable with lots of red plush, they provided a real show for a sixpenny matinee seat. This would include two films, the newsreel, and a short recital on the cinema organ. On Saturday evenings the queue wound right round the building no matter what the programme.

My earliest recollection of radio was listening to *Children's Hour* when still quite small. Those were the days when Uncle Mac held sway. His Birthday Club gave birthday greetings to anyone who wrote in. He would say "Happy Birthday" and one received an enamelled badge in the design of a clock – the hands at five and the words "BBC Birthday Club" round the edge. I can still recall his distinctive voice when greeting a twins' birthday with the words: "Hello twins!" He could be heard again on Mondays when we received our weekly dose of the great Toytown saga.

Stephen King-Hall was our weekly informant on current affairs. After his talk each week he would say: "Be good, but not so good that they say, now what have you been up to?"

Later on, there were shared programmes with the grown ups. I don't believe any TV thriller series has gripped as hard as the Paul Temple mysteries. We discussed them avidly next day, following each episode. Then Valentine Dyall chilled us all with his series *The Man in Black*, each one a complete story. Comedy was in abundance. *ITMA* with Tommy Handley really belongs to the war years. Before that was Arthur Askey's *Bandwagon* and many lively and colourful programmes like Harry S. Pepper's *Kentucky Minstrel Show*. *Music Hall* was usually on Saturday evenings with favourites like comedian Rob Wilton and singers Webster Booth and Anne Ziegler.

Some entertainments were "home-made" of course. Village events included the annual operettas produced by the Sunday school pupils, and prize-giving concerts were held on Shrove Tuesday. The Young Men had their annual revue and there was always the Christmas pantomime at the town theatre, my only experience as a child with the professional theatre.'

DOUBLE SEATS

'I remember the back row of the Ritz cinema in Selby, now demolished. It had very cosy double seats!'

OUR CONCERT PARTY

'My father would not have television, that "anti-social timewaster" in our home, so at the age of ten, as many children were beginning to view regularly, six of us formed a concert party. We were three girls and three boys with an odd assortment of dubious talents – between us we could dance, play the piano, write and perform sketches, tell jokes and sing – and how we sang! We had a wonderful selection of Mums and Dads who cut out, stitched, glued and chauffeured us around.

Practices were frequent and joyful occasions and spread around the district, as I doubt if any one family could have put up with us all the time. Once we got going the "bookings" came thick and fast. We performed on Saturdays, usually at church bazaars and community events around Poppleton, and were paid in tea and cakes. Any money collected went to a charity. Unfortunately it all came to an end in September 1951 and homework took over.'

THREE ACT PLAYS

'A succession of schoolmasters at Thornton Watless who were interested in drama kindled in me a love and interest in amateur dramatics that has stayed with me all my life. It wasn't just the children – the grown ups joined in too. After the 1939–45 war we aspired to three-act plays running for three nights, with such plays as *See how they run* by Philip King, and Arnold Ridley's *Ghost train*. The train noise off, was made by running a garden roller over corrugated iron in the schoolyard behind the stage, and after the second night, an old inhabitant of the almshouses which backed on to the schoolyard sent a message round to the schoolmaster to say that he was sick of that Goat Train, he couldn't get to sleep for it. The schoolmaster's wife was prompt, sitting in the porch wrapped in a blanket, because of the cold.

What fun we had, and what encouragement we got from the people who came to see us.'

SPORTING TIMES

'Sports and recreation held a significant place in village life at Preston under Scar. On Whitecroft field, to the east of the village, lay a tennis

232

Amateur dramatics were a popular attraction at Thornton Watless during the war.

court, while football was played prior to 1919 on the site of Preston Quarry. There was also a badminton club, and Lord Bolton had provided a fives court at the west end of the village. Lady Bolton presented a silver cup for a billiards competition, and quoits was played regularly, either near to the smithy or by the ford near the lane to the manor house.

On the cobbled road up to Scarth Nick there were motorcycle scrambles; and along the Stanney children built dens, hid and chased.'

'Football has always been a popular sport for players and spectators in Wensleydale. Carperby Rovers team has been in existence since the 1950s. In the 1930s boys would go in their dinner break from school to a field at the west end of the village, and 20 years later this field witnessed the official opening of Carperby playing fields by Lord Bolton. On the two and a half acre site there was one football pitch, two hard tennis courts and a bowling green. Even prior to this people had come to Carperby to play on the grass tennis courts here. Quoits was, and still is, played in July and August, weather permitting.'

'There has always been a good following for football and cricket in Spennithorne. In the 1930s it was possible to travel by special train to see Middlesborough play football for one shilling and ninepence return.'

A quartet of bathing beauties at Scarborough in the 1920s, when holidays by the sea were a real treat.

'My grandfather was a very good quoits player, playing at all the villages in the Easingwold area, where many had a good clay pitch on which to play. He won many prizes including beautiful copper kettles and brass candlesticks, and when each member of the family got married they were given a copper kettle. I still have the one my father "won" in 1935, but when the last of Dad's sisters got married the kettles had run out so her gift was a pair of candlesticks.'

'Village cricket matches were played every Saturday at Snainton and were nearly always "derby" matches. The older men, consisting of butchers, farmers, dealers, teachers and retired folk, always had the "grandstand" seats, as we called them. They shouted, clapped, swore, anything that would urge their team on. We also had a ladies team and they got the same treatment. The ladies played their matches in the evenings and travelled a radius of about 15 miles. All the supporters came with us, plus a few boyfriends. It was a wonder they had any voices left after shouting for 20 overs. No wonder they left us to have supper while they went to the pub.

The wicket always had to be rolled with a very heavy roller by the players, men and ladies alike, after every match. Our field was cut by horse-drawn cutter and sheep grazed it as well, it was always very well looked after.'

HOLIDAYS AT HOME

'After the war money was quite tight, and by no means every family could afford a holiday away. So during Bank Holiday week (the first week in August) we had "Holiday at Home" events in our local park.

Sheepdog trials were always held on the first Saturday, and we all took picnic teas so as not miss any of the action. Sunday saw band concerts. Then during the week a variety of entertainments were provided, to suit just about all tastes. There was an amateur boxing night one year, and Bruce Woodcock (the British champion) came along to give away the prizes. Displays were given by the police dogs and Army motorcyclists. The Magic Circle gave us a rare treat, and I well remember one member who with a circle of felt of little larger than the brim of a hat, with a hole cut out of the middle, created many characters from history, including Napoleon. On another evening we had a concert party. The culmination was the final Saturday when there was a fancy dress procession through the town, led by the town silver band, and ending up in the park. There were sideshows and swings and ice cream and pop. Then for me the main attraction – the races. Every single year I managed to augment my pocket money by winning my race for my age.

The evening highlight was a beauty competition, where the chairman of the council was on the panel of judges and got his picture in the paper the following week, putting the sash across the winner's shoulders.

The whole week finished in a cloud of glory with a mammoth firework display, which sent us all home happy.'

SPECIAL OCCASIONS

Royal coronations and jubilees were always a good reason to celebrate in towns and villages across North Yorkshire, but there were also other occasions we look back on with pleasure. The 1951 Festival of Britain in particular inspired many villages to put on their own pageants, using local talent.

A PAGEANT OF HISTORY

'After the war, in 1946, Horbury put on a pageant of the town's history right from the 7th century until the present day. All organisations took part, and this included our school. Our girls' school had a good choir and along with the boys from the other town school we were given the Elizabethan period to portray. Dressed as village swains and maidens we sang songs from Shakespeare's plays – such as "Blow, blow thou winter wind" and "Ye spotted snakes with double tongue"; and we also did a maypole dance. The boys performed the little playlet of Pyramus and Thisbe from *A midsummer night's dream*.

The pageant went on for a whole week, repeated each night, so many people wanted to see it; it was also mentioned on the wireless in a Northern magazine programme. Each night we returned to school in time to be clothed in our costumes and made up, and then marched the 100 yards to the chapel hall just in time for our particular part in the proceedings, with blankets draped over our shoulders to keep us warm. Immediately we had done our bit we were whisked away back to school, for with a cast of hundreds, there was not enough room backstage for all the performers. On the Wednesday night instead of returning to school we were allowed to sit at the back of the hall and see the rest of the performance, so we never got to see the beginning. I was disappointed because I had wanted to see our churchwarden all dressed up in chain mail.

Following this the Pageant Players were formed; an amateur company performing three or four plays a year, and I hardly missed one of them. The first play I remember was *Busman's Honeymoon*. I got in to see *Night must fall* free, because being a Girl Guide I was selling programmes on the door and stayed on to see the performance. The group went from strength to strength, and the last play I saw them do, before leaving home in the late 1950s was *A man for all seasons*.

On every occasion we went home happy to the accompanying strains of the Trumpet Voluntary by Purcell.'

PAGEANT OF BEDALE

'Bedale was granted a market charter in 1251, and for quite a few years plans had been in the pipeline to have a celebration when this 700th anniversary came round. Although there were great celebrations throughout the country that year for the Festival of Britain, Bedale's own celebrations were not to be outdone.

Although it is usual in a big production to say there was a cast of thousands, it is true to say that on this occasion there was indeed a cast of hundreds. Choirs from Bedale, Richmond, Crakehall, Newton le Willows, Kirklington and Thornton Watless; an orchestra drawn from Bedale, Darlington and Northallerton, and members of the bands of the Royal Dragoons and the Royal Corps of Signals provided the music.

The actors in the pageant were drawn from local people, and rehearsals began; they went on for weeks beforehand and then at last it was time to put it on – the 17th, 18th and 19th of July 1951.

Music played a large part in all the scenes in the pageant. First the presentation of the charter to Alan of Bedale was played out, followed by a hunting scene where he and King Henry III join together to follow the hounds. Next, in celebration of the part played by Bedale men in Edward III's wars with France, the siege of Calais was reenacted, and a scene showed Sir Miles Stapleton of Bedale being created one of the first Knights of the Order of the Garter by King Edward.

A scene of medieval enjoyment was seen next and the portrayal of the Pilgrimage of Grace. The scene then changed to the battle of Marston Moor and the rout of the Royalist troops; Bedale men were accused of Royalist sympathies but on putting their case to Parliament were cleared.

May Day celebrations then took over and there were exhibitions of sword and morris dancing and maypole dancing.

Finally the coming of the railway was celebrated, and a most authentic railway engine had been constructed around a Ferguson tractor.

The whole pageant was an enormous success seen and enjoyed by hundreds of people and living long in their memory.'

OUR FESTIVAL OF BRITAIN PAGEANT

'To mark the Festival of Britain in 1951 the people of Helmsley put on a pageant, depicting a story from the 12th century. This concerned the Lord of Hamelake (Helmsley) and his son the young Walter L'Spec. His mother the Lady Adeline dreamed of his death in the hunting field, but her son would not give up the sport. Walter was killed in a fall at Kirkham, on which spot his father built a church as he turned to religion for comfort after the death of his only son. Later he was to give land at Rievaulx to a group of French monks and thus began Rievaulx Abbey. All this was depicted in a simple but colourful pageant in the grounds of the now ruined Helmsley castle, where the family had once lived.

There were 200 performers, all local people. I was one of the children in the crowd and village scenes. Only the narrator, Robert Speaight, was a professional. We rehearsed for six months and the 200 costumes, including 24 monks' habits, were made by local people. One lady made 24 pairs of felt shoes. As children, we thought it was great fun, but were often "shushed" by the more serious performers when we began larking about. I remember we spent a lot of time catching rain beetles, and trying to put them in the monks' hoods. Unfortunately, the performance in July coincided with some very wet weather. People arrived at Helmsley station by train from long distances. We were not on the tourist map in those days, there were no cafes in the town and the town hall had to be opened for the WVS to make tea for the poor wet visitors. But when the showers cleared, the audience did enjoy a spectacular entertainment, against the magnificent backdrop of hills and woods.'

ROYAL MEMORIES

'We got a wireless for Christmas in 1935. It was the year of the first Christmas broadcast by the King, George V, following his Silver Jubilee the previous May. We had great festivities for the Jubilee in Topcliffe, starting with a church service in the morning and with a fancy dress parade and sports in the afternoon. I won third prize (two shillings!), dressed as an anemone. After the sports, held on the bottom field behind the Angel Hotel, there was a tea in the schoolroom for all the children and we were each given a commemorative mug. George V died the following year, so we were soon celebrating the coronation of George VI, when we had similar festivities as well as a huge bonfire on the Angel field down by the river Swale.'

'For George V's Jubilee we had a children's party in the school field at Middleton St George, with games and sports afterwards. I won a

All ready to celebrate George V's Jubilee at Thoralby in 1935.

tin of toffees and I still use the tin as a "pin box". We all got a Jubilee mug. Two years later we had the same kind of party and games for the Coronation, and a Coronation mug!'

'Here in Carperby in May 1935, the biggest celebration since the end of the war in 1918 was in progress. Races were organised for the children in the field behind the village institute. Then followed a traditional Dales tea of home-baked savouries and cakes, and gallons of tea to drink. Later on out came the men's patent leather shoes for a good airing at the Jubilee Dance in the village hall.

In 1953 schoolchildren and adults were invited to the house of the chairman of the parish council in Carperby to watch the Coronation on television. This was the first time many villagers had seen pictures on the TV and even now when some of the locals come into the house they make towards that particular room and say: "This is where we all watched the Coronation!" Each child was given a Coronation mug and we had a splendid traditional tea.'

'Celebrations for the Jubilee in 1935 and the Coronation in 1953 were both held in the granary of Manor Farm at Spennithorne, funded in part by house-to-house collections. Whist drives were held in the granary for the Coronation funds and of course, on the day we had a television to see the ceremony.'

'The physical division between Aiskew and Bedale is Bedale beck and to celebrate the Coronation in 1953 it was arranged to have a tug of war between the two towns. The venue was to be the bridge over the beck, and the winner the team which succeeded in pulling the opposition into its own town. Hundreds of people gathered to watch the "battle of the bridge", and a BBC commentator was there to describe the struggle for radio listeners. Bedale were the winners.'

'The only family with a television set in our street at Brandsby were the owners of the corner shop, so every day all the children in the area would gather in their front room to watch *Children's Hour* on the tiny screen. After it had finished and was switched off we would all sit in silence until the white dot faded away.

On Saturday nights during the build up to the Coronation in 1953, whole families would crowd into that same room to watch a film or the Saturday serial, and then we would have supper, for which we had all taken a contribution, and pay a shilling into the fund for the Coronation street party.'

A MEMORABLE DAY

'When I was nine years old it was the year of the coronation of Queen Elizabeth II. At school at Haxby each teacher tried to make the lessons relate to the occasion. We wrote stories and drew pictures of kings, queens, and flags to decorate the school.

Everyone was talking about the street parties and what we were going to wear as we were going to have a fancy dress parade. There were plenty of fairies, cowboys and pirates as these costumes were easy to make. My sister and I wanted something different to wear. Mum suggested that my sister Doramy should go as Britannia and I could go as a hula girl. As we were having a hot summer this seemed to be a good idea, the only thing to spoil it was some of my friends had German measles, and my sister got it in the weeks leading up to the coronation.

The making of the costumes went ahead; Doramy's dress was easy to do and my Dad made her a shield and a spear, but Mum came up trumps making her helmet out of old cornflake packets and covering it with silver paper. I had a top made out of Grandma's silk scarf and we spent a few days making crepe paper flowers to hang around my neck. Mum made my grass skirt from raffia from the artist's shop in the Shambles and it looked quite good.

All the ladies had been baking and making all kinds of goodies for the day. Everyone was so busy; then I started with a runny nose and sore eyes. It must be the dust from the crepe paper and raffia, Gran said, it would be all right by tomorrow. My sister was up first in the morning; and all I heard was, "Our Sandra, look at your face!" You've guessed it, I had German measles. I was covered. I started to cry and Mum said, "Well, you can't join with the celebrations today." I was so upset, but I hadn't reckoned with my Grandma. "We will have our own party," she said, and so we did. We sat in front of the open front door with the picnic table, all dressed up. I wore my costume and Gran sat with me. When it was time to judge the costumes they even came to see me. I was thrilled and more so when they awarded me the first prize in my age group. I won a lovely story book about Lassie the sheepdog, and I still have it along with my mug and propelling pencil which we all received for the coronation!'

CELEBRATIONS THROUGH THE YEAR

Each year brought its regular 'red letter days', from the Whit Walk to Harvest Supper. Christmas had its own well loved traditions, such as the eating of frumenty on Christmas Eve or 'lucky birding' round the village.

RED LETTER DAY

'The red letter days of my childhood were not days of national importance like coronations and royal weddings, but the village highlights of a Yorkshire child's life in the 1930s.

The one I recall most vividly was Whitsuntide. Of all the church's festivals this is now the one most neglected, since we altered our Bank Holiday to the end of May. But in my youth it was a great feast day. The Methodist church Sunday school at Scriven held its annual Anniversary, which meant augmented choirs, great "sings" and special teas. The Church of England to which my family belonged celebrated with an early attempt at ecumenicalism in joining with the two nonconformist churches in the village in the Whit Monday procession of witness through the streets led by a brass band, and choirs.

The most important part of the weekend for the children, however, was our new "Whitsuntide clothes". These consisted of new dresses and straw hats for the girls and new suits and shoes for the boys. It always seemed to be warm enough to wear our new dresses without coats. This was the time when we girls emerged from our long black winter woollen stockings into short white socks and if our parents' money or clothing club ran to it there were new sandals as well, for Whit Monday spelled Sports Day as well as processions.

Of all my successive Whitsuntide clothes the one I remember most vividly was a pale green crepe de chine dress with cap sleeves, sprinkled all over with tiny sprigs of pink and blue flowers. Along with that went a broad-brimmed straw hat which had flowers round the brim and black patent ankle-strap shoes, the height of sartorial elegance in 1935. I remember stopping frequently on my way to church to dust them carefully with my handkerchief so as to make sure they lost nothing of their brilliance.

Once church duties were fulfilled, the next ritual was our

"showing". This meant visiting family and friends to give them the benefit of our sartorial splendour and in return to have threepenny or sixpenny pieces pressed into our eager hands. This proved to be a very worthwhile operation, as I recall, and provided us with the means to really enjoy our Whit Monday revels.

Whit Monday was not entirely devoted to games. First we assembled for our Whit Walk. Each place of worship, in turn, led the procession. When it was the C of E's turn our vicar insisted we led with church banners, cross and candlesticks, often to a mutter of "popery" from the more die-hard members of the chapel community. On the whole, however, these occasions were amicably conducted. We paused, en route, to sing from our hymn sheets, to the accompaniment of a local band. I remember crowded pavements as we passed by. It seemed that the whole village population turned out to see us and join in the well known hymns. The one I most associate with this occasion is "Jesus shall reign where e'er the sun, doth his successive journeys run".

After tea in our own Sunday schools we all met again in the recreation field for our sports. These included egg and spoon, sack and three-legged races – all the usual tests of young children's athletic prowess, or lack of it! Funny that I cannot recall a wet Whit Monday but I suppose there must have been some. The only weather memory I have is of standing to sing and finding when we moved on that the melted tar on the road had stuck to our new sandals, so hot was the day!

These events at Whitsuntide serve to emphasise the strong sense of community that existed in my village in those years before the war. There was much real poverty and unemployment. We had none of the modern amenities that make life so comfortable today. There was much sickness in children, now thankfully largely eradicated. One summer saw a serious outbreak of diphtheria which depleted our child population, another of polio, but in spite of these disadvantages my memory of those years is of a warm and caring environment and a feeling of growing up in safety.'

MAY DAY AT UGTHORPE

'Our church at Ugthorpe used to hold an annual procession each May in honour of Our Lady. Children, priests and parishioners walked through the village and carried a statue on a sedalia. It was decorated with flowers and greenery and the little girls carried baskets of flowers. One of the older girls was made May Queen and had two small attendants.

Until about 1933, each year on 29th June, the feast of St Peter and St Paul, the Roman Catholic mothers and children were all taken to

The May procession was an annual event at Ugthorpe.

Runswick Bay beach for the day. We were very excited about it as we travelled by horse and waggon. There would be about five waggons following each other along the narrow lanes. We all enjoyed paddling in the sea, beach games and our packed food.'

ROSE QUEENS AND CHURCH FESTIVALS

'After the war the "Rose Queen" ceremony was revived at Wharram le Street. A teenage girl was chosen to be Rose Queen and various attendants were also chosen. There were usually two boys as pages, aged about ten years old. They were dressed like flunkeys in satin breeches and white socks with black shoes. They had matching satin jackets with a lace jabot at the neck. I'm amazed that they managed to persuade the "macho" boys of that era to wear such an outfit! There would be two small girls to carry the Queen's train and the rest of the village girls as attendants. There was also one girl chosen to carry the crown on a pink satin cushion to the crowning ceremony. I carried the crown at least once. There was a procession through the village to the rectory garden (if wet the ceremony was held in the school). A local person of some social standing was usually asked to do the crowning and then we all had a splendid tea afterwards. Unfortunately this colourful ceremony fell through sometime in the 1950s and I never reached the longed for pinnacle of being the Queen.

We also had a garden party on the rectory lawn most years, all the traditional stalls and sideshows followed by the inevitable tea. Sometimes there was a fancy dress parade too. Mother was very ingenious at making us unusual costumes for this.

In those days (after the war) every village had its own cricket team. There were lots of young lads working on the farms then before everything became so mechanised. Mother was a great cricket fan and we often went to watch the matches. We also travelled to away games in a coach organised for the purpose.

The church festivals were all highlights in my year. I loved Easter with its wonderful message of hope. The church always looked lovely with masses of daffodils and primroses everywhere. To this day the smell of daffodils instantly reminds me of Easter in our village.'

HIGHLIGHTS OF THE YEAR

'Pancake Day was the first bright spot in the year, when school at Topcliffe closed for the afternoon after the ringing of the pancake bell from the church. The next morning, Ash Wednesday, the whole school walked to church for a service to mark the beginning of Lent, which also meant that whips and tops were brought out again together with marbles and glass alleys by those fortunate enough to have them.

At Easter, we rolled our dyed hard-boiled eggs on Manor Hill or on some other slope. My mother made the first rhubarb pie and custard tarts for Easter. As we often had deep snow lying for a long time, a clump of rhubarb had to be covered by an upturned bucket in good time to protect it from the winter weather. Easter also heralded the approach of springcleaning when carpets were carried outside and beaten with carpet beaters or an old tennis racquet, floors were all scrubbed and cobwebs and dust removed from walls and ceilings by long brushes. Then all the paintwork was washed and the furniture cleaned with a solution of vinegar and water and then polished. All the curtains were washed and feather beds, eiderdowns and pillows were taken outside on a sunny day for an airing. My mother also gave her family a springclean! My brother and I were given a teaspoonful of treacle and brimstone (sulphur) every morning for a month to purify our blood. I can still remember the grittiness of it just as I can feel my Grandma's horse-hair sofa on my bare legs.

At Whitsuntide my mother made the first gooseberry pie and curd tarts. At this time of the year, when eggs were plentiful and cheap, several dozen eggs were "put down" to keep until winter when hens went "off the lay" in the cold weather and so preserved eggs could be used. The eggs were packed carefully in a large enamel bucket

Aiskew's village fancy dress competition in 1948 brought out young and old.

and covered with a solution of waterglass and water which formed a white jelly-like coating over the eggs. I can remember Mother buying eggs at 16 for a shilling, probably in 1933.

On 29th May, Royal Oak Day, we made sure we wore a sprig of oak or else the older boys would inflict punishment by using a bunch of nettles on our bare legs. Next in our year came Sports Day and the pleasure of playing hide and seek in hayfields full of haycocks.

A highlight of our year was the annual fair held on 18th July, when we had a holiday from school. There were a few sideshows and stalls on the field near the bridge, but it was primarily a horse fair and horses were raced up and down the village street all day by their owners to show their speed and stamina. A lasting memory is of the colourful clothes worn by the gypsy women on fair day compared with their rather drab everyday clothes. Many were resplendent in orange, purple or emerald satin dresses, richly coloured shawls and heavy gold jewellery. They came up to the village to the pumps for water which they carried in wonderful polished cans with copper or brass bands. As a child, I saw many bargains struck between dealers and farmers when a horse would be bought for a wad of notes and a slapping of hands. The smell of wood smoke permeated the village for the three or four days that the fair people stayed.

Beach huts at Filey in 1908, a popular seaside resort.

Once the summer holiday began there was the annual excursion for a day at the seaside (Redcar) which was officially a Sunday school outing but anyone else could go on payment of the bus fare, usually half a crown. This day was the only holiday for the majority and for many the only time they left the village during the year, so the excitement was intense. The village was very quiet that day.

The Harvest Supper was not to be missed! In fact, many people attended two by going to both the church and the chapel. The same lady cooked a whole ham in her copper each year and this was carved by the vicar on the Friday afternoon in the schoolroom where a team of helpers soon produced huge meat dishes full of sandwiches. My mother also made several apple pies, one farmer's wife provided fresh cream sponge cakes whilst another brought a butter basket full of home-made teacakes which were delicious and there were those who specialised in fruit cakes or perfect puff pastry, so there was always a sumptuous spread and everyone could eat until satisfied or beyond! The church was always full for the Friday evening service and the Harvest hymns were sung with great gusto, but no doubt the thoughts of a good supper to follow helped the attendance. I can remember the charge for supper being one shilling. Later it rose to one and sixpence and by 1960, it was half a crown.

We had "tatie scrattin' or potato picking holiday in October for a fortnight when the majority of the older children were employed by local farmers and the money they earned was used to buy winter boots or shoes and warm clothes.

Another annual event was the school concert, usually held before Christmas, performed by the schoolchildren, when the majority of the villagers crowded in as audience. My mother made huge jugs of cocoa and home-made biscuits for the children before going home. There were also socials held in the wintertime.

Christmas brought its own traditions in our family, but for many there would be little to celebrate, a highlight being the Sunday school party when there was a good tea, a present for everyone and an apple and an orange to take home. We always had frumenty (a spiced milk pudding made from wheat), eaten by candlelight on Christmas Eve, followed by Yule loaf and Wensleydale cheese. On Christmas morning we awoke to the sound of the "lucky birds" calling at the houses where they would expect to be given money.

This custom went on until the 1950s, but, I suppose, died out with the coming of a better standard of living. Another custom which was in use for a long time was for a large group of children to go "Yuling" at noon on Christmas Eve. They went to the Angel Inn where a shovelful of hot pennies was thrown out, to the doctor's house, the vicarage and to the shops, all of which gave out oranges, apples, nuts and sweets, as well sometimes as pennies. The children shouted "Youling, Youling" at the tops of their voices until the doors were opened and the gifts distributed.

The next celebration was on New Year's Eve but we were not part of that until we were grown up. Our own "lucky bird", usually a dark-haired man belonging to the family, knocked at the door after the church bells had tolled out the Old Year and were beginning to ring in the New Year after the last stroke of midnight. He brought for every member of the family a coin, usually an old silver threepenny piece, a piece of coal and a sprig of evergreen to ensure enough money, health and warmth for the coming year.

Fitting in amongst these highlights of our year were the annual thrills connected with the countryside around us. On Mothering Sunday afternoon, my friend and I always went to the same field to gather the first violets. The bank under the boundary hedge was a carpet of purple or white sweet violets. At about the same time, we went to a certain bank where primroses grew in great profusion. It was not until I grew up that I realised that the bank and the damp area at the bottom were the outer moat of the castle, long since ploughed up and levelled. A little further along the same lane was the spot to find harebells which always graced the tea table on my birthday.

One field we always went to in May was a wonderful spot for wild flowers and we always referred to it as "Fairyland". The ground was carpeted with wood anemones and cowslips and just one patch of oxlips. There was a small wood at one side where bluebells, primroses, stitchwort and dog violets grew in multitudes, and along the middle of the field was a drainage ditch where marsh marigolds and water avens grew. That lovely field was ploughed up in the Second World War but never produced decent crops. We had our special places to go for pussy willow, crabapple blossom and lilac. One particular piece of ground was flooded during the winter but transformed in the summer by masses of meadowsweet, blue cranesbill, and willow herb and there were always poppies along the field edges. I probably did a good turn to one farmer by collecting thistledown to fill the mattress and pillow for my doll's pram. When autumn came, we paid our annual visit to a field where the meadow saffron or autumn crocus grew – a sight to remember – and after that came brambling.'

THE MUMMERS CAME

'At Christmas time in the 1930s the mummers would visit us on our farm between Malton and the coast. They had blacked faces and held their lanterns high as they sang carols at our door, after which they were invited in for supper.'

'On Christmas Eve mummers came round to every house in Romanby. They had black faces and performed a play. My mother recalls being frightened of them when she was young. The village shop gave away to each of their customers, two candles and some wheat to make frumenty. Christmas dinner was either goose or chicken followed by plum pudding with rum sauce. Christmas cake was always eaten with Wensleydale cheese.'

FRUMENTY ON CHRISTMAS EVE

'Ever since I can remember my mother has made frumenty on Christmas Eve. She started to "cree" the pearl barley in water two days before Christmas and then on Christmas Eve she separated the sticky grains. Pints of milk and a cinnamon stick were stirred in and cooked slowly all day, adding milk as required. In the early evening she added casein and sugar to taste. The frumenty was served with rum and cream.

Before sitting down to frumenty, a yule log (the best dry log to be found) was placed on the fire and the oldest and youngest persons then lit the candles which were on the festive table, from the yule log. All other lights were extinguished and after the toasts were drunk the frumenty was eaten in silence, and then Christmas cake, ginger cake and cheese were eaten. Many sittings followed with the lights extinguished and silence observed each time the frumenty was eaten.

I still make frumenty on Christmas Eve, but find it very difficult to maintain the silence these days!'

'The highlight of the year was surely Christmas Eve and all the family gathered for the evening at our farm at Ugthorpe. Mother had been cooking the cracked wheat in the oven, slowly for several hours. The table had to be set with candles, silver and glasses, the Christmas cake, gingerbread and large cheese placed in the centre, awaiting the arrival of the large tureen full of piping hot frumenty, to be eaten with syrup and cinnamon. The youngest members of the family lit the candles. Father cut the cake, Mother poured the wine, and starting with the frumenty, the meal commenced. Father tasted all the goodies first and we followed suit and enjoyed a lovely merry evening, until it was time for bed and Christmas Day itself.'

THE BOXING DAY SHOOT

'Christmas was a wonderful time at the farm at Easingwold and all the family were there for Christmas Day when there was always a goose for lunch. On the farm there were geese, ducks, chickens and turkeys, many of which had to be plucked, dressed and trussed for regular customers. Boxing Day was the day all the menfolk in the family went round the farm with their guns and ferrets to catch pheasants, partridges and rabbits, before coming back to the house for lunch, after which they went back round the rest of the farm. If they had a good shoot there would be braces of pheasants and couples of rabbits everywhere, which were given to members of the family. If there was a surplus, it would be taken to market.

During the morning and afternoon of Boxing Day the women members of the family prepared for the Boxing Night festivities, which consisted of a large "knife and fork" supper with every kind of sweet imaginable. Family, friends and neighbours were invited and the farmhouse would be bursting at the seams. We younger members of the family were always allowed to stay up on that evening, when we had games, Christmas snowmen and Christmas houses with presents and gifts in them. When Christmas was over it was back to the toil!'

Index

251

252

List of Contributing Institutes

Contributions were received from the following WIs:

North Yorkshire East: Acomb, Alne, Askham Bryan, Barkston Ash, Barton-Le-Willows & Harton, Borrowby, Brandsby, Burn, Burniston and Cloughton, Byland-with-Wass, Cawood, Carlton, Carlton and Faceby, Carlton Miniott, Claxton and Sand Hutton, Copmanthorpe, Crathorne, Cropton, Dalton-on-Tees, Danby Wiske, Dishforth, Dunnington, Easingwold, Ebberston and Allerston, Farndale, Farndale Low Mills, Fryup Dales, Fulford, Fylingthorpe, Girsby, Glaisdale, Great Edstone, Gristhorpe and Lebberston, Helperby, Hemingbrough, Heworth, Hinderwell, Hovingham, Huby, Hutton Bonville, Hutton-le-Hole, Huttons Ambo, Ingleby Arncliffe, Ingleby Greenhow, Kilburn and Oldstead, Kirby Knowle and Upsall, Kirbymoorside, Kirby Sigston, Kirk and Green Hammerton, Lastingham and Spaunton, Lealholm, Long Marston, Middleton, Aisleby and Wrelton, Myton-on-Swale, Newton-on-Ouse, Normanby and Marton, North Duffield, Norton, Osbaldwick and Murton, Ouseburn, Pickering, Poppleton, Rievaulx, Romanby, Scalby and Newby, Sheriff Hutton, Snainton, Sowerby, Staithes, Stillingfleet, Stillington and Farlington, Stockton-on-Forest, Strensall, Stutton-cum-Hazelwood, Swainby and Potto, Thornton-le-Dale, Ugthorpe, Whixley, Wiggington and Haxby.
North Yorkshire West: Austwick, Beckwithshaw, Bedale, Belmont, Bilton, Bolton Abbey, Brompton-on-Swale, Carperby, Catterick, Constable Burton, East Witton, Farnley Estate, Follifoot, Gargrave, Giggleswick, Glusburn, Goldsborough, Grewelthorpe, Gunnerside, Hampsthwaite, Harmby, Huby and Weeton, Hunton, Ingleton, Knaresborough, Leyburn, Marske, Marton-cum-Grafton, Newton-le-Willows, Otley, Pannal, Preston-under-Scar, Ravensworth, Richmond, Ripley, Salterforth, Scriven, Settle, Skelton-on-Ure, Snape, Spennithorne, Starbeck, Sutton-in-Craven, Thoralby, Thornton Watless, Well, West Burton, West Witton.